D1617013

THE REASON OF FOLLOWING

RELIGION AND POSTMODERNISM
A Series Edited by Mark C. Taylor

ROBERT P. SCHARLEMANN

THE REASON OF FOLLOWING

Christology and the Ecstatic I

The University of Chicago Press
Chicago and London

ROBERT P. SCHARLEMANN is Commonwealth Professor of Religious Studies at the University of Virginia. His most recent books include *The Critique of Modernity* and *Inscriptions and Reflections*.

The University of Chicago Press, Chicago 60637
The University of Chicago Press, Ltd., London
© 1991 by The University of Chicago
All rights reserved. Published 1991
Printed in the United States of America

00 99 98 97 96 95 94 93 92 91 5 4 3 2 1

Library of Congress Cataloging-in-Publication Data
Scharlemann, Robert P.
The reason of following: Christology and the ecstatic I / Robert P. Scharlemann.
p.   cm. — (Religion and postmodernism)
Includes bibliographical references and index.
ISBN 0–226–73659–8 (cloth)
1. Jesus Christ—Person and offices.   2. Self.   3. Christianity—Psychology.   4. Knowledge, Theory of (Religion)   5. Theology—Methodology.   6. Reason.   I. Title.   II. Series.
BT205.S25   1991
233—dc20   91–11615
                                                                              CIP

Contents

Introduction

IN EVERY ACTIVITY OF REASON, whether it be scientific cognition or aesthetic appreciation or some other such activity, there is a definite configuration of the self's relation to its other. Each kind of configuration has characteristics which define it over against other kinds. Thus, we speak of scientific objectivity or of aesthetic distance, and we mean by it not some accidental characteristic of scientists and artists but an essential feature of the relation between knower and known in the scientific act or between observer and observed in the artistic act. We can speak of scientific observation as well as artistic observation, but we know that the objectivity of the first is not the same as the distance of the second. The aesthetic distance, which is shown, for example, when audiences at an opera do not come onto the stage to take part in the action by helping sympathetic characters, is not the cognitive objectivity shown when investigators of data do not manipulate the data in order to arrive at favored conclusions or to support hopes or awaken fears. The cognitive relation and the aesthetic relation are constituted differently; the way in which subject and object, the self and its other, are related to each other is different in each of them.

Recognizing the difference is not the same as defining it; and finding the right concepts to grasp what is essential to the various relations or determining how many such distinct relations there are is not an easy accomplishment. What we now know as aesthetics is of a later date than theory and practice. Our understanding of theoretical and practical reason owes its beginnings to Greek philosophy, as does our understanding of a certain kind of poetics; but aesthetics, as a sensuous rationality different from the rationality of theoretical science, does not emerge until Alexander Baumgarten in the eighteenth century, and even today aesthetics and poetics are often treated as though they were different expressions of one form of reason—as though, for example, the play of form that is sensuously perceived in the sounds and rhythm of poetry or in the colors and shades of a painting is artistic in the same way as is the making of a world that is done by the imagination in the writing and reading of a poem or novel or in the painting and contemplation of a work of visual art.

Such matters may seem at first to be irrelevant to a treatise on Christology. But they are not so if what has been developed under the title of "Christology" is not only the articulated confession of a faith but also the recognition of a form of reason with characteristics of its own. If it is the expression of a form of reason different from theory, practice, making, and sensuous appreciation, then we ought to be able to identify its characteristics and compare them with those of other forms of reason. The present study is an effort to provide such a definition and comparison. The title, *The Reason of Following*, suggests the substance of what will be presented. The christological relation, constituted by the self's "following" of another, is distinct from science, morality, and art; it is a rational form of its own. As such, it is the configuration of a self-to-other relation whose characteristics prevent it from being reduced to knowledge, moral action, artistic creation, or sensuous appreciation. But to speak of the self at all is to open questions besides those having to do with the construction of rational forms. Above all it requires a consideration of the theories of the self that have arisen out of the meditation on the self associated with transcendental reflection. In particular, clarification is needed with respect to three problems: the universality of the self contained in the meaning of "I"; the being of the self that appears in the connection indicated by the copula between the "I" and a particular person; and the capacity of the self to be outside itself, its ecstatic capacity.

First, that there is a universality in the self is understood as soon as we understand the meaning of saying or thinking "I." But understanding the meaning is not the same as finding the concepts with which to define what is meant, and the nature of this universality has presented problems, with elusive solutions, whenever the effort has been made to grasp it in concepts adequate to the meaning. In the analysis provided in his Gifford lectures of 1939, *The Nature and Destiny of Man*, Reinhold Niebuhr set out some of the difficulties.

He associated these with the philosophies of idealism and naturalism which lay at the roots of the then-prevalent scientific understanding of human nature and destiny. Of idealistic philosophy, Niebuhr said that it has the advantage over naturalism in appreciating the depth of the human spirit, for idealism recognizes that the self has the capacity of transcending not only the natural processes but also its own consciousness. But he went on to remark that it "usually sacrifices this advantage" by "identifying the universal perspective of the self-transcendent ego with universal spirit" so that the self of idealism is "both less and more than the real self"; the "actual self is absorbed in the universal."[1] Idealism recognizes the universality but can conceive of it only by absorbing the individuality of the real self into a universal self or universal mind; naturalism, on the other hand, can conceive of it only by ignoring the subjectivity of the self in the effort to reduce the self to a biological organism.

Second, the being of the self, the being of that entity which is not only conscious but also self-conscious and even conscious of its self-consciousness, is expressed in the traditional definition of man as a rational animal. Although the being of a thing is not simply identical with a concept of *what* it is, because being makes reference to the "is" that connects a subject with a predicate that defines it, the formulation of such definitions does also express an understanding of the being of what is defined. Modern existentialism in particular has called into question the understanding of human being contained in the traditional definition of man as rational animal. The most notable result of this questioning is the recognition that human being can be defined not by saying "what" it is but by saying "where" it is. "Man is a rational animal" can be replaced by the definition " 'I' am here." The word *here* in such an existential definition indicates both a temporal and a spatial location; it indicates that the being of the self, the being of that entity whose presence is shown by the word *I*, involves the connection of a particular with a universal not by means of a general concept and specific difference (the genus animal, and the difference of rationality) but by means of a place that has both temporal and spatial dimensions. Descartes's method of doubt leads to the recognition that "I am when I think"; existentialism adds that the "when" is both a time and a space. One can, of course, still say

<hr>

1. Reinhold Niebuhr, *The Nature and Destiny of Man: A Christian Interpretation*, 2 vols. (London: Nisbet & Co., Ltd., 1941–43), vol. 1, pp. 79, 80.

that the entity called human being belongs to the genus of animal and is distinguished from other animals by the capacity for reason; it is the "living thing" that "has the capacity for language and reason." But such a definition falls short of exposing that aspect of the being of human being which emerges in the existentialist definition of the self as "I am here." The importance of this change is far greater than can be stated briefly, and it accounts for the fact that two of the longest chapters in the present volume, chapters 1 and 2, are devoted to explicating its significance, while another chapter, chapter 3, is occupied with its ramification into the meaning of the "thinking" of being. This ramification brings with it the necessity to make clear the connection of "thinking" to such forms of reason as science, morality, and art. It brings with it as well the obligation to set forth an understanding of what has been called, in a formulation coming from Augustine and Anselm, "faith seeking understanding" and to do so in a way that reflects the extent to which phenomenology and existentialism have affected the manner in which such a formulation can be appropriated.

A third problem is that of the ecstasis of the self. There is a long tradition of reflection on the self that is shut out of the conception of the self-positing self. A reflection having the character of Descartes's method of doubt, particularly when pursued to Kierkegaardian lengths, shows unmistakably that the self cannot but posit itself in the place indicated by the word *I*. But is the place so indicated the same as the time and space of the person who says and thinks the word? Or can the place be split between two chronotopes, two personal times and places, so that the "I" can be ecstatic and can thus do such things as be beside itself or come to itself or gain itself by losing itself? That the soul can be distended in *memoria* between the past it remembers and the future it anticipates in its present action is a temporal extension of the I between having-been and about-to-be, but this is not yet an exstantiality that makes possible the self's being outside its own "here." If the self can be beside itself, the being of the self is not only indicated by the copula that connects a self as "I" with a place but also includes the possibility of the self's being outside its place ecstatically. In the present study, this possibility is used for an interpretation of the form of reason called following. It provides the basis for understanding the self not only as a substance of attributes but as an "exstance" of different places.

These are three basic problems that appear in the delineation of christological reason as the form of reason exhibited by acts of following in which the follower and followed are identified by an "I am." In the explication of this form of reason, which is undertaken in chapters 4 to 6 (while chapters 7 and 8 are reserved for the two specific questions of textuality and theology), a decision had to be made about the material to be used for clarification, exemplification, illustration, and analysis. If, as is contended here, Christology is a form of reason and can be explicated as such, there is in principle no necessity to draw materials only from the Christian theological tradition. But two considerations seemed to make it advisable to do so. One is that a greater diversity of cited material could well make the line of thought unclear. The second, and more decisive, one is the interpreter's need to have a sense of the inner power of materials in order to provide a credible interpretation of them; and scholarship in the world's religious traditions is still not at a stage to make it possible to become intimately familiar with more than one body of such materials. In these circumstances the use of materials from traditions other than one with which an author has a living acquaintance cannot avoid appearing (and being) superficial and probably unhelpful. Some such materials have been used in the present study, but they are used with the recognition that they cannot but seem superficial to those who have an intimate acquaintance with the dynamics of those materials in their own settings. In the main, however, the counsel followed in the choice of materials was to remain with what was most familiar to the author. This will be most evident in chapter 6, which undertakes the explication of this form of reason by reference to the relation between Jesus and his disciples in the New Testament gospels. The cost of doing so is the risk of leaving behind readers who may have an interest in the topic but do not have any familiarity with, or interest in, the biblical materials used for the explication, to say nothing of the lesser risk of having the exposition appear biblicistic in a manner not intended. There did not seem to be any way to avoid paying the cost of this risk.

Measured by standard expositions of Christology the present one is idiosyncratic. But the nature of the subject matter and the interest lying behind the posing of the questions have made a more conventional exposition inadvisable. The hope is, therefore, that the idiosyncrasy will be seen as a positive rather than a negative value or at least not as a distraction.

1

The Subjectivity of the Self: The I as Such

MUCH CONFUSION IS PRODUCED
in our understanding of the self if we fail to make clear the distinction between the individual and the I. One evidence of such a confusion is the way in which critics of existentialism have over the years criticized its concern with authenticity—the propriety or *Eigentlichkeit* of the self—as being individualistic and unconcerned with community or the social dimension of human being; yet there is a basic difference between the propriety of being a self and the individuality of a person. This confusion is of consequence, moreover, not only to ethics or to social theory, which are not the concern here, but also to our conception of rationality and to the branch of Christian theology that is entitled Christology. For Christology contains an understanding of selfhood that has been obscured not only by modern theories of the self but also by the ways in which theology has treated Christology. Christian theology differs, on the one side, from Jewish and Muslim theologies in its acknowledgement of a concrete deity and, on the other side, from Hindu theologies by its affirming only one concrete deity, only one "incarnation" of the *logos* of God. This double difference is theologically located in Christology, which in this sense has no strict counterpart in any other theology. But Christology is more than a moment in a doctrine of God; it is also and, in historical terms, probably more originally an articulated understanding of the nature and constitution of human being. This phase of Christology has by and large been lost to view, although Barth did his part to recover it in his own fashion in the doctrine that "every man as such is the fellowman of Jesus," who is "the concrete event of the existence and reality of justified man in

whom every man can recognize himself and every other man."¹ At
least it has scarcely done more than to begin to express itself in conversation with the modern and postmodern understandings of selfhood. Declamations against the self-centeredness of the "Cartesian"
self will hardly do; for the very word by which the christological self
is identified is the same as that of the egocentric self—"I am," *ego
sum, ego eimi.*

The certainty of the self in the modern understanding is connected
with time and possibility. The temporality of the self appears already
in Descartes's meditations on doubt, although the theme is not pursued as such. For the certainty of the "I think" is there connected
with time: *when* I think, I am.² It is not until Heidegger's *Being and
Time*, however, that the connection of the self's time with possibility
and end is brought into the foreground. For what manifests the I on
its own is the thought of the end that is the possibility most "my"
own: death is that which I, as I, always "can" but never "do" do. The
propriety, the reality or "ownness," of the I appears with this double
qualification—as the end that is my-death and as a pure possibility
forever debarred from "my" actualizing it. By "certainty" is meant
not just a state of mind, as though certainty were only subjective, but
an appearing reality whose presence cannot be dislodged. The traditional example of immediate certainty is sense perception, whose
objects are the *certa* in this sense. When I see a tree directly in front
of me, I am immediately certain of seeing something as a tree. Even
if, because of lighting conditions or other optical illusions, it turns
out that what I was seeing was not a tree but something else, this
result does not negate the immediate certainty of my being certain
of seeing something as something when I beheld it.³ Can there be a

1. Quotations are from Karl Barth, *Church Dogmatics: A Selection,* selected and
edited by Helmut Gollwitzer, translated and edited by G. W. Bromiley (New York:
Harper Torchbook, 1961), pp. 168, 169. There are two different strands in Barth,
one a genuine debate with modernity and the other a kind of theological isolationism,
which make his real contribution always somewhat elusive.

2. "This proposition: I am, I exist, is necessarily true each time I pronounce it, or
that I mentally conceive it" (René Descartes, "Meditation on First Philosophy," *The
Philosophical Works of Descartes,* translated by Elizabeth S. Haldane and G. R. T. Ross
[New York: Dover Publications, 1955, from the 1931 corrected ed.], vol. 1, meditation II, p. 150).

3. As Descartes shows by the example of the wax that changes in the heat, this
is not purely a *sense* certainty but a certainty of understanding (*Works,* vol. 1, meditation II, pp. 154f.).

mediated certainty, as well as an immediate certainty? Can certainty apply to cognition as well as to sensation? Can we be certain not only of our being aware of something but also of its being a definite kind of thing (a tree, for example)? That certainty can be mediated is one of the results of the Cartesian method of doubt. But such a mediated certainty, when it pertains to the I, is peculiarly connected in the Cartesian reflection with the I in its temporality. It is initially the certainty expressed in the statement that *when* I think, I am. How does this phenomenon appear?

The Mediation of Self-Certainty in the Method of Doubt

The I is a phenomenon. It is something that shows itself from itself, and phenomenology is the discourse which shows the phenomenon in the very talk about it.[4] Thus, a stone is a phenomenon in the sense that when we have it in full view it shows itself as a certain kind of thing—we cannot see it as something other than a stone. The world of a poem is also a phenomenon, in the sense that what the poem is about shows itself to our imagination as we read. The emotion of anger, likewise, is a phenomenon in that it shows itself in our inward state when we are angry and through our expressions or actions to someone else.[5] A "phenomenology" of the stone is a discourse, whether written or oral, which presents the stone to us in the very language that speaks about it. In the case of objects such as stones and trees, there is no difference between phenomenology and talk. Properly, therefore, phenomenology is not of stones and such objects but of realities that appear not to sense perception but only in language (or, in Husserl's form of phenomenology, as essences to eidetic intuition). Phenomenology reflects the phenomenon in language, in *logos*.[6] The I is a phenomenon to the extent that it can show

4. These phrasings are adapted from Martin Heidegger, *Sein und Zeit,* 10th unalt. ed. (Tübingen: Max Niemeyer, 1963), §7, p. 34.

5. Martin Buber called attention to the problem of objectifying such emotional states and proposed the solution of doing so by recalling the living moments in which they manifested themselves. See "What Is Man?" in *Between Man and Man,* translated by Ronald Gregor Smith (New York: Macmillan, 1965), pp. 118–205.

6. In Kantian philosophy a "phenomenon" is contrasted with a "noumenon." A phenomenon is an object as we perceive it (with our senses); a noumenon is an object as we conceive it (in an abstract thought). Thus, the concept that we form of a tree when we read a dictionary definition is a noumenon; the tree that we actually see is a phenomenon. According to this Kantian theory of knowledge, we can *know* some-

itself from itself, and a phenomenology is possible to the extent that the I as such can be manifested in a discourse that articulates it.

But *can* the I appear? The answer is less obvious than it may seem to be since the word *I* means the one *to* whom things appear. It raises a problem similar to the one that Gassendi put for Descartes. How can the eye, "incapable of seeing itself in itself," nonetheless see itself in a mirror?[7]

In one way, the self appears as the phenomenon of the I in the very understanding of the word *I*; it appears not as an object sensibly perceived (as it would in the Kantian sense of phenomenon) but as a meaning understood. The word *I* carries a meaning that is simultaneously a reference to something most concrete and most universal; when I say "I," I am the only one meant, but the same is true for anyone who speaks the word. To think or to say the word is to show the phenomenon of the self from its own self, not as an intuition, an *Anschauung*, but as an understanding of a meaning. The I is, thus, something that appears not to our sense perception but as a meaning. It appears whenever the meaning that is borne by the word *I* is thought.[8] To show itself, the phenomenon requires that we are able

---

thing (instead of merely sensibly perceiving or abstractly conceiving it) only when we connect the two with each other. If a noumenon cannot be "exhibited" in an object, we can have no "knowledge" of it; we can only have a concept of it. And if a phenomenon cannot be subsumed under a concept, we can have no "knowledge" of it either but only a sensation. In the present context, the contrast is being made not between phenomenon and noumenon but between phenomenon and *logos,* the appearing thing and the appearing thing reflected in an articulated language. Phenomenology thus involves the two questions of (1) where and how the thing appears and (2) how it is reflected in the language that articulates it. The "thing" at issue in the present discussion is the I as such.

7. Gassendi's Fifth Objection to the *Meditations.* Descartes, *Works,* vol. 2, pp. 162ff. See also Louis Dupré, "Alternatives to the Cogito," *Review of Metaphysics* 40, no. 4 (June 1987): 689.

8. This seems to me to be a more adequate way of indicating the subjectivity meant by the word *I* than Peter Caws's identifying the ego with the body. But his analysis of subjectivity as "what permits the integral, continuous, and repeated apprehension of the object" (p. 141) is a nice analytical account of Heidegger's contention that the self (Dasein) is from the start always in some way in the world. "It is not that I *inhabit* my body, rather as a conscious subject I *am* it," he writes (p. 149); and he characterizes subjectivity in this sense as idiosyncratic (I know subjectivity only as my own), linear ("I trace [the *me*] as if it were a continuous line through [the] network of subjective states" [p. 150]), and arbitrary (there is no answer to the question why there should be just the subjectivities in the bodies here and now that there are). Farther back, as it were, we also need to ask how we know the difference of the "I"

to understand the meaning of the word, or that we are able to think the thought that is contained in and conveyed by the word when we use it in the course of our speaking.

What is the *logos* of this phenomenon that might make a phenomenology of it possible? Here we are referred first of all to the *cogito ergo sum* of Descartes. In the context of thinking, the I is articulated, or structured, in its certainty. A modern discourse on the self is one in which the self is reflected in the medium of thought and in relation to the question of certainty. Of what can I be certain? Of what can I know both what it is and that it really is? Descartes's method of doubt is the form of thinking which is directed toward answering this question, and it can be said to inaugurate the modern understanding. Certainty is not just a subjective conviction; it is the form in which the real appears in its reality. I can doubt that I am thinking, I can doubt that I am doubting; but I become aware, when carrying out this doubt methodically, that I who think or I who doubt cannot be expunged even by the most radical doubting. The modern I is, thus, the I that appears as a phenomenon in the midst of the impossibility of its being eradicated by the activity of its own thinking; I cannot think the I of myself away. What is meant by thinking in this context is the activity of presenting something to mind as it is on its own; and what is meant by doubting is the activity of asking whether what we have presented to our mind as the thing on its own is really the same as what we have presented it to be. If what is present to me is something as a tree, then my doubting it involves my asking myself whether what appears to me as a tree is "really," that is, on its own part, a tree and my thinking that it possibly is not what it appears to be.

To think of it as being a tree is to present it to mind as it is on its own. But I can also doubt whether that is what thinking is. I think *of* my own thinking *as* a presenting to myself of the object as the object is on its own. I can then doubt, or call into question, whether my way of thinking accords with the real relation between my thinking and that about which I am thinking. I can endeavor to think that my thinking does not accord with the reality of which it thinks; or I

---

from the "me" that "I trace." Hence, I suggest here that the I as such appears just in our understanding the meaning of the word *I* even in its difference from the meaning of the word *me*. See Peter Caws, "The Subject in Sartre and Elsewhere," in *Descriptions*, edited by Don Ihde and Hugh J. Silverman (Albany: SUNY Press, 1985), pp. 141–51.

can endeavor to think that I am not really thinking. The method of doubt makes it possible to call into question every object of thought including the very activity of thinking. If I can doubt that an object is what I think it to be, I can also doubt that I am engaged in the activity in which I think I am engaged when I am immediately aware of it. I can call into question the validity of that awareness. I can ask: Am I really thinking or, rather, only imagining or thinking or dreaming that I am thinking? I can ask, "Is thinking really what I think it to be?" Followed even further, the path of doubting turns upon itself. I can doubt whether I am doubting. I can think that, when I think I am doubting, I am not really doubting. Not even my doubting of my doubting is free from doubt. However, the one phenomenon that can never be dislodged through such doubt is the I as the one who does it. What remains indubitable is I who am doing the doubting or the thinking or the calling into question. The I, thus, shows itself from itself not only in the understanding of the meaning of the word *I* but, more radically, in the doubting that is turned methodically upon itself. By putting into play the thought that is meant by the word *doubt*—the play of swinging between the yes and the no of being and nonbeing by thinking that what is is not—I bring into view the ego in its existence as the "I" that I cannot but assert. Unlike the reality of objects and unlike the validity or reality of the *activity* of thinking, which do not remain certain in the process of doubting, the reality of the I as I is ineradicable. This method of doubt is, then, one means by which the certainty of the phenomenon of the I is mediated. If it is asked, "Where do we see the phenomenon of the I just as I?" the answer is that we look in the direction indicated by the method of doubt.

But this self-certainty is temporal: *when* I think, I am. Or, to put it into different terms, the element of the self that is meant by the word *I* exists as such at those times when one thinks the meaning of the word and thus instantiates the one meant. This temporality gives the phenomenon a certain erratic character. What becomes of the I as I at other times? Where is this pure subjectivity when we are not thinking the meaning of the word *I* at all? Such questions are only skirted in the Cartesian meditation.[9] With the existentialist

9. "I am, I exist, that is certain. But how often? Just when I think; for it might possibly be the case if I ceased entirely to think, that I should likewise cease altogether to exist" (*Works*, vol. 1, meditation II, pp. 151f.).

analysis in *Being and Time*, Heidegger will later answer: in *das Man*, so that the phenomenology of Dasein must also be hermeneutical.[10] In a preliminary way, we can say that, at times other than those when the self is instantiated by thinking the meaning of the word, the self as I is hidden in the generality of the *one*, or the "they," as in: "one does not do such things" or "one never knows" or "they say . . . ," and the like. The temporality of the I is, thus, the double temporality of the everyday (when the I is hidden) and the proper (when the I appears as such). In the everyday, the I exists submerged in the subjects of any time. When I think "I," I am the self as I; at other times (when I do not think "I"), I am the self as anyone. The self as I has these two times, the time of being as an I and the time of not being as an I. We can call them the times of wakefulness and forgetting, or of obviousness and obliviousness. These are times of being and not being; the I both can be and not be *as I*.

The Uncommon Singularity of the I in the Attack of Conscience (Anfechtung)

Descartes's exposure of the ego in the self, which appears in the *cogito*, occurred not in connection with the search for a theory of the self but rather as part of an effort to become free of prejudice or received opinions and to secure a firm knowledge. Once that had been attained, Descartes was not further concerned with the meaning for the self of the discovery that its being is connected with the temporality of the "I think." Even so, the method of doubt, which laid part of the foundation for the autonomy characteristic of modern thought, always contained the potential of making one ask again who is the I who can "think" and who, when thinking, "is." The *pronunciatum* "I am" is "necessarily true each time that I pronounce it or that I mentally conceive it."[11] But the Cartesian meditation is only one root of modern self-understanding. The other root lies in another figure at the dawn of the modern age, one for whom doubt played an equally fundamental but different role. "*Quid enim incertitudine miserius?*" Luther wrote in 1525 (*WA* 18; 604,33)—"What is worse than uncertainty?"[12] Here uncertainty is a different prob-

---

10. "Phänomenologie des Daseins ist Hermeneutik," *SuZ*, §7, p. 37.

11. *Works*, vol. 1, meditation II, p. 150; see note 2 above.

12. See Gerhard Ebeling, "Gewißheit und Zweifel: Die Situation des Glaubens im Zeitalter nach Luther und Descartes," *Wort und Glaube*, vol. 2 (Tübingen: J. C. B.

lem. It is the uncertainty of salvation, the uncertainty whether the accusations of conscience, by having the last word, amount to an unending destruction of the self.

In Luther's case, as in Descartes's, it was in connection with doubt and certainty that the subjectivity of the self emerged. The dissimilarity in the two cases cannot be denied. In Luther, doubt comes in the form of an attack, which one suffers, and it comes unpredictably. In Descartes, doubt is an intellectual activity taken up at leisure in the interest of freeing the mind of prejudice and bondage to the world of sense. In Luther, the subject overtaken by doubt is accused and condemned by the attacker. In Descartes, the subject undertaking to doubt assures itself of itself. As Descartes wrote in his *Discourse on Method*, "The setting in of winter detained me in a quarter where, since I found no society to divert me, while fortunately I had also no cares or passions to trouble me, I remained the whole day shut up alone in a stove-heated room, where I had complete leisure to occupy myself with my own thoughts."[13] The self which seeks out a quiet place for itself at the beginning of winter in order to devote itself at leisure to the search for a method is clearly in circumstances different from those of the self that is attacked at unpredictable times by the power of doubt. Despite this great difference in the kind of experience that doubt involves, the similarity is that in both cases the phenomenon of the I is associated with the movement of doubt and certainty. It is doubt that brings to the fore the self in the form of a first person singular, which can do nothing but assert itself, even in its attempt at its own denial.

If temporality is decisive for the I of the *cogito sum*, it is the feature of unmediated singularity that defines the I attacked by conscience. The intensity and the inescapability of the attacks of conscience have to do with the way they isolate the self in a singularity that does not permit the I to be subsumed under anything common. This is not a case of theologically construing the ordinary understanding of con-

Mohr [Paul Siebeck], 1969), pp. 138–83. The quotations from the Weimar edition (*WA*) of Luther's works are taken from Ebeling's essay.

13. "Le commencement de l'hiver m'arrêta en un quartier où, ne trouvant aucune conversation qui me divertît, et n'ayant d'ailleurs, par bonheur, aucuns soins ni passions qui me troublassent, je demeurais tout le jour enfermé seul dans un poêle, où j'avais tout loisir de m'entretenir de mes pensées." English translation in *Works*, vol. 1, p. 87. See also Ebeling, "Gewißheit," p. 150, n. 31.

science as the voice of God. The one who is thus attacked is attacked, as it were, without the protection of a common humanity, or of what Luther in this connection called *ratio*; one is attacked not as *a special case of* something common or an *individual case of* something special but as single and alone. Hence, the battle is waged "within you alone" and "with God alone," a battle of the self (as *fides*) against itself (as *fiducia operum*) to win God against God (*deum contra deum vincere*).[14] Conscience represents a flight, not from the deceptions of sense perception or prejudice, but from "works."

What Luther portayed, in countless variations, as the interior battle of the self exposed in its isolated singularity, Kierkegaard analyzed in connection with the monstrosity of faith that appears in Abraham, when "God tempts" Abraham by telling him to offer his son Isaac as a burnt offering. "When I have to think of Abraham, I am as though annihilated. I catch sight every moment of that enormous paradox which is the substance of Abraham's life, every moment I am repelled. . . . To be able to lose one's reason, and therefore the whole finiteness of which reason is the broker, and then by virtue of the absurd to gain precisely the same finiteness—that appalls my soul, . . . it is the only prodigy."[15] There are echoes here of Luther's language. "Faith says: I believe you, God, as you speak. What does God say? Things impossible, mendacious, stupid, uncertain, abominable, heretical, diabolical—if you consult reason. . . . They are monstrous, reason says; they are diabolical. Faith puts such reason to death and kills the beast that neither heaven and earth nor any creatures can kill."[16] Faith believes God when God speaks, but *ratio* calls the things God says monstrous. But Kierkegaard goes on to identify what makes the paradox monstrous or unthinkable and the sense in which "reason" is defied by it. It is the fact that there is no

14. "Non enim ideo tentaris desperatione seu turbinibus conscientiae, ut ad operum fiduciam curras, sed contra ab opere avocaris, quia spiritualissima etsi acerbissima haec pugna est intra te solum cum solo deo consummanda, sola spe sustinente et expectante, deoque causam totam commendante deumque contra deum vincente . . ." (*WA* 5; 167, 11–16 [1519/21]). Quoted in Ebeling, "Gewißheit," p. 168.

15. S. Kierkegaard, *Fear and Trembling,* translated by Walter Lowrie (Garden City: Doubleday Anchor, 1954), pp. 44 and 47.

16. "Fides dicit sic: Ego credo tibi deo loquenti. Quid loquitur? impossibilia, mendacia, stulta, infirma, abhominanda, heretica, diabolica,—Si rationem consulis. . . . Monstra sunt, dicit ratio; dicit ista diabolica. Fides hanc rationem occidit et mortificat istam bestiam quam coelum et terra non possunt occidere nec omnes creaturae" (*WA* 40, 1; 361, 1–4. 7–9 [1531]).

mediating term between Abraham and God and therefore no concept, no interpretation, which might make the deed intelligible. "Abraham is . . . either a murderer or a believer. The middle term which saves the tragic hero [namely, the concept of sacrificing a private good for the greater good of the nation], Abraham has not. Hence it is that I can understand the tragic hero but cannot understand Abraham . . . "(p. 67). The "ethical expression" for what Abraham did is that he "would murder Isaac"; the religious expression is that he "would sacrifice Isaac"; the "dread which can well make a man sleepless" lies in the contradiction between those two (p. 41). There is no concept between murder and sacrifice by which the contradiction can be mediated—as there might be, for example, in the case of having to do an evil for a greater good. There is no mediation; the I is instantaneous. Faith is a "paradox that no thought can master" (p. 64), the paradox that the "particular is higher than the universal" in such a way that "the individual, after having been in the universal, now as the particular isolates himself as higher than the universal" (p. 65).[17] If that is not faith, Kierkegaard concludes, then Abraham is lost, and there never was any such thing as faith (p. 65). Such a faith can be described only by silence because there is no concept common to or mediating between murder (ethically) and sacrifice (religiously). The pseudonym Johannes e Silentio for the author of this piece indicates that recognition, and Kierkegaard later clarifies it in the figure of Frater Taciturnus in *Stages on Life's Way*.

First the individual is in the universal; one understands oneself in one's humanity, as subject to a universal ethical law—for example, "Thou shalt not kill." But then the I—not the "individual," as Kierkegaard has it—stands out; it stands not above the universal, but outside it. In this analysis, it is the summons that isolates Abraham, bringing to view the phenomenon of the I in its uncommon, or unmediated, singularity in the person of Abraham. As representing

17. "Faith is precisely this paradox, that the individual as the particular is higher than the universal, is justified over against it, is not subordinate but superior—yet in such a way, be it observed, that it is the particular individual who, after he has been subordinated as the particular to the universal, now through the universal becomes the individual who as the particular is superior to the universal, for the fact that the individual as the particular stands in an absolute relation to the absolute. This position cannot be mediated, for all mediation comes about precisely by virtue of the universal; it is and remains to all eternity a paradox, inaccessible to thought. And yet faith is this paradox . . . or else there never has been faith" (*FT,* p. 66).

faith, Abraham has nothing in common with anyone else and cannot say anything to communicate what the event and deed of his faith were. To the trial by God he responds alone and unprotected, unmediated by any universal concept under which his deed can be subsumed and made intelligible. He can speak of it only by silence.

Kierkegaard's analysis here contributes in part to the confusion between individuality and egoity. First the individual is subordinated to the universal—a self becomes one instance of human being. Then, "through the universal," that is, by means of being a human being or by means of being conscious of one's humanity, one's theoretical and practical rationality, the individual becomes "the individual who as the particular is superior to the universal" and does so because of standing "in an absolute relation to the absolute" (p. 66). The individual is subordinated to the universal: there is something common to him and to others as particulars of the same universal, and individuals can understand one another by reference to that commonality. An Abraham unaware of any ethical universals would have no problem. But in faith something else happens. The individual, the I that I am, becomes, as Kierkegaard puts it, superior to the universal. It is not that the individual is ignorant of the universal, but that the individual, qua individual, is universalized.

The categories that Kierkegaard employs may obscure the point, for they suggest that it is only a matter of determining which is superior to which—the individual to the universal or the universal to the individual—rather than a matter of showing how the I as such is both universal and individual, belonging to a quite different category. But there can be little doubt about Kierkegaard's insight itself, namely, that in Abraham the phenomenon of the self as I appears in its uncommon singularity. It is not that in Abraham the *individual* becomes superior to the universal (humanity as such) but rather that the absolute singularity of the I as I appears in the individual. The man Abraham is not made superior to the whole human race, he does not become *the* one universal human being. Rather, he is the one in whom the singularity of the I as such manifests itself in the call he hears. Abraham cannot answer for what he does by appealing to general principles or by reference to a reason or cause that will make his deed intelligible to anyone else or even to himself as a thinking being. He can answer for it only in the form of himself as a self alone. If any reason can be given for the deed, it can be given only in a language of silence, not in the language of causality or intentions or norms. "I did it because God told me to do so" is not an answer that makes the deed intelligible. For one could then ask, "How do we know it was God talking to you?" If there is anything else to which we can appeal in order to confirm that it was God talking, then the case is lost.

The transcendental ego in Kantian philosophy, the ego who is the rational subject as such, is, thus, not the same as the ego in its uncommon singularity. Nothing illustrates this difference more succinctly than the comment Kant made in the *Streit der Fakultäten* upon just this story of Abraham. If he, Kant, were to hear a voice commanding him to kill his son, he would, he explained, have replied differently from Abraham. He would have said that, while he was not sure whether a voice speaking from the clouds was the voice of God, he was sure that a father ought not to kill his son.[18]

With the *cogito* of Descartes and Kierkegaard's analysis of the temptation of Abraham, we have two ways in which the subjectivity of the self, or the I as such, appears: its temporality and its singularity. I am I *when* I think, and I am I *as* an uncommon singularity. The doubt about reality, which in Descartes's method leads to the certainty of the I as the ineradicable "who" of reflection (the one who does the thinking, doubting, dreaming, and so on), and the doubt about salvation, which leads to the certainty of the I as the "who" of trust (the one who does the trusting involved in the question of the certainty of salvation), show the temporality and the uncommon singularity of the I as such. The most radical doubt about the reality of the world and the self cannot but reassert the ineradicability of the I as the "who" of the doubting, just as the deepest fall from the ideal of human perfection cannot but reinstate the I as the "who" of trust (that is, the one who has always already been brought back). These two appearances of the egoity of the self come together in a certain way in Heidegger's analysis of the call of conscience in *Sein und Zeit*, §§54–60 (hereafter referred to as *SuZ*). Conscience is there analyzed as the voice, coming from the futurity of the ego, that summons the self to answer for the "not" (to become *schuldig*), and the I appears in connection with what is a pure potentiality, a "can" that can never be turned into a "do" in the first-person singular, the potentiality of not being. The "owing" that we do when we have a debt to pay is traced back to an "ought" that is a modality of

18. Immanuel Kant, *Streit der Fakultäten* (Hamburg: Felix Meiner, 1959), p. 62.

our being; and the proper form of this modality, the form in which I appear as I, has to do with the possibility of death.

The Appearing of the I

Heidegger's analysis can be used to show more than just the phenomenon of the I-can-die. A few observations about his procedure may help us to see how these connections can be made, or, in other words, to see how the phenomenon of the I appears, though not yet as such. The starting point is provided by the everyday (*vulgär*, popular) understanding of conscience. This everyday understanding is taken back to its existential ontological basis; the popular understanding is given an existentialist interpretation. The existentialist interpretation is, in turn, confirmed by reference to the popular conception of conscience as an understanding which expresses an ontological phenomenon in ontic terms. Whether, as Heidegger says, the theological interpretation of conscience (God speaking to us through an inner voice) can only be seen as a version of the popular understanding is a question we can defer for the moment.

At all events, what Heidegger's analysis of conscience makes clear is the way in which the I appears not in relation to being or thinking but in relation to *non*being. The I of conscience is not the I of "I am" but the I of "I am not." At first, this seems to contradict the result of the method of doubt. For it seems to disclose the I in a way that it cannot be disclosed, namely, as one who am *not*. If the method of doubt shows anything, it shows that the I who thinks cannot not be. It is the I which cannot but in some way assert itself as real. Yet the contradiction between the I appearing in reflection, as incontrovertibly self-assertive, and the I of conscience is only apparent. What is often overlooked in Heidegger's analysis of the voice of conscience, and the existential possibility it implies, is that the I appears in relation to the *not* only in the form of potentiality for being, a *Seinkönnen*, a can-be. We cannot lose sight of this aspect of the analysis if we are to see how it is that the I appears in the voice of conscience.[19]

---

19. David Wood provides a general evaluation of Heidegger on conscience in *The Deconstruction of Time* (Atlantic Highlands: Humanities Press International, 1989), pp. 179–219. But he approaches Heidegger in so different a way that one loses sight of the relation between the self and its being, which seems to me to be the issue in Heidegger's own account.

The experience that is at the basis of interpretations of conscience is that of feeling guilty, that is, answerable for an obligation; and the obligation can have the form of *not* having done what should have been done or of having done what should *not* have been done. This combination of the *should* and the *not* is what constitutes the distinguishing feature of the experience of conscience. But this basic feeling—"feeling" is used here in a general sense—is interpreted in one way in the popular understanding and in another way in an existentialist analysis. Characteristic of the popular understanding is that it puts this feeling into what Heidegger called "ontic" terms. Hence, it understands conscience as having the structure of someone calling someone else to account for not having done what was right or for having done what was wrong. From this, the popular understanding can also move on to think of conscience as the voice which informs me about the right thing to do and which judges me when I have not done it. This is to say that the popular understanding identifies the *elements* of a whole existential structure as though they were things on the order of actual *persons* being related to each other. Conscience as a whole then becomes a kind of juridical forum, a court in which one's deeds are judged as good or bad.

What is left out of account in this popular interpretation (and in the theological variation which construes it as a relation of man to God) is the fact that the voice of conscience is heard only within and that there are no "ontic" entities corresponding to the elements of the experience of conscience. We may owe someone some money. That is an ontic relation. The one who owes, the one to whom it is owed, and the money (or favor, and the like) are all temporally and spatially distinguishable entities. That ontic relation is different from the relation implied in the experience of conscience. The voice of conscience is not the voice of another person addressing me; what conscience says cannot be put into writing or into words; and the I who hears the voice of conscience is not a person distinct from the voice of conscience. This difference between conscience and ontic relations is part of the experience of conscience itself, but it is suppressed in the popular interpretation. Thus, the task for existential interpretation is to show the *ontological structure* which is implied in the experience of conscience and which is interpreted ontically in the popular understanding. The ontological interpretation shows the experience of conscience not as the relation of one entity (one person) to another entity (another person) but as a structure of the being that is the being of human beings—in other words, a structure of *Dasein*.

Let us follow Heidegger's analysis a bit further before drawing together the results. That Dasein is the being of the entities that we human beings are means that "be-ing there" is what we are implicitly always doing in whatever particular actions we are taking. (In the later Heidegger, the Heidegger of poetic interpretation, "be-ing there" is by and large replaced by "thinking of [*An-denken*]," but this is a terminological variation more than a change in the understanding of Dasein.) Our writing or reading a book, our talking to someone else, our walking and running, and everything else we do are all ways in which we are be-ing there. The character of that being is identified as care, or *Sorge*. In be-ing there, we are always caring in one way or another—taking care of tasks, caring for others, caring about causes. Thus, Heidegger identifies care as the being of Dasein as such. The *meaning* of that being, the meaning of care as the being of Dasein, is temporality. In this way, the temporality of the I, which Descartes mentions but does not develop, becomes a theme for Heidegger's discussion by way of care as the being of existence and by way of temporality as the meaning of the being of existence. The significance of the distinction between the "being" of something and the "meaning" of that being we can leave undiscussed here. But it is worth noting, parenthetically, that in connection with other things there is no difference between their being and the meaning of their being, whereas in connection with us as human beings there is a distinction not only between our being and the meaning of our being but also between the *Dasein* that is our being and the care, *Sorge*, that is our activity of be-ing.

Heidegger's designation of the modes of being is by this time familiar. The being of tools, like hammers when we use them, is a being-at-hand (*Zuhandensein*); the being of objects, like trees or electrons when we are observing or investigating them, is a being-on-hand (*Vorhandensein*); our own being is just a being-here-now (*Dasein*); and the being of other human beings is a being-there-too (*Auch-mit-dasein*). In connection with tools and objects nothing is made of a difference between their being and the meaning of their being. But there is an express difference between our being and the meaning of our being. Temporality is the meaning of our being, and *Sorge* is the being of our being as a being-here-now. That is to say, if we are comparing the being of objects with our being, it is sufficient to say that objects are *vorhanden* and we are *da*. But if we ask what we are "doing" when we are be-ing here and now, the answer is that we are "caring" in one way or another; we are taking care of, caring for, caring about this or that.

But how do we move from the experience of conscience to an analysis of the existential structure it expresses? Heidegger's steps are rapid. Conscience "discloses" something, and that is reflected even in the popular understanding of it. It is, thus, related to that aspect of Dasein which is called its *Erschlossenheit*, its "disclosedness," or its openness. What the popular interpretation of conscience takes to be the disclosing of something by one entity (speaking through conscience) to another entity (me) is, ontologically interpreted, something that Dasein is always doing by its very being. Conscience is one expression of its be-ing, just as writing and reading and talking and listening and the like are other expressions. "Disclosing" is what we are always doing when we are be-ing at all. Moreover, as an earlier part of Heidegger's analysis indicates, the constituent elements of this disclosing are *Befindlichkeit, Verstehen, Verfallen*, and *Rede*. Where we *find* ourselves (where the "here-and-now" is), that we already *understand* ourselves and our world in a certain way, that we understand ourselves as one *case* of people in general, and that we have a certain way of *talking* about things—these are the four constituents of the disclosing that we do by our be-ing at all. What are we disclosing? We are disclosing being, as a particular here-and-now of being.

This is the first step in moving from the experience of conscience to understanding it ontologically—conscience belongs to the disclosing aspect involved in our be-ing. But conscience does its telling or disclosing in the form of "calling"—conscience calls to us. The voice of conscience is not an actual voice, as are the voices of people around us. In that sense it is the voice of silence. It addresses us in the form of calling to us; it belongs to *Rede*, discourse, the fourth of the four constituents of disclosure. Conscience refers to the discourse which is an original discourse of the self with itself, and a discourse in which the self calls to itself. This understanding obviously involves a partial correction of the popular understanding. Conscience is popularly understood as telling us what to do and judging whether what we have done is good or bad, right or wrong, and the judgment is always related to what we have already done—a bad conscience comes from our having done what we know we should not have done. Yet a closer inspection of the experience of conscience shows that this popular understanding is superficial. Conscience never tells us what to do, and the accusation of conscience, which is popularly understood as a judgment of what we have done, is, if we look more closely at the experience, not a verdict upon the quality of our action but a voice addressing us and summoning us to be willing to answer for the *not*. In Heidegger's terms, conscience calls upon us by summoning us to become guilty, *schuldig werden*. But what activity of be-ing is meant by becoming "guilty," or becoming one-who-owes? It is the activity of answering for the *not*, or, in a certain way, *not* being. What first appears as a judgment passed by conscience upon the quality of our actions is upon closer inspection not a judgment upon actions at all but a summons to answer for something, and, in this case, to answer for the negative that is expressed in the combination of *not* and *should* (doing what one should not, or not doing what one should). Conscience, in its proper function, is not the voice that judges the deed as *not* being what it should be; rather, it is the voice that calls upon us to be the one who owes, the one who will answer for the negative indicated by the word *not*. "Conscience," as Heidegger formulates it, "is the call of care from the uncanniness of being-in-the-world—the call which summons Dasein to its ownmost potentiality-for-being-guilty" (*SuZ*, §59, p. 289).

Conscience is, in other words, the attestation of not being at home in the world. What is experienced in the talk of not having done what one should have done, or of having done what one should not have done, is the more primordial "guilt" of not being at home in the world. What is it that conscience is telling me in the reflection "I should not have done what I did"? It is giving me to understand that I am to answer for ("should") the *not*; it is, in other words, calling to me to be willing to answer for *not* being in the world. The uncanniness, the *Unheimlichkeit*, of the world is the worldly quality that discloses the being of the self *as an I*. As "an entity" or "a self" one can very well be in the world; but the I as I is not a thing in the world, and it is just this that conscience makes known. To a judge one might very well answer as one human being to another; to the voice of conscience one can only answer as *I*. Only I *as I* can hear or respond to the voice that is the voice of conscience; the only form in which one can be addressed by the voice of conscience is the form of the first person singular.[20] It is the call *of care*, that is, of the being of Dasein. It is the call of being, not just of any being, but of the being of Dasein—the call issued by that which we are doing when we are be-ing in the world at all. It is the call coming from being in the world, in which care—that is, our being—summons us to be in the world on our own, that is, as *I* exposed to the world; and this occurs when the self can see itself related to the negative.

Significantly, the I appears here in relation to *not* being. What we are doing (how we are be-ing) when we listen to the voice of conscience by being willing to have a conscience (*Gewissen-haben-wollen*) is be-ing not, that is, being as the one who answers for "not" being there (in the world). The willingness to have a conscience is the willingness to let ourselves be connected with the negative, and that is simultaneously to be a self as *I*. Conscience attests to the fact that we *can* answer for the negative as well as the positive, that being in the world involves our caring not only by the using of what is in hand, the investigation of what is on hand, and the solicitude for others who are there too, but also by answering for *not* being.

This existential interpretation corrects the popular interpretation of conscience, but it can do so because the popular interpretation already contains a recognition of what the existential interpretation makes explicit (such as the fact that only I can hear my conscience, and the only conscience I can hear as a voice of conscience is my own) and because a closer inspection of the experience of conscience shows the features of it which do not become clear in the popular interpretation. In conscience the self calls to itself; the self that is occupied with care calls to itself to be itself as *I* in the world (in Johannine language: to be in the world but not of the world).

The full dimensions of the I which appears here in relation to the negative come out, however, only in the *Entschlossenheit*, the decisive kind of openness, that is connected with being at the end, *Sein zum Tode*. The possibility of death, the can-be that is indicated in "I can die," is the possibility that radically isolates the I from being in the world and thus makes it whole.[21] Here the I appears in relation to a can-be ("I can die") that can never be converted into a do-be. Dying (being not) is what I always "can" do but never "do" do as "I." The uniqueness of the being-not that is designated as "my" death is that it is something I always can do but never do do as I; it is the *not* that I always can. "I can die," just as anyone and everyone does; but the occurrence or doing that is projected in the "I can die" is one that, when it occurs, is no longer what "I" do nor is it something that has befallen "me." I "am" no longer "there" as the one doing it or the one to whom it is done. Hence, the *I* appears as a whole in relation to the end (my death) and it appears in the form of a pure possibility, that is, a genuine "I can" that can never become an "I do" or "I did." Ending is not like taking a trip. Of taking a trip, we can say "I can do it" and "I am doing it" or "I have done it." Of ending (my-death), we can always only say "I can end" but not "I have ended."

Through the method of doubt, the I appears in reflection as the one who cannot but assert itself; it appears as ineradicably certain, although the certainty is connected with a temporality. The other side of doubt is the call of conscience. In doubting I endeavor to deny the reality of anything and everything and in the process un-cover the I as the one whose reality cannot but be asserted even by the most radical doubt; the I appears as indissolubly connected with an "am." By contrast, the I as it appears in the call of conscience is related, not to being, but to nonbeing. For conscience is a witness

21. In *Speech and Phenomena*, where he is assessing the end of metaphysics in relation to Husserl's epistemology, Derrida throws another light on the meaning of my-death. Metaphysically, I imagine the ideal world, which the empirical world is always approximating but never achieving, as still being there when I die, which means, in effect, that "I" am somehow still there or that my presence can be reenacted infi-nitely by the word *I* just as the ideal object, in Husserl's account, can be represented infinitely by the word that names it—the ideal can always be recalled to mind. But if absolute knowledge means, not the coincidence of the infinitely repeatable I and the infinitely repeatable ideal, but a finite appearing of the infinite *différance*, then history is closed. It is so because something appears—the relation to my-death—which bursts the metaphysical oppositions. "The appearing of the infinite *différance* is itself finite [in the relation to my-death]. Consequently, *différance* . . . becomes the finitude of life as an essential relation with oneself and one's death. *The infinite* différance *is finite.* It can therefore no longer be conceived within the opposition of finiteness and infinity, absence and presence, negation and affirmation" (Jacques Derrida, *Speech and Phe-nomena*, translated by David B. Allison [Evanston: Northwestern University Press, 1973], p. 102).

to the negative possibility of the self. It attests to a possibility (a can-be) that is uniquely *eigentlich*, uniquely appearing in relation to the pronoun of the first person singular. Death, existentially understood, is the "can" that is inconvertible into a "do" when it is referred to the self as "I." As the end, death is the possibility of having no possibility of being in the world. As such, it reveals the I of the one who is in the world and reveals it as the "who" of what is purely a can-be. In the method of doubt and in the call of conscience, we have, then, the phenomenon of the I in relation to being and in relation to being not. In the act of negating (the world and itself), the I appears in its ineradicable being; in hearing the call of conscience, the possibility of being negated (the I-can-come-to-an-end), the I appears in relation to, as answerable for, the "not."

If the I can thus appear in the reflections of one person alone, it can also appear in the meeting with other persons. For this aspect of the phenomenon we can take as a guide the ethics of the theologian who stands between historicism and dialectical theology, Wilhelm Herrmann.[22] The terms in which he explicated this phenomenon in his *Ethik* are those of a *Lebensphilosophie* and a neo-Kantianism which associates the egoity of the I especially with practical reason or the will; and there are good reasons, some of which were indicated in the misunderstandings of conscience that Heidegger mentions in his analysis, for not accepting the notion that the I of the self is really apparent only in practical reason. But the analysis of trust that Herrmann gives can be understood, independently of the neo-Kantian framework in which it is expressed, as a phenomenology of the I which adds to what appears in the Cartesian meditation and in Heidegger's analysis of conscience.

The context of Herrmann's account of the self in his *Ethik* is the question how there can be an ethos other than an ethos of self-assertion, for self-assertion is the natural drive in things.[23] One might

22. The continuity and discontinuity are nicely epitomized in the inscription that was Herrmann's last direct communication with Barth: "Nonetheless, with best regards from Wilhelm Herrmann." See Karl Barth, "The Principles of Dogmatics" (1925), *Theology and the Church: Shorter Writings 1920–1928,* translated by Louise Pettibone Smith (New York: Harper & Row, 1962), p. 239. Barth's testimony to his being a "disciple" suggests the same kind of continuity. "I cannot deny that through the years I have become a somewhat surprising disciple of Herrmann," he remarks (ibid., p. 238).

23. Wilhelm Herrmann, *Ethik* (Tübingen: J. C. B. Mohr [Paul Siebeck], 1901, 1913⁵).

even say that the inescapable self-assertion that appears to thinking in the method of doubt is a reflected form of this natural drive. The natural drive is attested by the self-assertion in reflection as the possibility of not being is attested by conscience. If negation is the dynamics of life, then the effort to negate, as in the method of doubt, is an expression of those dynamics, and the unavoidable assertion of the I which the result of that method discloses is the basic drive in nature itself. On the face of it, another ethos seems impossible. Both nature and reflection inescapably assert the ego even in the attempts to deny it. The appearance of an I that is other than self-asserting depends, therefore, upon something other than nature and reflection. It depends upon something that can break into the circle of self-assertion.

This something is an event and an appropriation. The event takes place when it *happens* that someone we meet fills us with "respect" and "trust" (p. 109). In meeting a person whom we can trust, we are freed from the "unlimited power of natural life," and there "arises in us" the thought of "a value that is independent of our interest" (p. 39). That experience takes place, as Herrmann puts it, in certain thoughts, which make the one who is thus filled with trust *selbständig*, or which, in other words, show the I of the one who, in response to the meeting with the other, finds it possible to trust (pp. 39, 110). The three thoughts are those of a value independent of us, of an inner autonomy in the other, and of a free obligation which is ours (pp. 39ff.). The one from whom the trust is elicited by being "filled with" respect for the other is not a dead or passive recipient of an action but is rather the one who becomes a free self, an I, in the thoughts formed as one's own response to the other. To respect a person is to "bow before something [invisible and unprovable] in him" (p. 40). The thought of the unconditional demand, which in Kantian terminology means the thought that something is to be done just because we are enabled to do it, is the thought that is awakened in the relation of trust, but it is a thought that we need to produce within ourselves in order to become the free I that the relation brings about. In another formulation of Herrmann's, the thought that we are to produce in ourselves as the end goal (*Endzweck*), which is humanity, is the thought that makes us stand on our own in the experience of being filled with respect and trust. In one sense we are dependent; for we cannot become one who trusts without the encounter with someone who instills the respect in us. But

in another sense we stand on our own at the same time; for the
movement of trust (which takes place "in" the thought of humanity
we form) is one in which we come to stand on our own, or become
selbständig.[24] And what is this *Selbständigkeit* of which Herrmann
speaks if not the *Eigentlichkeit* that Heidegger contrasts with the generality of human subjects? What appears in the act of trust is the
phenomenon of the I. The experience of being filled with respect
shows what we *can* be. The thoughts that we form (to use Herrmann's phraseology) make the possibility our own. That we *can* be
freed from the self-assertion natural to the I is the content of the
experience of being filled with respect for the other; that we *do* become someone other than a self-asserting I is the content of our
forming the thoughts which appropriate that possibility and which,
therefore, show the self as the I who trusts. "This consciousness,
given with the ethical willing, of an independent and inexhaustible
life is freedom" (p. 65).

How are we to compare the I of "I trust" with the I of "I think"?
When I think, I am. That is what Descartes has shown; it is what is
always shown in the method of doubt when we try to enact the
thought that we are not thinking. For in the thought that we are not
thinking, what is incontestable is the "I" who does the thinking or
dreaming or anything else. How is the "I" of trusting related to the
I of this doubting? We can approach this question by recalling how
two different traits of the I appear in the method of doubt and in the
audition of conscience. The I of the *cogito* is the I in its actuality;
and, if what we are always doing when we think or dream or sleep
or eat, and so on, is in one way or another be-ing; if, in other words,
"be-ing" serves to designate the fundamental action of a subject, then
the actuality of the I is also the action of "I am." In that sense, the
method of doubt shows the inescapability of the "I am." The *actuality* of the I appears, and it appears as the actuality of the one who
is doing the be-ing in all of the particular actions. It relates the I to
being. Hearing the voice of conscience, by contrast, discloses the
pure *possibility* of the I, an "I can" which is never convertible to an "I
do." This possibility appears, however, not in relation to being but
in relation to a "not," for the possibility of having no possibility of
being in the world, or the possibility expressed in saying "I can end,"

24. In the movement of trust we are "abhängig und selbständig zugleich"
(p. 110).

shows the I as the one answerable for the "not" contained in the idea of no longer being there. This "not" is the existential ontological aspect of the ontic owing that we do when we have a debt or an obligation.

What appears in trust is a third trait: the I in its *freedom*, not just the practical freedom of morality but the freedom of the I to be as such. By the concept of freedom we mean what is just the edge, or the boundary, the dividing line, between actuality and possibility. When we think of a boundary, like the boundary between two states, we recognize that the boundary itself is "invisible." We cannot, literally, stand *on* the boundary between two countries. When we cross from one country to another, the boundary between them refers, strictly speaking, to what we shall be crossing or to what we have already crossed but never to a place where we are or can stand. There is no time or place that belongs to the boundary, the dividing line itself. Thus, being "on the boundary" means moving from one side to the other side; it does not mean being at a place or time other than on one side or the other of the boundary.[25] This conception of boundary can help us to place the trait of freedom in relation to actuality and possibility. The I is always either actual or possible. Its freedom is the boundary between its actuality and its possibility. Crossing from the "I just am (I just *do be*)" of actuality to the "I always can not (I can *not be*)" involves passing through freedom. From one side, freedom is the limit upon actuality; from the other side, it is the limit upon possibility. Freedom is what separates actuality from possibility, when viewed from one side, and possibility from actuality when viewed from the other side. It is beyond actuality for the "I just am" and beyond possibility for the "I can not."

The concept of freedom is, in other words, related to the concepts of actuality and possibility differently from the way in which a generic concept (ground) is related to specific concepts (differences). A generic concept contains what is common to the specific concepts, appearing in all of them, and we can state that common content apart from the specific expressions of it. (We can say, for example, what belongs to being a tree as such, apart from whether the tree is a maple or an oak or of some other species.) A boundary concept has no content of its own; its only content is to separate and join the

25. Thus Kierkegaard's analysis in *The Concept of Dread:* there is nothing between the state of temptation and the state of having fallen.

two concepts which it bounds. Thus, we cannot say what the free-dom of the I itself is, as though it were a general concept having the specific forms of actuality and possibility. Rather, freedom is the line that one crosses when moving from the "I do" to the "I can" and back again. It is what makes actuality and possibility other than each other although inseparable from each other. From the side of pos-sibility, actuality looks like necessity; from the side of actuality, possibility looks like nothing. From the side of I-can-be, actuality looks like an I-must-be; and from the side of I-am, possibility looks like an I-can-not-be. Thus, the call of conscience, which is related to the possibility at the edge of the pure actuality of the I-am, can only appear as a call to answer for a "not"; and from the side of self-assertion, or the will to be a self, the method of doubt appears to disclose only a blind or unintelligible necessity, the "I just am" ap-pears to the "I can be" as an "I must be."

How, then, does freedom appear as a trait of the I? Here Herr-mann's *Ethik* proves helpful, for it shows that the I of *trusting* is the I in its existential freedom. Viewed from the side of pure ac-tuality, trusting is what I, as I, *can* do (and do do) but never *must* do. It both is and is not possibility, when possibility means the feature of the I that appears in the "I can end." Viewed from the other side, the side of pure possibility, trusting is what I always just do do but never have the power to do. It both is and is not actuality, when actuality means the feature of the I that appears in the "I am" through the method of doubt. The free I appears as the "one who" of the act of trusting. Heidegger provides an account of this trait of freedom in his later thought about the *Er-eignis* (self-appropriating event) that is connected with the *Es gibt* (a giving). It will be to our advantage here, however, to follow a less Heideggerian description.

Herrmann identifies the experience of trust as the one in which appears a self free of the network of cause-effect connections to which the concept of nature refers. Freedom is not the absence of causality but something other than the whole of cause and effect. Characteristic of the experience of trust is that its occurrence is, at one and the same time, something that happens to me and some-thing that I do. I can trust only because something happens to me which enables me to do so (by, in Herrmann's terms, filling me with respect for the one who elicits trust); but it is also true that I can trust only because, again in Herrmann's terms, I form the thoughts that make the act of trusting my own free act.[26] Trusting is, therefore, both an event and an appropriation. In it gift and giving are so closely interwined that their occurrence is simultaneous. It is, in other words, an experience of something that both is and is not an action or a passion, a possibility or an actuality. It has the characteristics of the occurrence and the doing that are the boundary, or edge, between the actuality and possibility of "I am" and "I can not-be."

What is it to trust? The "trust" meant here is different from the acting on assumption which Richard Swinburne calls trust in his investigation of the nature of faith.[27] "To trust a man," Swinburne writes, "is to act on the assumption that he will do for you what he knows that you want or need, when the evidence gives some reason for supposing that he may not and where there will be bad consequences if the assumption is false." To act on an assumption is "to do those actions which you would do if you believed" that what is assumed is true. For example, a patient "who trusts a doctor to cure him acts on the assumption that the doctor will do for the patient what he knows that he needs him to do." The reason for supposing that the doctor may not do so may be, for example, that "attempts to cure are not always successful," and the "bad consequences" are that the patient will remain ill if the doctor does not cure him. The action of trust does not itself require that one believe the assumption to be true; it requires only that the action taken is the action one would take if one believed it to be true. The "belief that in fact guides you is the belief that there is at least a small, but not negligible, probability" that the doctor will cure you. In that sense, to "act on the assumption p is to do those actions which you would do if you believed that p." Or, to cite another example, an "escaping British prisoner of war may have trusted some German by telling him of his identity and asking for help." The assumption here is that the Ger-

---

26. This is different, of course, from the Kantian notion of the practical I. But it is also different from having recourse to the feeling or relation of love, as is done in Francis Jacques, *Différence et subjectivité* (Paris: Aubier-Montaigne, 1982), for example, p. 99. Quoted by Louis Dupré, "Alternatives to the Cogito," *The Review of Metaphysics* 40, no. 4 (June 1987): 703.

27. Richard Swinburne, "The Nature of Faith," in *Faith,* edited by Terence Penelhum (New York: Macmillan, and London: Collier Macmillan, 1989), pp. 207–25; quotations in this paragraph are all from p. 214. The essay is reprinted from Richard Swinburne, *Faith and Reason* (Oxford: Clarendon Press, 1981), chap. 4.

man "will do for him what he knows that he wants (viz., provide help), when many Germans are ill-disposed towards escaping British prisoners."

In this account Swinburne assigns trust to the sphere of action. To trust is to act on an assumption. The assumption can be stated as a proposition about what the one you trust will do for you; the patient assumes that the doctor will cure him. But not every acting on an assumption is an act of trust. It is so only if there is reason to believe that the assumption may not be true (the doctor may not cure the patient) and that bad consequences will follow its not being true. Noteworthy here is that Swinburne does not say that the action is an attestation of trust but that trusting is the action itself—"to trust a man is to act." One might modify the definition by saying that the action attests a trust, or is the practical expression of the trust, rather than that it is the trust itself. Even with this adaptation, however, the "trust" that Swinburne describes is different from the trust which is made possible by an encounter and appropriated by the formation of the thought of what one can be. To see that difference, let us try to work out more exactly the conception of trust that appears in Herrmann's ethics.

We can start with a description of what occurs when one person trusts another person, when trust is defined not by reference to another kind of experience of which trust might be a deficient form but as a mode of being of its own. This, in essence, is what Herrmann's account provides. When we "trust" a person, we do not do so with the thought that, having investigated the person's history and abilities, we conclude there is a high correlation between what he says he will do and what he does do. That we may use the word "trust" in such a sense no one would deny. But trust as an original mode of being a self is something else. It is a relation between persons of such a kind that the very presence of the other person elicits from me a response of trust. In Herrmann's neo-Kantian terms, what radiates from the other person is pure "good will." The meeting is one in which I am "filled with" respect and I appropriate that gift by forming the thought of doing something good or right just because I can do so and for no other reason—that is the thought of "humanity." That I just can do so is not, strictly speaking, a reason for doing so. It is an expression of the originating of an action that is purely free, neither caused nor uncaused, neither motivated nor unmotivated, because its characteristics are those of the boundary between caused and uncaused, motivated and unmotivated.

THE SUBJECTIVITY OF THE SELF: THE I AS SUCH   *27*

Because it involves an "I can," trusting is related to possibility, and hence to the possibility of coming to an end. But it differs from that pure possibility because the "end" to which it comes is not non-being (the possibility of my being-not) but rather the end of the *self-assertion* that is inescapable for the I either in its actuality or in its pure possibility. It represents a genuine *self*-negation that my-death does not represent. Trusting is a self-negation, that is, a negation of the self-assertion that characterizes the pure actuality of "I am."

This provides us with a preliminary description of the experience of trust. It is a description of trust in ontic terms, as a relation taking place between one person and another. But we can give an ontological interpretation of the experience by showing the structure of the self that is contained in the person-to-person relation. Is there a guideline for doing so? In the analysis of conscience, the experience of the voice of conscience provides a guideline for interpreting an actual relation of debt in ontological terms. The experience of conscience is midway between the experience of owing something to someone and the existential understanding of being finitely (being as the one who always can end) in which I appear as the one who answers for the "not." Is there, similarly, an experience between the ontic experience of trusting another person and the existential understanding of being freely on one's own?

That intermediate experience seems to be the one Buber analyzed as the encounter of I and thou. For we recall that the "thou" of which Buber speaks cannot be equated with another person. I can encounter a tree as a "thou"; I can also encounter transpersonal powers (spiritual powers) as a thou. What differentiates among these encounters is not whether the "thou" is really encountered but the relation to language. Encounters with the "thou" in a tree or other objects are sublinguistic; encounters with the "thou" in other human beings are linguistic; and encounters with the thou in transpersonal powers are language-creating. In Herrmann's account, this "thou" of which Buber speaks is the "good will." Although this account makes no allowance for our encountering the "good will" in entities other than persons, and although Herrmann identifies it with the personality of the person, still it is more than just the person.[28] In any case, however, the kind of experience which serves as a guideline for interpreting the experience of personal trust ontologically—in chapter

---

28. One who lives according to the kind of ethical willing that contains the consciousness of inexhaustible life and freedom is called a "person" (*Ethik*, p. 5).

3, we shall consider why, strictly speaking, this will be a theological rather than an ontological interpretation—is an experience in which something other than another person instills the trust.[29] That anything *can* enable trust as does an encounter with persons is the indication that trust is not only an ontical relation, an ontical phenomenon, but also an existential (ontological or theological) phenomenon. Thus, I who appear as the one who trusts is the I as such in its freedom.

The I that shows itself in the method of doubt is, then, the I of pure actuality; the I that shows itself in the anticipation of death is the I of pure possibility; and the I that shows itself in the evocation of trust is the I of pure freedom. Does this exhaust the traits of the phenomenon of the I? Let us leave this question provisionally unanswered in order first to take a look at some pertinent texts. Heidegger notes that what is shown in dying (*Sterben*) is that death is ontologically constituted by *Jemeinigkeit* and *Existenz* (*SuZ*, §45, p. 240), the former referring to the way it is always related to the self in the form of "my" own and the latter referring to the "who" of whose own death it is. "Seiendes," Heidegger had written in an earlier section (*SuZ*, §9, p. 45), is "ein *Wer* (Existenz) oder ein *Was* (Vorhandenheit)"; an entity is either a "what," something that is on hand (*vorhanden*), or a "who," something that projects itself upon a possibility (*existierend*). "To exist," in this existentialist sense, means to project oneself as a can-be that is one's own; and that projecting means, in turn, to be able to understand oneself in the being of the entity that is uncovered in the projecting (*SuZ*, p. 263). In other words, "to exist" means to be able to understand oneself "in the being of" the entity that is uncovered by projection. In the case of death, what is uncovered is the possibility of being one who has no possibility of being in the world. To exist as the one-who-can-die is to project oneself as the "who" of not being able to be in the world. "Projecting" a self is the counterpart of "objectifying" an object. The being of *Existenz* is a project; of *Vorhandenheit*, it is an object. To objectify an entity is to answer the question what that entity is; and to project an entity is to answer who the entity is. If death as a

29. The ontological has to do with the structure of the self as being in the world; the theological has to do with the structure of the self as trusting the other. Being in the world is illuminated as an understanding of being, and hence ontological; trusting to the other is illuminated as a faith in God, and hence theological.

possibility of being has the characteristic of *Jemeinigkeit*, then the answer to the question "Who can die?" is given properly in the form "I." Does the I, then, which appears in its *actuality* in the method of doubt, in its *possibility* in the project of the end, and in its *freedom* in the evocation of trust, have yet another trait with which it can appear? What projection of the self can show more than has already been shown in these three? One possibility is that the freedom shown in trust has another aspect by virtue of which it can be *finite* freedom. Actuality is finite when measured by possibility, and conversely; freedom is finite when measured by something else. Our task is to uncover what that is. We can do so by contrasting the freedom of trust with the freedom of "following"; for the I who trusts is the self come into its own freedom to be on its own, whereas the I who follows is the self free to be finitely. We are free to trust when another fills us with respect. When are we free to follow?

"Following" has from early Greek and biblical times on carried an existential meaning along with its physical sense.[30] It can mean following a speaker's thoughts or following a wise man (as in Aristotle's ethics) or a friend or a loved one (as in Plato's *Phaedrus*). In religious literature it meant following a god. In Old Testament usage the verb came over time to designate a following after false gods and was used less and less of Israel's relation to Jahweh. In New Testament usage, it occurs only in connection with Jesus—as in Mark 8:34 (and parallels): "If anyone will come after me, let him take up his cross and follow me." That a disciple follows a master is a widely attested usage of the term; but this use too undergoes a change in connection with the disciples of Jesus in the New Testament, a change which suggests that the "who" of following shows a trait of the phenomenon of the I different from the traits of actuality, possibility, and the freedom of trust. This may also be shown by the fact that "following" never

---

30. See Gerhard Kittel's article ἀκολουθέω in *Theologisches Wörterbuch zum Neuen Testament*, edited by G. Kittel (Stuttgart: Kohlhammer Verlag, 1933), vol. 1, pp. 210–16. The word is used by Plato, as a verb or adjective, to refer to the way one state of affairs or one proposition follows from another; the noun (ἀκολουθία) appears but not in a technical sense. Aristotle uses ἀκολούθησις rather than ἀκολουθία. In the Stoic usage it has both physical and logical senses, but with the Latin translation (*consequentia*) the differentiated senses in Stoicism are lost and the Aristotelian sense becomes dominant. See E. G. Schmidt, "Akoluthie (ἀκολουθία)" in *Historisches Wörterbuch der Philosophie*, vol. 1 (Darmstadt: Wissenschaftliche Buchgesellschaft, 1971), col. 127f.

appears in a nominal form. Although the noun form already existed in the Greek language, the word appears in the New Testament only as a verb and only in connection with the action of following Jesus.

A consideration of some texts from Luke will show the features characteristic of "following." Luke reports Jesus as saying publicly ("to all"), "If any man would come after me, let him deny himself and take up his cross daily and follow me. For whoever would save his life will lose it; and whoever loses his life for my sake, he will save it" (Luke 9:23f.). Again, Luke reports one person as responding to Jesus' "Follow me!" by expressing a willingness to do so after first going home to bury his father. To him Jesus replied that the dead should be left to bury the dead, but "as for you, go and proclaim the kingdom of God" (Luke 9:60). Another person is willing to follow, after first saying farewell to those at home. To him Jesus said, "No one who puts his hand to the plow and looks back is fit for the kingdom of God" (Luke 9:62). The "following" of Jesus is, as these texts indicate, a spontaneous action to be done immediately (in response to the "Follow me!") and heedlessly of social or familial ties.[31] The call to follow calls one out of the everyday concerns of the world. Just after these events, Luke reports the commissioning of the seventy (or seventy-two), sent out two by two, who were to announce "peace," the possibility of being whole, or the coming of the kingdom of God, and who were to carry no provisions for their future needs (no purse, no bag, no extra sandals) but were to live from whatever was provided by those who responded with peace to the message of peace. If nothing else, these texts do indicate an isolating of the self of those called from any worldly or social connections. The "Follow me!" calls the hearers to disengage themselves from the cares of being in the world.

On the face of it, this is a call to the self to come to its own, to be "I," in the midst of being in the world by dwelling in a message of peace. The *Unheimlichkeit* of Dasein is its peace. The self is summoned to be wholly itself in the message that is borne. At least with the commissioning of the seventy, this is clear. Those who are sent are to be nothing other than ones who announce peace. If there is no response to the announcement, they must go on. If there is a

---

31. Although one might suppose that the word *immediately* is peculiarly associated with following in the New Testament, its usage there is not thus delimited and cannot be taken as a technical expression of the spontaneity of the following.

response, they are to live in the community disclosed or made possible by the message itself. They are not to live in the daily conventions; indeed, contrary to convention, they are not to greet anyone along the way but are to go directly to a house to which they speak peace. The existence peculiar to those who are sent is an existence in a message. They are who they are only in the message they bring; they exist only as ones who speak and hear a peace in and with the words; they are who they are in the words in which they dwell by saying and hearing.

Finally, we can note that, especially in John's gospel, the one who calls disciples to follow him identifies himself with the words "I am." The voice of the burning bush which once sent Moses to Egypt is the same as the voice of Jesus which summons and sends disciples and apostles. The self-identification of Jesus is the identification of the I before all time ("Before Abraham was, I am"). The power of the voice which summons and commissions is, thus, not an alien authority; it does not subject the ego of the disciple to the ego of Jesus. It is, rather, the power by which the I comes to itself, although in a manner different from heeding the call of conscience.[32] The call to follow is from the "I" of "I am" to the "I" of "I am." How so?

The manner in which this occurs through a human relationship is nicely depicted, if in a somewhat romanticized way, in Joachim Wach's "religio-sociological" analysis of the master-disciple relation. In a study first published in 1924, Wach delineates, in an often eloquent manner, the difference between the teacher-student and the master-disciple relation.[33] The former is based on a common interest in a subject matter; the latter is based on the personalities of the two. In the former, "the entire relationship is born and lives by means of the common interest in the object of study," and the persons of each are replaceable by others (p. 1). In the latter, "the significance [of the master] for the disciple rests in the master's personality, whose very character and activity are individual and irreplaceable," and the disciple's choice is correspondingly "grounded in the master's inclination, which grows out of a deep conviction regarding his 'calling'

32. See chapter 6 below.
33. Joachim Wach, "Master and Disciple: Two Religio-Sociological Studies," *Journal of Religion* 42, no. 1 (January 1962): 1–21. Translated from the German of 1924 by Susanne Heigel-Wach and Fred Streng. Wach's interest in this essay was to uncover some universal structures in these relations. But the essay itself is mainly confined to the description.

to discipleship" (p. 2). The master is unlike a prophet too; for, "while the person of the prophet in itself is not of decisive significance for the proposed mission, the master is the carrier of a metaphysical meaning" (p. 8). The "most sacred moment" comes when "the master finally turns the disciple back to himself," and it is "the specific tragedy of the master's life that he is destined to direct everything toward this parting" (p. 3). The disciple "follows after" the master until "the hour of decision" comes, an hour that "always must be the hour of parting"; the disciple must either choose himself and "take leave of the master, who was dearer to him than all things" or "deny himself, continuing to love the master, and so destroy completely the master's labor" (p. 3). To be a student belonging to the school of thought which is the same as the teacher's is "a unifying experience"; being disciples of the same master "is no basis for mutual love" but "often the basis for hate"; for to a disciple "it seems impossible that someone else should have a part in the relationship that ties the disciple to his master" (p. 5).[34]

Wach documents, from Buddhist, Greek, Islamic, and Christian materials, the many facets of this master-disciple relation. But it is the theme of the parting of the master that touches most closely on the ecstatic quality of the self that appears in the relation. Whether the term "tragic" is the right one to apply here, as Wach does when he writes that the knowledge which the master has is "a tragic one" (p. 9), may be disputed; for tragic freedom is a freedom defeated by its very greatness, whereas the freedom in finitude that "following" implies is a freedom reconciled with finitude. It does seem incontestable, however, that there is an element of self-sacrifice contained in being a master and that "the last great temptation" is "to remain a savior for one's self" (to use the "words of the Buddhist teachings"), a *pratyeka-buddha*, instead of becoming a redeemer of all, a *sammāsambuddha*. This self-giving on the part of the master corresponds to the self-giving on the part of the follower. In both cases, the ontological basis for being able to do so can be existentially interpreted as the "ecstatic" possibility contained in being a self. The sadness of the master as well as of the disciple in view of the necessity

---

34. Matters change after the teacher or master is gone. The students of a teacher's school of thought then break up into disputing factions, whereas disciples "are brought together through the image [of the master] which is sacred to each of them" (p. 5).

to take leave of each other might very well be common, if not universal, features of the master-disciple relation. But these emotions, expressing the sadness of finitude, are possible in the first place because the self has ecstatic capacity. That one *can* be called and *can* follow is the freedom in finitude.

If this is the nature of the relation at work between the caller and the called, the I calling to itself to be free in finitude, then the call to follow the master is the same as a call to be a self of one's own. When the call is heard as the voice of a true call, following is not different from coming to oneself but is, instead, a coming out of the world (or to one's self on one's own) that is *enacted* by the call of the summoner.

To this point, however, the call to follow may not seem to be different from what Herrmann analyzes as the awakening of trust. In both cases the deed that is the self's own is made possible by a happening which can be appropriated. It *happens* that another person fills me with respect and trust; I *appropriate* the freedom thus offered in the movement of my own thought by which I form the concept of the humanity of my being. Similarly, it *happens* that the voice of another summons me to follow, and I *appropriate* what is offered by my bearing the message of peace. What is the difference between the trust evoked by respect and the response called forth by being filled with the message of peace?

The analysis of trust provided thus far has not been sufficiently nuanced to make the difference clear. We need to introduce a distinction between hearing the voice of the other as an encounter with the thou (as in Buber) or, in neo-Kantian terms, with a pure good will and hearing the voice of the other as the confrontation of the I with the I in another place that is the self's own peace, its own being whole. The voice of the "I am" which comes from another person and can call me into being myself on my own by following it, not harbored by the worldliness of the world, sounds not from the thou but from the I. Following is, therefore, as different from trusting as the respect with which the other "fills" me is different from the summons, coming from elsewhere, that "sends" me. In the act of trust, the one trusted is other than the one trusting; in the act of following, the one followed is the same as the one following. We trust one whom we can address as "thou"; we follow one whom we can never address as "thou" but can hear as the "I" of our own peace or wholeness. The Jesus whom the disciples followed as a person other than their own persons "had to" die and be taken away from them; that is part of the following which leads them back to themselves on their own. A person whom one trusts has no such need to be taken away from the one who trusts; indeed, a trusting relation always includes both the one and the other. A following of the "I am" terminates not in there being the one and the other, the follower and the followed; it terminates in the follower's coming to be as "I" in the fullness of being I.

It is not coincidental that the message of the disciples is also the message that the kingdom of God is near. For does this not say that, existentially interpreted, the ontic relation of a disciple's following the master (when the master is the voice of "I am") is an ontological (more precisely, a theological) relation? that, in other words, the (ontic) relation of person to person—of a follower to one followed—can be given an ontological (theological) interpretation because there is in the ontic relation itself a guide to that understanding? The difference between the ontological and theological can be deferred to a later chapter. Here the purpose is to be clear on the difference between an ontic relation between two persons and an understanding of the structure of being a self at all which makes possible (and is thus contained in) the ontic relation. How can the I as I "find" itself by losing itself through following a call and a commission? It can do so insofar as, in addition to having actuality, possibility, and freedom, it shows itself as capable of being outside itself, that is, as capable of *ecstasy*, as the prodigal son can disown himself by his wandering until he comes to himself again. The ecstasy of the I is its being away from itself so that it must or can come back to itself in order to be whole. But this being whole is different from the *Ganzseinkönnen* connected with the possibility of not being in the world (Heidegger's *Sein zum Tode*). The call to follow is a call to become in fact what one already is. One person is capable of following another person and of becoming free in the process because the ownness of the I can be presented in the person of another. To the extent that the disciples of Jesus were "followers" of the "I am" of Jesus, the one they encountered in his person was not their "thou" but their "I," and in losing themselves in him, they came to themselves on their own. In attaching themselves to him, they attached themselves to one whose death left them on their own. His *exousia* ("authority," literally, "being-out," "ex-entitas") is not the power of a lord over a servant but the "being-outside," the appearance "without," of the egoity of the I of which we are normally aware "within" ourselves. That the I *can* so call and be followed is its ecstatic trait.

How is the ecstasy of the I related to its freedom, possibility, and actuality? It is most directly related to freedom. For it represents the freedom in finitude as possibility represents the finitude (the "endingness") of actuality. The self can be whole not only by projecting itself onto the possibility of its own not being (the anticipation of death, the possibility attested by the voice of conscience); it can be whole by projecting itself entirely onto one actuality (or, more exactly, by being retrojected upon itself by one actuality). This, again, is a theme that will require further elaboration. For purposes of the present chapter it is sufficient to take note of this ecstatic feature of the self—the feature described when we say that the I can appear to itself outside itself so that it comes back to itself by following the one whose voice is that of "I am."

We can, then, distinguish a call to follow from the call of conscience. Conscience calls us to answer for the "not" of being, and it attests the possibility of *Sein zum Tode*. The summons of "I am" is a different call; it is related to the possibility of being freely and wholly in the world and, that is to say, a way of being worldly other than through care. If death represents the be-ing that the self as I always *can* but never *does* (a pure possibility never convertible to an actuality), life represents the be-ing that the self as I always *does* but never *can*.[35] We always *can* but never *do* die; we always *do* but never *can* live, for we are never outside of life presented with it as a possibility to be actualized. The acoluthetic summons is the call to be in the world freely; it is the call of the voice of freedom in finitude, of the freedom to be in the world wholly.

Is there an attestation of this freedom comparable to the attestation that conscience gives of the possibility of not being in the world? There seems to be such an attestation, not only in the free creation of meaningful works, but also in the voice that tells us of our "vocation." Following a vocation is different from pursuing a profession. Like the voice of conscience, the voice of a vocation is one that can only be heard in the first person singular. "I" cannot tell

---

35. Herrmann remarks that the highest stage of consciousness is one at which it is possible to hold together the claim to an autonomous life and the fact of death, or, as one could say in more existential terms, the "can live" and the "must die" (*Ethik*, p. 64).

"you" what your vocation is; what "my" vocation is I can hear only as an inner call. Like conscience, then, vocation provides an attestation of a mode of being for the I. But there is a difference. In the case of conscience, the call is connected with the *not* of being that underlies the ontic relation of debt or owing; in the case of vocation, or one's "calling" in the world, the call is connected with the freedom to be that underlies the ontic relation in one person's following another person. The ontic relation of master and disciples, attested by a vocational call, is affiliated ontologically with the call to follow, just as the ontic relation of debtor to creditor is affiliated ontologically with the not-being that is attested by conscience. The ontological (or theological) structure which explicates how a disciple follows a master freely, a following in which the disciple becomes autonomous through following, is the structure of the self related to its own freedom to be whole in the world. The difference between the freedom that comes to be through trusting and the freedom that comes to be through following is the difference between freely being with another and freely being whole. In trust we are with the other in freedom; through following we come to be whole on our own in the world. A community of trust is correspondingly different from a community of peace. The former is based on the freedom to be; the latter is based on the freedom to be finitely or to be in the world wholly.

2

The Being of the Self

THE SUBJECTIVITY OF THE I, AS
analyzed in the preceding chapter, is not the same as the being of
the I—the "am" of "I am I" or "I am this-one-here" (*Da-sein*).
The difference between the two is related to, but not the same as,
the distinction between self-consciousness and self-relation (or self-
definition).[1] Self-relation expresses the being of the I (just as the
relation of a predicate to a subject expresses the being of an entity);
self-consciousness is the awareness of the subjectivity of the self (the
"I"). Descartes formulated the being of the I when he said that "I
am a thinking thing [*res cogitans*]"; his thus defining the self was
different from his showing the ego of "I think," the ineradicable "one
who" of the thinking activity. In *The Sickness unto Death*, Kierkegaard formulated the being of the I when he wrote that the self is
the relating of the self to the self, or it is that in the relation which
relates the self to itself.[2] There are other ways of formulating the
being of the self. But these formulations indicate the sense of the
word *being* that comes into play here: being means a *connection* of
some kind.[3] In propositions, or logical judgments, "being" means

1. On this see Ernst Tugendhat, *Self-Consciousness and Self-Determination*, translated by Paul Stern (Cambridge, Mass.: The MIT Press, 1986).
2. "The self is a relation which relates itself to its own self, or it is that in the
relation [which is that] the relation relates itself to its own self. . . . A synthesis is a
relation between two factors. So regarded, [as a synthesis of infinite and finite,] man
is not yet a self" (*Fear and Trembling and The Sickness unto Death*, translated by Walter
Lowrie [Garden City: Anchor Books, 1954], p. 146).
3. The word *being* can have other meanings, ranging from the word's being a
virtual synonym for God, especially when capitalized as Being, or for ultimate reality,
on the one side, to its being treated, on the other side, as a function in logical calculus.

the connection of individual with universal that is expressed by the copula in a judgment ("*A* is *a*"). In the case of the self, this embraces both "I am I" and "I am this-one-here." We can use this idea of the link between a subject and a predicate as a guide for delineating the sense of the concept of being and for considering how the being of the self shows itself as unconditional positing (Fichte), as care (Heidegger), and as gift (Herrmann).

Personal and Nonpersonal Being

We can begin with a distinction between personal and nonpersonal ("natural," "objective") being. The being of a person can be expressed in the judgment "I 'am' (you 'are,' etc.) this-one-here." This is, in Heideggerian language, Dasein. Nonpersonal being can be expressed in the judgment "This-thing-here 'is' a stone." In the first case, the universal term serves as the subject of the predication; in the second case, the universal is the predicate-term. As we shall see, this grammatical and logical feature indicates something about the mode of being that is expressed; for this difference provides a clue for distinguishing the modes of being. The being of a stone, for example, appears as the connection we can make between a particular percept, the object as pointed out by the adverbial demonstrative "this here," and the concept of a stone as such; it is the unity of individual and universal (or particular and general) which we apprehend when we understand this-thing-here "as" a stone. The word *as* designates nontemporally what the word *being* (*is, was, will be, has been*, and so on) designates with a temporal modification. For present purposes, it will not matter whether we work with four terms (individual, special, general, universal) or two terms (particular and general, individual and universal, or a similar pair) in designating

---

As the word is used here, it means a third element in addition to the perceptual and conceptual aspects of things; it refers to what is the object of "understanding" in contrast to the concrete individuals that are the objects of perception and to the abstract universals that are the objects of conception. "Being" is what we always "understand" but never "see" or "define," never sensibly "perceive" or abstractly "conceive." Kant's epistemology distinguishes understanding (*Verstand*) from intuition (*Anschauung*) and reason (*Vernunft*). In that terminology *Verstand* is closer to what is here called "conception (conceiving through an abstract thought)" than it is to "understanding," which is related properly to the "being" of things.

what is linked in our understanding of being.[4] In a brief formulation we can say, in this example, that the being of a stone appears as the connection of what we see as a stone with what we conceive as a stone, a connection made when we understand that the thing before us *is* a stone. "Being" is, thus, the proper object of understanding, rather than of perception (which is of singulars) or of conception (which is of universals). The same sense of the word is intended when we speak of personal being ("I am this-one-here") rather than of natural being.

The difference between the being of persons and the being of natural things, or *Existenz* and *Vorhandenheit* in Heideggerian language, is not a difference in the meaning of the word *being*.[5] Rather, it is a difference indicated by the change in relation between the general (or universal) and the particular (or individual). In the being

4. "The ancient philosophers called these [general names of qualities applicable in the same sense to individuals] universals or predicables . . . : *genus, species, specific difference, properties*, and *accidents*. Perhaps they may be more" (Thomas Reid, *Essays on the Intellectual Powers of Man*, edited by James Walker [Cambridge, Mass.: John Bartlett, 1850], p. 293). In the *Prior Analytics* (43A 25–44) and the *Posterior Analytics* (81B 10 to 84B 3), Aristotle makes the following distinctions among individuals, species, genera, and universals. *Individuals* are things that cannot be predicated of anything, but other things can be predicated of them. "PLATO is wise" and "SOCRATES is snubnosed" are two examples provided by Thomas Michael Tomasic in "The Logical Function of Metaphor and Oppositional Coincidence in the Pseudo-Dionysius and Johannes Scotus Eriugena," *Journal of Religion* 68, no. 3 (July 1988): 361–76. *Universals* are those things of which nothing can genuinely be predicated but which can be predicated of other things. "Socrates is HUMAN" or "Fido is a BEING." *Species* and *genera* are those things which can be predicated of other things and of which other things can be predicated. "Socrates is a man" and "Man is an animal." It is not clear to me why Tomasic thinks that, to Aristotle's Greek-speaking contemporaries as well as to "English-only" readers, it would have been "mystifying" why, according to Aristotle, "Plato is wise" ("Socrates is snub-nosed") is correct but "Wise is Plato" ("Snub-nosed is Socrates") is incorrect. Greeks as well as English speakers, Tomasic points out, use predicate adjectives, as in "Bewildered . . . am I." The matter with which Aristotle is concerned is not, however, whether there are predicate adjectives (nor even how to "support his antidualistic ontology") but whether, even when we say, for example, "The white thing is wood" (ὅταν τὸ λευκὸν εἶναι φῶ ξύλον) (*Post. An.* 83A 6), it is wood that is being predicated of white or the color white that is being predicated of wood. To this Aristotle answers that even in such cases, despite the grammar of the sentence, it is "the white" that is predicated of wood and not "wood" that is predicated of "the white."

5. The rationale of Heidegger's terminology is the fact that natural objects (*Vorhandenheit*) are on hand before "me," whereas the self (before whom objects are on hand) has to stand out (ex-sist) from the self to appear to the self (*Existenz*).

of a natural thing (such as a stone), the universal is found in the abstract concept of the thing which appears logically as the predicate of a subject; in the being of persons, the universal is in a pronoun which serves as the subject of a logical predicate.[6] Despite its grammatical form of first person singular, the I as such has the meaning of a universal, whereas the concretely perceptible this-one-here, the one whom I can see in a mirror and whom others can see, is the individual. "This-thing-here 'is' a stone" formulates an understanding of the being of the stone by predicating a general concept of a perceptible particular. "I am this-one-here" also formulates an understanding of being. But in this case it does so by predicating a concrete location, an embodiment as a placing and timing, of a universal idea. The location defined by "this-here-now" is always unique; it is the radically individualizing side of being. The general or universal indicated by the concepts of stone or entity-as-such or by the idea of I, by contrast, has applicability to an indefinite number of instances. "I am this-one-here" joins the universality of the thought "I" with the particularity of an embodiment; "this-thing-here is a stone" joins a particular sense-perception with the abstract concept of a stone.

The center of orientation for both is the "this-here" (or, more fully, the "this-here-now") which serves to indicate an individual entity uniquely. In the one case, the "this-here," serving as the subject-term of the judgment, is subsumed under its general concept, and our act of subsuming is the form in which we express the understanding of the being of the thing. In the other case, the "this-here," serving as the predicate-term of the judgment, designates the concrete location at which the named subject is found. In this latter case, illustrated by the judgment "I am this-one-here," the understanding of being does not involve an act of subsuming. Subsuming a particular under a general, or (in Kantian language) an intuition under a concept, ascribing a general predicate to a particular subject, including a particular in a universal—these are different ways of describing the act of understanding involved in such judgments as "This is a stone." With the judgment "I am this-one-here," the act of understanding does not subsume what is indicated by the subject-term

---

6. Pronouns (like demonstratives) show an entity; proper nouns (names) individualize in a name the entity shown; common nouns group individuals in a name; generic concepts define what the pronouns and nouns point out and group.

under what is conceived in the predicate-term; rather, it is an act of ascribing to the subject-term an assumption of the here-now indicated by the predicate-term. Our understanding of the being of a nonpersonal thing thus reflects a subjecting of the thing as perceived here and now to the thing as conceived generically, whereas our understanding of the being of a person reflects the taking on of a particular embodiment (here-now) by the subject of the thought. In brief, understanding the being of a natural thing means subsuming the particular under a general; understanding the being of a person means assuming a particular to the universal. The terms "subsuming" and "assuming" can, in other words, serve as guides for seeing the difference in the modes of being involved. When I understand myself as here-now, the action of understanding is one of taking on—the I takes on a particular here-now—so that the "this-one-here" is a particular location and temporalization of the I. In existentialist terminology, the way in which "I" assume the "here-now" is my "self-understanding." This is to say that the technical sense of self-understanding, or *Daseinsverständnis*, is that of joining the universality of the I as such with a particular embodiment that represents the here and now that the I has taken on. Strictly, we should not speak of "the I," since the universality of the subject is not given in the third person but in the first person—as "I" which can be said and thought at different times and different places. But for expository purposes, it is convenient to use phrasings such as "the I," "the ego," and "pure subjectivity."

What constitutes the particularity of a person's embodiment is not only the physical body. It is also the psychical body, that is, the nexus of memories, encounters, experiences, thoughts, skills, perspective, desires, and whatever else, which configure the individuality of a subject and prevent it from being interchangeable with another. The psychical and physical body makes each personal subject unique but does not alone constitute the being of a person. This being is, instead, the unity of that body with the pure subjectivity of "I." We can say *what* a physical or psychical body is in the same way that we can say what an individual tree is. But, strictly speaking, we cannot say what a person is but only who, where, and when it is. Personal being, so understood, is the unity of the idea of subjectivity (I as such) and a finite location (a psychic and physical embodiment that locates the here-now). From this it should be clear that the being of a person is not the same as the existence of a person.

Does the contrast just drawn between personal and natural being amount to the same as Heidegger's contrast of *Existenz* (the being of that entity of which we can say *who* it is) with *Vorhandenheit* (the being of that entity of which we can say *what* it is)? Not entirely. But what existence does mean in relation to being we can make more definite by beginning with a concept of existence broader than the existentialistic one.

Being and Existence

In systematic terms, existence can be defined as one mode of being: to exist means to be in a world (for [or to] someone). In a more restricted sense, this can mean being in the physical world; and then trees and stones can be said to exist but not ideas and geometric figures. In a less restricted sense, it can mean being in any kind of world; and then ideas and geometric figures, along with the imaginative figures of literature or art, exist as much as do trees and stones, but in some world other than the world of physical perception. They are in the world of the pure intuition of time and space (to use Kantian language) or some other world, even though they are not material objects. When one asks whether unicorns or similar things "exist," the intention is to determine whether there are any animals in the physically perceptible, spatiotemporal world that have the characteristics of unicorns, any empirically perceptible object of which one can say, "That is a unicorn." Such a question presupposes the more restricted sense of being in a world, since unicorns obviously do exist in the world of imagination. In the present context, where we are defining the basic concepts, nothing depends on the question whether the sense of "world" is the more or the less restricted one. In either case, existence can be defined as the mode of being that is a *being in the world (for [or to] someone)*.

The reason for adding the parenthetical "for someone" becomes clear when we ask whether "I" exist. At first, it seems that obviously I do exist, and I even exist in a material way—I am in this world as much as are trees and stones and other things. Indeed, does not Descartes's method of doubt show that, when thinking, I cannot but exist? Yet, strictly speaking, I do not exist, and neither does the world, and the Cartesian proof does not show that I "exist" but only that I "am" (somewhere and somehow in the act of thinking). I am the one *for whom* the world is world, and the world is that *in which*

what exists does exist, but neither I nor the world as such is one of
the things in the world. That is the unforgettable truth that emerges
from the Kantian analysis of the three ideas of self, world, and God.
Whatever can appear as an object or person in the world, appears to
"me"; but "I," the one to whom everything in the world appears, do
not appear to myself.[7] Even the reflection that I see when I look into
a mirror is not I, for "I" means the one to whom the reflected vis-
age appears. Similarly, the world as world does not appear, because
everything that exists does so in the world. Even if a particular world
exists—the world of science or of art, let us say—it is not the world
as such. The whole world, the world as such, is that in which even a
particular world would have to appear.

   In that sense, I and world are infinite ideas, not concepts of existing things. In a looser sense, of course, we may say that I do exist,
and then we mean that this-person-here, the one I am, is an entity
among other entities in the world. But in a stricter sense, when existence denotes being in the world, "I" do not exist because "I" am
not in the world. This does not preclude the possibility that something in the world might mirror, even perfectly mirror and objectify,
not just an outward appearance but the I as such (so that, to pursue
Gassendi's question to Descartes, the I to whom the world is world
could encounter itself in something or someone in the world in the
way in which the eye that sees can see itself in the physical reflection
of a mirror); nor does it preclude the possibility that something
which exists in the world may also perfectly embody the worldliness
of the world itself and, in that sense, be the existence of the world.

   7. Karl Heim, *Glaube und Denken* (Hamburg: Furche-Verlag, 1957[5]), pp. 100–
105, has a lucid presentation of this relation. A more elaborate phenomenological
description, along the lines set out by Merleau-Ponty, can be found in Paul Ricoeur,
Fallible Man, translated by Charles Kelbley (Chicago: Henry Regnery, n.d.), pp. 32–
37. In this phenomenological sense, my "origin" is not the chronological time at
which this person was born but the I as the "here-from-where" of all actions and
passions. As Ricoeur puts it: "My birth is an event for others, not for myself. For
others I was born in Valence; but I am here, and it is in relation to here that the others
are there and elsewhere. My birth as an event for others assumes a position in relation
to that 'there' which for another is his 'here': thus my birth does not belong to the
primordial here, and I am not able to call up all my 'heres' starting from my place of
birth. On the contrary, beginning from the absolute here, which is the here and
now—the *hic et nunc*—I lose track of my earliest 'heres,' and I borrow my place of
birth from another's memory. This amounts to saying that my place of birth does not
appear among the 'heres' of my life and cannot therefore be their source" (pp. 36–37).

There may exist such symbols of the I and the world. Those possibilities allowed, however, the place of the I and world as such is not in the world; neither of them "exists." The being of the I, which is the unity of pure subjectivity with some embodiment, or the being of the world, which is the unity of all particular things with the concept of entity as such, is different from the existence of either of them. As strictly defined, then, "existence" designates that mode of being which excludes the being of myself as I and the being of the world as a whole.[8]

Whether this delineation of the basic concepts of being and existence corresponds with what Heidegger meant by *Sein* and *Dasein* in his *Being and Time* is open to question. It does, however, seem to make sense out of the way in which Heidegger's development of the question of the meaning of being comprises both the meaning of the word *being* and the meaning of an entity's being the entity it is. It does make more sense, in any case, than the account given by Tugendhat.[9] Missing in that account is a clarification of how being, understanding, and existence are interconnected. Tugendhat takes Heidegger's statement, to the effect that "we can only clarify *being* [the word] by recourse to the understanding of *being*, the '*Seinsverständnis*'" (p. 149), to express the thesis "that the understanding of a certain word—the word *being*—somehow underlies all other understanding" (149), a thesis which implies "that in relation to understanding only the understanding of sentences is at issue, since the word *being* only occurs in sentences" (p. 150). The problem that then arises from the fact that the word does not occur in all sentences Tugendhat treats by reference to a second thesis of Heidegger: "that there is only an understanding of being in conjunction with an un-

8. When "existence" and "being" are used denominatively, as subjects of predications, they refer to anything at all that exists or is something. Hence, such statements as "Existence is fallen" and "Being is essentially good" are statements for which any existing thing and anything at all can serve as examples. "Existence" refers to anything that is in the physical world or, more broadly, in some world (which is a world to "me"); "being" refers to anything that is anything definite at all, whether it is in the physical world or not. To say "Being is finite" is, therefore, to say that anything which is something at all is something definite and, as such, limited by something else. Similarly, to say "Existence is estranged" is to say that anything which is there, in a world (for me), is there in such a way that it is not all that, by its definition, it could be or should be; it is not identical with itself. Such statements are verifiable by reference to anything that is or that is there at all.

9. Tugendhat, *Self-Consciousness and Self-Determination*, pp. 149ff.

derstanding of nothing," which Tugendhat takes to mean, in non-Heideggerian terms, that "it is the connection between affirmation and negation—the yes/no—that underlies the understanding of sentences" (p. 150); and he adds that, if understanding extends further than understanding sentences, the affirmation and negation underlie that understanding too. This, Tugendhat says, is the "only attempt" he knows to have been made "to understand what Heidegger means by *being* in a way that can be intersubjectively checked" (p. 150). Farther along, in reference to what Heidegger means by the being of "a particular human being," Tugendhat remarks that what is meant "is obviously existence," and he objects to Heidegger's putting *Existenz* in "total opposition" to *existentia* (or being-present-on-hand). What is missing, he concludes, is a generic concept of existence which would apply to both forms (p. 153).

That Heidegger does put the two terms in total opposition is far from obvious, even in the texts that Tugendhat quotes. For in them, all Heidegger asserts is that the mode of being designated by the one term is different from the mode of being designated by the other; the one refers to a mode of being called *Vorhandenheit* (being on hand), and the other to a mode called *Existenz*. Tugendhat is, however, right in noting that a concept or term for what is common to *Existenz* and *Vorhandenheit* is absent and that Heidegger devotes no attention to defining the content of the term "mode of being" (*Seinsweise*) as such. Here I have attempted to identify that common meaning not, technically, as a genus of species but as the form of being called "being in the world." Both being on hand (*Vorhandenheit*) and being out-of, or ex-sisting (*Existenz*), are ways of being in the world. Some entities are in the world by being on hand, or present to "me"; others are in the world by being an "out-standing" of the I.[10] In both cases, however, the common meaning of the word *existence* is the mode of being definable as "being in the world (for me)."

In existentialist thought, both as symbolically expressed (in the myths of fall) and as conceptually formulated (in Schelling and Kierkegaard), the term *existence* has acquired the additional meaning of self-estrangement—inward conflict if not inherent contradiction. This is more than what is included in Heidegger's concept of ex-

---

10. The fact that in Heidegger *Dasein* seems more exactly to designate a mode of being, rather than a genus of entities, takes some of the force out of Tugendhat's objection to the use of the word on the grounds that it has no plural.

sistence and more than what is intended here. For estrangement or self-conflict means that being in the world (for someone) is also being in conflict with oneself. The conflict can be described, along with Tillich, as one between "existence" (or thatness) and "essence" (or quiddity, whatness).[11] Existence then involves an entity's both being and not being who or what it ideally is—it actually is not what according to its concept it could be or should be. The paradigmatic case of such an existence is human being.

How this sense of existence is connected with its more neutral sense of being in the world can readily been seen if we notice the difference in meaning between "There is a tree" and "I am this one here." To say that a tree exists (or that there is a tree) is to remark that there is something in "my" world that is a tree, something of which the predication "is a tree" can be made. To say, similarly, that human beings exist (or that there are human beings) is to remark that there are entities in my world which have the qualities of being human. But to say that I am this one here (or that I exist) is different. In one sense I do exist, because I am identified with an actual person (this one here) in the world (for someone); but in another sense I do not exist, because, strictly speaking, "I"—the I of my own—am inescapably the one *to* whom any world is world and who can therefore never appear in any world because every world is a world to "me." One can think of oneself as someone in the world; but the someone thus thought *of* is distinct, in the act of thinking, from the subjectivity of the one doing the thinking. I as such, as the zero point from which all actions and thoughts originate, am not fully identical with the person here now. "This person here," the one that bears my name, is somewhere in the world; it exists. But "I" do not exist. A contradiction seems, thus, to be contained in the very structure of my being in the world. I both am and am not in it.

Something similar is true of the existence of the world. On the one hand, the world seems obviously to exist because everything that

11. "Essence" and "quiddity" are often used as synonyms, both of them designating *what* something is (according to its concept) in contrast to its existence as meaning *that* it is there. The quiddity of a tree is its treehood; the existence is the individual tree as it is somewhere in the world. In other contexts, as here, a distinction between the essence and the quiddity of an entity needs to be made. Quiddity then refers to *what* an entity is (which can be given in the form of an abstract or generic concept), and essence refers to an entity's *being* what it is in a certain way. Essence is then a mode of being of the entity rather than an element of its constitution. The quiddity of something tells us *what* it is; the essence tells us *how* it *is* what it is.

there is is in some world, and if the world did not exist, nothing else would either; but, on the other hand, what is there is never the world as such but only the things that are in it. One manifestation of this two-sidedness is Kant's analysis of the idea of the world as containing an insoluble dialectic. If we ask whether the world has a beginning in time, we can show that it must have such a beginning (because otherwise an infinite series of moments would have had to elapse before the world began, and an infinite series is one that can never have been traversed) but also that it cannot have such a beginning (because, at whatever point one places the beginning, one can always think of a moment before it which is still part of the same series and therefore already the world). The idea of the world is one that must be thought of as a whole (and therefore as existing) and yet cannot be thought of as a whole (and therefore as not existing but existed-in).

"I" am always coming into existence but never exist; "world" is always existed-in but never exists. These are the marks of contradictoriness that apply to the existence of the self and world and that indicate the dialectical, if not the estranged, nature of their existence. One exists in contradiction to oneself as I; and the world exists in contradiction to itself as the whole. Things and persons may exist in the world without there being any such contradiction in their existence. They are there in the world (to a "me"). But I (the pure subject to whose view they exist) and the world (the infinity in which they exist) cannot be said, strictly speaking, to exist; neither of them is "in the world (to me)."

With this existentialist interpretation of the concept of existence, we can see the sense in the distinction Heidegger made between *Vorhandenheit* and *Existenz*. Both terms make reference to existence in the broad sense of being there in the world. And if we want to specify the meaning that is common to *Existenz* and *Vorhandenheit* it is the meaning of "being here now." But *Existenz* is applicable only to those entities whose being is connected with a personal pronoun—I am, you are, he or she is, and so on. Entities that are on hand (that is, present in our world) are those of which we can say "what" they are. The mode of being of such quiddities is the mode of *Vorhandenheit*, being on hand or, in the usual translations, being present-on-hand or present-at-hand. Entities that ex-sist are those of which we can say "who" they are. Their mode of being, that of *Existenz*, is defined by the fact that the entity which exists can project itself upon a possibility of being in the world. The I of "I am this-one-here" not only assumes a location but also projects itself as the possible "who" of that location. The one to whom the world is world is related to entities in the world not only objectively as things and persons over against it and with it but also projectively as possibilities of its own being in the world.

In the undifferentiated sense, "existence" means being somewhere (in the world). In the existentially differentiated sense, an entity is somewhere in the world either by being on hand there (*Vorhandenheit*) or by being a projection of the one (*Existenz*) for whom the world is world. Entities exist as objects or projects. If the mode of being that we as human beings have is ex-sistence, rather than on-hand-ness, then we, as in each case the I to whom the world is world, can be in the world by projection of that I—the persons in the world are projections of the I as such—onto possibilities of being in the world. (To anticipate the later Heidegger: the fourfold of mortals-divinities-sky-earth is a similar projection, a "worlding," of the world as such.) Accordingly, when we say, "I am this-one-here," and thus identify ourselves with the time and place of an embodiment, the bodily location is not an objectification of the I but a projection of it. I am never on hand in the world but always only projected into it from where I am I. And if I am in the world only in this form, that is, as projected into it from the I beyond it, then what is on hand, or objectively present, to me or anyone else is never the self in its propriety as I but only a projected entity. Hence, the subjectivity of another person, as well as of my own person, is for me a projection of the self into the world but not a being objectively on hand in the world.

The contradictoriness of existence is not specifically characterized by such Heideggerian concepts as *Existenz*. What is contained in them, however, is the recognition of the difference between the way in which any entity other than one identifiable by a pronoun, especially those of the first and second person, is in the world and the way that I am in the world (to me) and you are in the world (to you). Hence, the concept of existence as we find it in Tillich and existentialist theology is different from the *Existenz* of Heidegger's *Being and Time* but not incompatible with it. What does not enter into Heidegger's concept, but does into Tillich's, is the notion of a mode of being that can be characterized by the conflict between the way in which an entity is in fact what it is and the way in which it would be if it were what it could and should be. Such observations provide a basis for the existential understanding of human being not only as projective being but also as a living contradiction. To be human is to find oneself as the unity of "I" and this-one-here, a unity of what never can exist with what does always already exist.

Whether this unity of opposites involves a conflict (as it does in some existentialist conceptions of human being) or only a polarity is a question that can be left open here.[12] Tillich, as we know, distinguished the state of "essence," in which polar opposites are in tension, from the state of "existence," in which they are in conflict. It is conceivable that the opposition between the pure subject I and its embodiment, as well as between the world as such and any "worlding" of it or the sum total of ordered things in it at any moment, can have the form of polarity rather than of contradiction or conflict. In a polar relation, opposition does not serve to cancel but to sustain each of the related elements indicated by the terms. Thus, the opposition between our freedom, as our being one particular modification of the I as such, and our destiny, as our being a corresponding modification of the this-one-here, may initially seem to be a conflict, because we have no choice about when and where we are born or with what inherited talents or prospects. But it can also be a creative tension, when, on the one hand, the two are in agreement with each other so that, as it were, we would have chosen to be just the ones we in fact are and we continually choose to be just those very ones, or when, on the other hand, we create a new way of being in which the two are reconciled. Accordingly, it is not the opposition between pure subjectivity and its form as this-one-here that constitutes the self-destructiveness of existence but rather the possibility that the opposition, instead of being a productive tension, takes the form of conflict.

I both am and am not in the world. That is a formal statement of the opposition, whether a polarity or a conflict, that emerges when one asks whether I exist. But what about the "I" as said by another person? Does the saying "I" on the part of another person, who does exist as a personal entity in what is the world to "me," represent the existence of I as such in the world? And is the world of that existing I—the world for the subjectivity of the other person—the real existence of *a* world in *the* world? If the latter is the case, we can see how the "worlding" of a particular artwork, as the later Heidegger

12. See chapter 6 for a discussion of polarity as tension and polarity as conflict.

interprets art, can also be the manifestation *to* me of the "I." In the normal relations, I never come into view at all within the world, since I am the perspectival center from which everything is thought, sensed, done, acted upon and to which all appears; I can reflect upon my sensations and then upon my reflection, and so on ad infinitum, but at each turn I as such, the point of origin, am one step removed from all that appears. This constitutes the systematic elusiveness of the pure subject and a certain infinity of subjectivity itself. We can be aware of this subjectivity in all our acts as the subjectivity to which all things appear but which never appears itself. We can also be aware of its universality, for any person can think the meaning of the word *I* and by so doing become that kind of infinite subjectivity. Unreflectively, or un-self-consciously, we may equate the meaning of the I with that of the name of the person using the word, as though "I think" meant the same as "*N* (a proper name) thinks."[13] reflect on it, we become aware of the difference between the meaning of the pronoun and a proper name and likewise of the universality of the pronoun in the first person singular. The recognition can even come as a kind of revelation, as it did for Jean Paul Richter.[14] Anyone

13. As H. Reichenbach (*Elements of Symbolic Logic* [New York: Macmillan, 1947], p. 284) tried to do when he analyzed "I" as equivalent to "the person who utters this token." See Hector-Neri Castañeda, "Indicators and Quasi-Indicators," *American Philosophical Quarterly* 4, no. 2 (April 1967): 67, for a criticism of Reichenbach on this contention.

14. It is a revelation of the being of the I (that "I am I") that Jean Paul Richter reports in his *Sämtliche Werke* (Berlin, 1862), vol. 34, p. 26: "One morning, as a very young child, I was standing in our front door and was looking over to the wood pile on the left, when suddenly the inner vision 'I am an I' [Ich bin ein Ich] shot down before me like a flash of lightning from the sky, and ever since it has remained with me luminously: at that moment my ego [Ich] had seen itself for the first time, and for ever." Quoted in Herbert Spiegelberg, "On the 'I-am-me' Experience in Childhood and Adolescence," *Psychologia: An International Journal of Psychology in the Orient* 4 (1961): 135, from "Aus Jean Pauls Leben," *Sämtliche Werke* 34, p. 26. Roderick Chisholm, *The First Person: An Essay on Reference and Intentionality* (Minneapolis: University of Minnesota Press, 1981), asks how one comes to see this "I am me" and replies, "It would be correct to say: 'One has only to consider it to see that it is true.' But it is, apparently, something that many people never happen to consider" (p. 90). And if one needs an illustration of not seeing it, A. J. Ayer's refutation of the *cogito ergo sum* will supply the need. Descartes's cogito "must not here be understood in its ordinary sense of 'I think,' but rather as meaning 'There is a thought now,'" Ayer tells us; and he draws the conclusion that the principle *cogito ergo sum* is false because " 'I exist' does not follow from 'There is a thought now'" (*Language, Truth and Logic* [New York: Dover Publication, 1946], pp. 46f.).

can use the word *I* and become the place at which subjectivity is embodied; that is its universality. Descartes's *cogitans sum* applies not only to the person of Descartes but to anyone who thinks the meaning of "I." Each of us can embody, but none of us can exhaust, the meaning of the word; each of us in our individuality can be the place, but none of us the only place, with which the universal becomes identified. Hence the question arises whether the I in another person is an I that exists in the world for me. Yes, but not *as I*, not in the form of the first person singular; rather, in the form of the second or third person, as a you or a he or she (to me).

The relation between the I as said in my person and the I as said by another person involves both an identity and a difference. For my part, I know that there is a difference in place between the I as I say the word and the I as another says it; and I also know that this difference can never be eradicated. I in my person can never take the place of the other person, just as the I of the other can never take mine.[15] The identity, however, lies in knowing that what I am inwardly aware of as the pure subjectivity of the self is the same as what the other is also inwardly aware of. It is an identity of analogy: what I am to my own self in this person is analogous to what the other, as I, is to his or her own self in that person. Thus, despite the fact that I, as the person I am, can never take the place of the other person or be the subject that the other person is, I as purely subject can be understood by each of us through analogy. This recognition is the basis of one formulation of the Kantian categorical imperative—the imperative to recognize humanity, whether in my own person or in that of another, not merely as a means to an end but as an end in itself or, we might say, to recognize that no person is only an entity in a world but also a subjectivity to whom the world is world. There is in every person a subjectivity eliciting recognition as such by other persons. It is because we are aware both of the meaning of the word *I* and also of the different locations of the awareness of the I that we can recognize the legitimacy of the demand to respect the other unconditionally as a subjectivity.

This may seem to contradict Charles Peirce's explanation of the possibility of sympathy, when he said that man is a word.[16] Peirce

15. Heim, *Glaube und Denken*, pp. 85f.
16. See Vincent M. Colapietro, *Peirce's Approach to the Self: A Semiotic Perspective on Human Subjectivity* (Albany: SUNY, 1989), 102ff.

denied that the mind can be identified with only one bodily location. "Are we shut up in a box of flesh and blood?" he asks; "when I communicate my thought and my sentiments to a friend with whom I am in full sympathy, so that my feelings pass into him and I am conscious of what he feels, do I not live in his brain as well as in my own—most literally?" He answers by granting that "my animal life" is not there "but my soul, my feeling, thought, attention are"; for if that were not so, "a man [would not be] a word . . . but something much poorer. . . . A word may be in several places at once . . . and I believe that a man is no whit inferior to the word in this respect. . . . That he truly has this outreaching identity—such as a word has—is the true and exact expression of the fact of sympathy, fellow feeling."[17] But to say that a human being can, like a word, be in different places does not come to asserting that the I, as I am immediately aware of it in my own person here and now, can exchange places with another. It only raises the question whether our relation to the freedom of another, or to what being an I means to the other person, is only by way of analogy. There may be a sympathetic feeling of the I of another that is more than an analogical appropriation of it, and hence a different basis for mutual recognition. Phenomenological analyses which show how I do myself really feel another person's pain indicate such a form of sympathy. But even if there is such a direct feeling, sympathy is still not an identity—we may have a "reaching out" capacity that exceeds the capacity of analogical appropriation, but we still remain aware of the absoluteness of origin for each of us that the word *I* signifies.

The Self's Being

The being of the self is the unity of pure subjectivity with a location that is expressed in "I am this-one-here." The existence of the self is paradoxical. "I" do not exist, but the entity that I am does exist. How does this being come to be? How does the self come into being as the unity of I with this-one-here, the unity of the subjectivity of which we are aware when we understand the meaning of the word *I* and the location that is indicated by the designation "this-one-here"? That an entity is at all or is the kind of entity it is means that it has come into being by a process in which nonbeing is negated. But

17. Quoted by Colapietro, in *Peirce's Approach to the Self*, p. 103, from Peirce's *Collected Papers*, vol. 7, p. 591.

what is the nature of that coming into being? And what is the difference, if any, between the being of "I am I" and the being of "I am this-one-here"?

We should recall that the matter of the self's being comes up in post-Kantian thinkers in connection with the question of knowledge. To ask "What is the self?" is not the same as to ask "What is the basis of knowledge?" Yet the two questions come together in the speculative idealism after Kant. Fichte is a key figure, for it is his *Wissenschaftslehre*—a science of science—which shows the basis of knowledge in the being of the I, who is, in a sense to be carefully defined, the creator of the world.[18] Kant's critique had posed the question whether metaphysical knowledge is possible—whether, in other words, we can *know* about the I, the world, and God as we can and do know about triangles, trees, and dogs. In answering the question, he took his guideline from two cases, mathematics (geometry and arithmetic) and physics, clearly acknowledged as examples of knowledge. With that guideline, he analyzed knowledge to mean a unity of percept (*Anschauung*) and concept (*Begriff*) so that we do not "know" either phenomena (things intuited) or noumena (things conceived) but only things that are both phenomenal and noumenal, that is, a synthesis of the thing as perceived and the thing as conceived.[19] The question he left aside is the one the post-Kantians, Fichte among the first of them, took up: How do we know what knowledge is? This question is prior to any critique of knowledge. The work that Fichte entitled a *Wissenschaftslehre* thus had the character of a "science of what science even is [*Wissenschaft von einer*

18. Johann Gottlieb Fichte, *Grundlage der gesamten Wissenschaftslehre (1794)* (Hamburg: Felix Meiner, 1970). English translation by Peter Heath and John Lachs, *The Science of Knowledge* (Cambridge: Cambridge University Press, 1982). The present discussion follows the German text. There is more to Fichte's thought than his *Wissenschaftslehre*, even through its various editions; but it is only the Fichte of this work to whom reference is being made.

19. It only creates confusion when one describes the Kantian epistemology by saying that we know only phenomena and not noumena. Although there are phrasings in Kant's critiques which support such a description, it is more accurate to say that, in this epistemology, we do not "know" either phenomena or noumena. What we "know" is always only the synthesis of the phenomenal and the noumenal, that is, a synthesis of the object as given to intuition with the object as abstractly conceived. We can intuit (perceive) an object in its singularity, and we can conceive it in its abstract generality; but we can "know" it only in a synthesis of the one with the other. See chapter 1, note 6, above.

Wissenschaft überhaupt]"—a knowledge of what knowledge itself is.[20] The matter of the self's being comes into the picture because it is the self's positing of itself that provides the foundation for the whole of knowledge. The being of the self is the foundation of knowledge; and the self comes to be unconditionally or groundlessly. Fichte's ambiguous accomplishment lies in the way that egoism and ontology are intertwined in an original deed-act (*Tathandlung*). The nature of the self-positing which defines the being of the self will be the object of attention here. The way in which this provides an epistemological foundation will be left aside.

Fichte's analysis shows the being of the self as an unconditional positing. The being of the I is the being of a subject that posits itself unconditionally and does so in an act that Fichte names a deed-act, a *Tathandlung*, an occurrence that is activity and deed at once. In this deed-act, the self is both the agent of the action and the result of the action done. "The positing of the I through itself," Fichte wrote, "is its pure activity. The I *posits itself*, and it *is*, by virtue of this mere positing through itself; and, conversely, the I *is*, and it *posits* its being, by virtue of its mere being"; thus, the "action and deed are one and the same; and hence the 'I am' is an expression of a *Tathandlung*, but also the only possible one" (p. 16). Fichte thus decisively brings the origin of the I out of the sphere of objectifying, or mythological, conceptions of creation and makes clear the difference between the I and the individual person who "I" am; the self-positing of the I is not contemporaneous with the birth of a person or the emergence of self-consciousness.[21] The being of the I is here identified in its uniqueness. It is the only being that is both an activity and a deed in one, so that the activity is the deed and the deed is the activity—the I is the one acting and is also the one brought about by the action; and it is the only being that just is, groundlessly. This is the deed-act that is at the basis of all consciousness (p. 11).

What, then, is the being of the self? What is the nature of the connection, made in the *Tathandlung*, between the I and the this-

20. Quoted, from the first edition, by Wilhelm G. Jacobs in the introduction to his edition of the book: Joh. Gottl. Fichte, *Grundlage der gesamten Wissenschaftslehre (1794)* (Hamburg: Felix Meiner, 1970), p. vii.

21. The question "*What* was I before I came to self-consciousness?" implies that there is a "substratum" of consciousness that can be abstracted from the I. "But, without noticing it, one thinks the absolute subject along with it; one includes the very thing from which one has purportedly abstracted" (*WL*, p. 17).

one-here that is the being of the I? It has, so goes Fichte's answer, the nature of an unconditional positing, a *Setzen*, although that term itself remains undefined, and of a motion that is both an activity and a deed. It is a positing that is a being posited. What is meant by positing, and how is it that the self posits itself unconditionally? It will be helpful to trace the several steps of Fichte's own argument—steps which he does not identify as such—before formulating the conception of positing that defines the self's being.

According to his statement in the *Wissenschaftslehre*, Fichte was searching for a method by which philosophy could raise itself to the rank of an "evident science," one whose knowledge is not based upon other knowledge but is evident in itself. That search is, of course, different from an investigation of the being of the self. But the two matters become intertwined because Fichte's search is for what he called the "unconditional axiom [or principle, *Grundsatz*]" that expresses the *Tathandlung* lying at the basis of all consciousness. This deed-act is not itself one of the particular things one does or undergoes; it is, rather, the deed-act preceding all the particular, empirical activities or passivities of the consciousness. To uncover that principle, or axiom, Fichte proposes to start with any act of consciousness in order then, by reflecting on it (to determine whether it is what one initially takes it to be) and by abstracting from it everything that does not belong to it, to arrive at what one must necessarily think of as the foundation of all consciousness because one cannot think it away. The method is Cartesian—it proceeds by thinking away everything possible until it reaches the point at which something appears that cannot be thought away because the very act of thinking posits it.

One can start anywhere. Fichte chooses a starting point that is intended to reach the goal by the shortest route. He starts with the incontestable proposition "A is A," or, as he also writes it, "A = A." It is a proposition that everyone would grant, a proposition that we posit as certain, not a proposition that we would or could prove or find a reason for. But if no reason is needed for being certain that what the proposition says is so, and if it cannot be proved to be so in any noncircular way (since any logical proof has to make use of it in the proof), then our positing this principle shows that we can posit something without any further basis (*schlechthin*). There is, in other words, a positing that we just can do without any other foundation than the sheer fact of the doing.

This marks the end of the first step in uncovering the foundation. Starting anywhere, we arrive at the point of recognizing that there is a phenomenon of unconditional or groundless positing. The second step is to determine what is posited when we affirm that A is A. We do not posit that A *is*, or that there is an A. What we posit is that *if* A is (if there is an A), then it is A. This is undeniably a correct thought. The knowledge involved in this positing concerns the *form* of the proposition and not the *Gehalt*. The form has to do with *what* is known; the *Gehalt* is that *about which* it is known. Today we might say the form is the "sense" and the *Gehalt* is the "reference" of the proposition. This is to say that what we posit, without any further basis than our being able to do so, is a necessary connection (*Zusammenhang*) of the subject- and predicate-terms. Call this connection (Fichte says) *X*. Then *what* we can posit unconditionally is a necessary connection of some sort. In the first step, it was disclosed that positing is something we can do unconditionally; this second step discloses that what we posit is a connection between two elements. In other words, not Fichte's, we posit being.

The third step is taken when we ask under what condition A *is* A. What is the condition for eliminating the "if" in our saying "If there is an A, then it is A (or: If A *is*, then it is A)"? What changes the hypothetical to the thetical positing of being? The connection is initially made *in* the I and posited *through* the I; I am the one who says or thinks, "If A, then A is A." Moreover, there is no basis for the connection other than the thought of the one who thinks that A is A. The law (*Gesetz*) in the positing (*Setzen*) is given to the self through the I; no one tells me how or why that is so, I just recognize it. Of the positing of A we do not know how and whether A is posited; but we know that it is posited insofar as the connection of A with A, the *X*, is posited. *X* points to both the logical subject and the logical predicate of the proposition because it connects the two. What is posited, then, is that in the I there is something that is always one and the same. This assertion seems like a jump rather than a gradual progression in Fichte's argument. But the intention is not difficult to see. If we can posit unconditionally the connection *X* (which asserts unconditionally of anything a sameness and unity of the logical subject with the logical predicate), then the *X* can be expressed as I = I, or "I am I." The *X* is not the A. The *X* is the connection made between A and A. But that connection itself is the identity of the I with itself, the "I am I."

Thus, in step 1 the argument was that we can posit unconditionally. In step 2, it was that what we posit is a connection, having to do with the form (what is said) but not the reference (the about-which) of the proposition. In step 3, it was that A can be posited only insofar as the connection of A with A is posited. In step 4, it is now that the positing of this connection is the positing of an identity of the I with itself; what is posited, in positing the *X,* is that there is something in the I that is always one and the same. What is posited in positing *X* (the connection of anything with itself, of A with A) is the connection of the I with the I. Or, in other words, what is posited is the being of the self as the identity of I with I.

Finally, in step 5, we recognize the point at which we have arrived in step 4. The "I am" is an expression of an empirical fact (*Tatsache*), though not yet a *Tathandlung*; namely, the empirical fact that *X* is posited without any ground other than its being posited. It "just is" posited, or, in Fichte's term, it is posited *schlechthin*. To move from the empirical fact that I am to the deed-activity that underlies it, we attend to the difference between "A is A" and "I am I." Unlike "A is A," the proposition "I am I" always has a *Gehalt*, a reference, as well as a form—it not only says something about something (the form) but also posits that *about* which what is said is being said. "I am I" is a proposition that is not only valid but unconditionally true. It asserts not only that, if I am, then I am I; it also asserts that I *am* and hence that I *am* I. "A is A" has a reference only under the condition that the reference is posited—if there is an A, then it is A. All "I" can do is posit the connection. But "I am I" has a reference unconditionally. It not only asserts the connection that, if I am, then I am I; it also posits the I, with the predicate of being identical with itself. It is, thus, an empirical *fact* that "I am I" always has a reference as well as a form and content; "I am I" posits something about something and also posits the something about which it is positing it.

How, then, do we uncover the *Tathandlung* in this empirical fact? For this, Fichte takes a second start with "A = A." With the proposition "A is A" a *judgment* is made, and judging is an activity, something that we do. But the activity of judging is based on something, the "I am," that in turn is not based upon anything else. Hence, what is simply posited is the ground of a certain activity (the activity of judging, and, as Fichte says he will later show, of all activity) of the human mind. The pure *Charakter* of the human mind is this activity of itself. And the activity is both a *Handlung* and a *Tat*. It is an activity because it is something I do; it is a deed because it is something that is accomplished through the activity.

What is shown by Fichte's discussion? First, that "I" just "am," and, second, that I am I. What emerges here is not just the I of the *cogito* but also the being of the self as I. Fichte's interest lies in this being as the foundation for all knowledge. That I am, and that I am I, is the basis for knowing anything at all; for this is the one and only case in which the noumenon (the *thought* I) is also a phenomenon (an *appearance* in the world). Furthermore, what I know, including what knowledge is, is based upon the positing of the self in its identity with itself that is expressed in the "I am" and "I am I." To know is to judge that this perceptible phenomenon is a conceivable noumenon. I can know because I am such a unity. Everything else has a reason; that I am and am I has no reason other than that I am posited by my positing.

With this we are at the final question. What is meant by "positing," this crucial term which Fichte leaves undefined? The being of the self is a positing; positing precedes the active and the passive voices in our being related to the world in judgment. To posit is, clearly, to unite the phenomenal and noumenal aspects of a thing, that is, to judge, and it is to do so in such a way that the judging is simultaneously the realization of being. It is made possible by an unconditional occurrence which is both active and passive or which, more exactly, is activity and deed in one. It is a "being placed" by "placing" that is different from actions in which we act upon something else and passions in which we are acted upon by something. It is logically prior to the active and the passive voices of our being. To be a self is to be self-positing and self-posited; it is to "be" in the understanding of being (judgment). In all that is done to it, the self posits itself; in all that it does, the self is posited by the positing. Its doing is a being done to. In that sense the basis of all knowledge is the being of the self. That I am and that I am I is always implicitly contained in whatever we know of anything at all as the basis of that knowledge. What is inescapable is that I am and that I am judging.

Fichte's reduction of the empirical to the ontological uncovers something different from what is shown in Descartes's method of doubt. What the Cartesian meditation shows is that self-awareness, the awareness of the I as a point of origin behind which we cannot get and which we cannot escape, not only is immediate and unreflected but also can be reflected or mediated. Nothing is so immediately certain as the fact that I am. That this immediate certainty survives a reflection upon it is what is shown in the Cartesian reflection. Not only am I in fact certain of myself as I, but I cannot but be certain of it, for every attempt to dislodge the self-certainty only confirms it. Implicitly there is more in Descartes, since he also shows that the I is reflectively certain of itself *when* it thinks. The temporality thus introduced is a new aspect over against the immediate self-certainty. Fichte's reduction discloses, by contrast, the *being* of the self expressed in the judgment "I am I" in an act of positing that is also the deed of having been posited. In effect, the self shows itself to be the creator of itself and the world because its being is implicitly contained in all knowledge of the world. The otherwise pretentious characterization of the self as the creator of the world has here a definite sense that makes it not quite so pretentious.

Tugendhat has noted how the phenomenon of the self, which in modern philosophy is treated in part as self-consciousness and in part as self-determination (*Selbstbestimmung*), is really not one phenomenon but two. Self-consciousness, or the awareness of the I that emerges in the Cartesian reflection, is different from the defining or determining of the self that is carried out by Fichte. The "epistemic self-consciousness," which can be formulated as "I know that I . . ." (feel hot, am thirsty, and so on), is different from the self-determination that can be formulated as "I will do *X*" and "I can do *X* or *Y*" (p. 23). Tugendhat is undoubtedly correct in asserting that there are two phenomena involved, not just one, even though they were traditionally treated as one by Fichte as well as Descartes. But instead of joining Tugendhat in referring to the two as self-consciousness (the awareness of self) and self-relation (the relation of the self to itself), and then construing the two along the lines of knowing and doing, we can refer to them as the subjectivity of the self and the being of the self. The *subjectivity* of the self is the phenomenon that appears when we understand the meaning of the word *I* and is assured in the method of doubt; the *being* of the self is what appears when we understand the connection of that phenomenon with a time and space, an embodiment, in assertions that have the form "I am this-one-here." In Fichte's analysis, this being is always simultaneously the being of "I am" and "I am this-one-here." The self's being as shown in the "I am I" and "I am this-one-here" is in some sense an ungrounded being, both cause and caused, agent and deed. The self comes to be as one who is always already there. Its being, this paradox of givenness and doing, comes to be as eternally having been.[22]

The being of the self, the unity of "I" and this-one-here, as Fichte explicated it, is an unconditional positing without which science would not be possible; it is the being of the epistemological subject. Other characteristics of this being appear in the self of everyday talk and the self of trust. In everyday talk, the being of the self lies in its understanding. It becomes manifest in the way in which the self is always worldly. Even in the know-how exhibited by the use of tools there is an understanding of self as one who is worldly. That we know how to use a hammer to pound nails to make a cabin to dwell in is not a form of scientific knowledge. But it is a know-how that exhibits an understanding of the self as a being in the world. This being is not an unconditional positing but a matter of having been "thrown" somewhere. For what the use of tools in every know-how shows is that the self does not understand itself as eternally having posited itself and the world but rather as making a place for itself in the world into which it has been thrown.[23]

Like Heidegger's existentialism, the analysis of trust, as we have seen it in Herrmann's *Ethik*, shows the self's being as other than an

22. With such deictic words as *I* and *this*, the understanding of the being of the entity is simultaneously the assertion of its being in the world. Tugendhat, in opposition to Castañeda, thinks there is a difference between "I" and "this" as deictic terms. "When the word *I* is used significantly," he writes in agreement with Castañeda, "it is not possible that the entity referred to does not exist." The same is said not to be true for the word *this*, but the contention is immediately qualified in such a way to make it pointless; it is said not to be true "more precisely for the combination this so-and-so." It is possible to say "This beetle that I have in my hand is red" without there being any beetle there. That is, of course, true. But the question of deictic or indexical force in the word *this* is deflected by that qualification. Without the qualification, it remains true that the word *this* is deictic as much as is the word *I*. To say "This-thing-here is a beetle" is to assert the existence of something, even if I have falsely identified it as a beetle. In this respect, there is no difference between "I" and "this"—both words, when used significantly, assert existence simultaneously with understanding being.

23. *Geworfenheit* is, in Heidegger's usage, like the terms "objectivity" and "subjectivity" in being derived from the root meaning "throw" (*werfen, jacere*). To characterize human existence as *Geworfenheit* is to distinguish it from both objectivity and subjectivity (or even subject-objectivity), but it is also to distinguish it from self-positing. The self does not "place itself" but finds itself already "thrown" in a certain place. Its being is not a unity of substance and accidents but a *befindliches Verstehen*, an understanding that is shaped by one's "being found" or "finding oneself" in a certain way.

unconditional positing. It is more on the order of a creation, a being that is brought-to-be through the establishment of a relation of trust, rather than a self-positing. Such a self, as brought to be by the one who elicits trust, does not understand itself as always having posited itself unconditionally but as having been brought into being through a gift from another—from the one who can instill or evoke the trust.

Positing, understanding, and donation are, thus, the characteristics of the self in its being a knowing subject (Fichte), an entity with the know-how to be there in the world (Heidegger), and one who is freed to trust (Herrmann). With this, we can turn our attention to the question of the self as an ecstatic possibility, for the notion of ecstasy and ecstatic being does not readily fit under the notions of the self's being as it has been developed since Descartes. But it will be necessary to take a detour through some further considerations of ontology, theology, and rationality in the questions of the self and its forms of reason.

3

Modes of Thinking

THE BEING OF THE SELF IS THE unity of pure subjectivity with a location, which is manifested as the unconditional positing of the epistemological subject, as the self-understanding of Dasein, and as the gift of the self free to trust. It is the being of the I-who-know, the I-who-exist, and the I-who-trust. But the ego is never isolated and alone. It is always a thinking self, that is, a self *relating itself to* its other. It is this relating of itself to the other that we shall take up here under the headings of thinking and reason. Thinking is the openness of the self to what is other than thinking, and reason is the configuration of this openness.

Faith and Understanding as Two Modes of Thinking

Heidegger's question "Was heißt Denken?" carries, as we know, the double sense of the verb *heißen*. Understood in its most direct sense, the question means "What is thinking called?" or "What do we call thinking?" or "What does 'thinking' mean?" But since *heißen* also has the connotation of calling in the sense of "summoning," the question "Was heißt Denken?" can be understood to mean, at the same time, "What is it that summons us to think? To what are we responding when we find ourselves thinking? What or who is making us think?" There is also a double sense in the formulation "What does thinking mean?" In part, the question asks for a definition or clarification of the concept of thinking; in part, it asks what significance there is in that activity of thinking or in the fact that such an activity is possible at all. Although these two senses do not coincide exactly with the two senses of "Was heißt Denken?" they are closely enough akin so that we can take them as giving the same kind of direction for the delineation of thinking: thinking as an activity involves an openness to what is other than thinking. Here I shall follow that direction by describing the "faith" and "understanding" of the phrase *fides quaerens intellectum* as two fundamental modes of thinking, each of which has the hallmark of opening in it. For the sake of clarity, I shall speak of faith and understanding as two *modes* of thinking, in contrast to the *forms* of reason to be discussed later. Reason is taken here to mean the structure of thinking as distinct from the activity or process of thinking. The activity takes place either in the mode of faith or in the mode of understanding. A structure, or a relation of the agent and the terminus of the activity, is implied in the activity, and that structure is designated "reason." Thus, by "reason" we shall mean the relating of the self, as the agent of thought, to the other, as the terminus of thought. But there are several ways in which that relating is configured, just as there are two modes of the activity; these configurations of reason will be called "forms" rather than "modes." Apart from the need to keep clear the distinction between thinking and reason, the forms of reason could be called "modes" as well as "forms."

INTELLECTUS AS THE UNDERSTANDING OF BEING

In speaking of "faith" and "understanding" as the two modes of thinking, it will best serve clarity to designate explicitly the object toward which the activities are directed. Understanding is always an understanding of *being*, and faith is always a believing, or trusting, in *God*. This is a more limited sense of understanding and believing than they have in general usage; but it is the sense in which faith and understanding are modes of thinking. The way in which understanding is the understanding of being is apparent if we recall how percepts and concepts are united in judgments (propositions). In the compound judgment "This is a tree and a tree is a woody perennial plant with one main trunk," "this" is the deictic word, which directly points out the thing to which reference is being made, "a tree" is the common name, and "a woody perennial plant, etc." is the definition of the object pointed out. What the judgment accomplishes is a connection of a singular that is perceived with a general that is abstractly thought, and it does so by means of a middle term that is the common name. The making of that connection is an "understanding of being." In distinction from perceiving and conceiving, understanding has to do with "being" as the connection of singular (or individual) and universal (or general) by reference to some temporalization of being. From this description it should be evident what is meant by saying that understanding is always an understanding *of being.* In one way, it is, of course, the phenomenon, not just the being of the phenomenon, that we understand. But to understand it means to be able to make a connection of it in its singular aspect with itself in its general aspect. The difference between a thing and the being of that same thing may play only a small role in everyday matters. That is also true of the difference between a thing as it is perceived and the same thing as it is abstractly thought. If we need to trim a tree, we do need to be able to recognize something as a tree. But in the trimming we do not need to make a distinction between treating it as a perceptible object and treating it as a conceivable object, even though that distinction is in the background when the tree is trimmed in accord with what species of tree it is and not only as a cuttable individual thing. Still less do we need to make a distinction between the being of the tree and the tree. It would not make any sense to say that we want the being of the tree trimmed but not the tree itself. Although such distinctions play a negligible role in the everyday dealing with the world, they are significant for purposes of delineating the scope of thinking and the forms of reason.

How are we to fit this notion of understanding (as always having to do with being) with the familiar Kantian notion of *Verstand* and with Dilthey's contrast between understanding and explaining, *Verstehen* and *Erklären*? In Kant's critique of reason, understanding is midway between intuition (*Anschauung*) and reason (*Vernunft*). The forms of intuition synthesize a sense-manifold into objects (the tree as an object is a synthesis of sensations); the concepts of the understanding make connections between the objects (the sun's shining "causes" the stone to be warm); and the ideas of reason unify the whole. There are only three ideas of reason, representing the subjective unity (the idea of self, the I), the objective unity (the idea of the world), and the absolute unity (the idea of God). Nothing in Kant's critiques connects understanding distinctively with being in the way delineated here. Indeed, when Kant speaks of the being of something, as he does in his much-discussed assertion that being is not a predicate, he means something's givenness as an object, its real existence independent of its idea. To ascribe being to an object is, in this Kantian sense, no more than to say that such an object can be found in the world. This, clearly, is a notion of being different from the one involved when it is made the object of understanding. In fact, there is no clear counterpart in Kant to the notion of being as just that connection between singular and universal which is indicated by the copula and which is the object of understanding in contrast to perception and abstract conception. Being, as different from existence and as more than a verbal copula, appears in Kant in connection with the transcendental imagination. For the transcendental image of a thing is neither a replica of an individual sense object nor a picture of what is contained in an abstract concept; rather, it is intermediate between them. The transcendental image—Kant's example is the image of a dog as dog—makes it possible to connect the sense perception of an individual dog with the abstract concept of the genus dog. The image is not a reproduction of an actual dog, and it is not the visualization of the abstract genus; it is intermediate. How the imagination worked was a puzzle that Kant did not pretend to be able to solve. But he did acknowledge its being distinct from sense intuitions and abstract concepts. If we draw out this line of thought in Kant, then it is in the transcendental image that we find a representation of the being of an object, in the sense the word *being* has in the present context, as distinct from its perceived and its conceived aspects. Such a transcendental image would, in that case, be the work of what here is called "understanding," but it would not be the object of what Kant called *Verstand*. In other words, the sphere of what Kant called the transcendental imagination is the same as the sphere of what is here called understanding. By calling it understanding, we maintain a continuity with the meaning in the Latin word *intellectus* or *intelligere* (literally, "reading between," or "gathering between") and also with its meaning as shaped by Heidegger's renewal of the question of the meaning of being.

Dilthey's distinction between understanding and explaining is located in a different context. Yet both understanding and explaining do there have to do with the relation of particulars or singulars to universals or generals. The difference is that if we subsume something under a law, it is a matter of explanation. An object falls to the earth, for example, because of gravitational attraction. If, on the other hand, the universal is not a law but subjective agency, then it is a matter of understanding. To understand, for example, the actions of Napoleon means to be able to identify oneself with the one who acted in that way. Such understanding is not a matter of subsuming a particular instance under a general law but of bridging the gap between the awareness of the self in one's own actions and the self that is the agent of actions other than one's own. What happens when we can put ourselves into the place of the other agent, when we can see ourselves as ones who could do those very things done by the other, is that the actions of the other are brought into the sphere of the subjectivity (the self-awareness) that is interior to us. This, too, is an employment of the notion of understanding different from the one in which understanding is always the understanding of being, that is, of that which unites singular and universal.

Is there a direct intuition of being as the object of understanding? Some of Husserl's remarks in *The Idea of Phenomenology* would suggest that there is.[1] Husserl adduces the matter in connection with epistemological theory. He identifies as the main problem, even the enigma, of cognition this question: How is it possible for knowledge to "reach the transcendent"? (The transcendent here does not mean God or ultimate reality but rather that which is beyond, or outside of, the mental process itself.) Ordinary knowledge of things as well as scientific knowledge of nature presupposes that such a reaching of the transcendent, or knowledge of what is outside the mind, is possible because it is actual. We do know that in fact some things are so and others are not so, regardless of how we might wish to think of them. But the question which was paramount for Husserl was to know how this is possible at all. To see *how* it is possible is to understand it. We cannot understand its possibility, in this sense, by constructing arguments based on its actuality or by acquiring more actual knowledge of the world. Rather, we can understand it only if "the essences of this relation [which is implied in the wording 'reaching the transcendent'] were somehow *given* to [the knower], so that he could 'see' it and could directly inspect the unity of cognition and object" (p. 30, emphasis in text). That unity of cognition and object is what is meant by the phrase "reaching the transcendent." This is to say that we can understand how cognition of a reality transcendent to the mind is possible only if we are able to "see" something that is the unity of the act of knowing and the thing known. Husserl's problem is not, in other words, whether we know the world—no sensible person doubts the existence of real things—but

1. Edmund Husserl, *The Idea of Phenomenology*, translated by William P. Alston and George Nakhnikian (The Hague: Martinus Nijhoff, 1973), pp. 30ff.

rather *how* we do so; and how we do so can be understood only if the relation between cognition and its object is itself a "given," something that can be "seen" and not just an inference or a conjecture. To understand how knowledge can reach the transcendent is to be able directly to see, as a given, not just the object or the cognition but the relation between cognition and its object.

The meaning of this kind of understanding emerges clearly in an illustration that Husserl provides. A person who is born deaf may very well know that there are sounds and that there is a musical art, but "he cannot understand *how* sounds do this, how musical compositions are possible." He cannot imagine such things; he cannot "'see' and in 'seeing' grasp the 'how' of things" (p. 31). The person's knowledge that sounds and musical art do in fact exist will not help; for one cannot explain the possibility by "drawing conclusions from nonintuitive knowledge" (p. 31). Although Husserl's purpose in this passage is not to explain what "understanding" means but to show that only a direct seeing, rather than inferences or "transcendent pre-suppositions," can make it clear how knowledge or anything else is possible—only a direct seeing can elucidate any possibility—he does apply the word *understanding* to this act of seeing how something is possible. To understand is to see; it is to see how something is possible; and it is to see how it is possible by seeing directly into it. That we *can* know the world, or that cognition can "reach the transcendent," can be derived from the fact that we *do* know the world—in the natural knowledge that we acquire just by living in it as well as in the scientific knowledge of nature. But *how* we can do so cannot be derived from the fact of our doing it. How it is possible has to be seen in direct intuition.

To "understand" something means, then, to see how it can be what it is or to see how something that is so can be so. Understanding is a matter of seeing-how. Husserl is concerned with seeing how it is possible for cognition to reach its real object. But the same sense of understanding can be included in the notion of understanding as the uniting of percept and concept. Then Husserl's position amounts to saying that we cannot understand *how* we make a connection of singulars with generals by assertions of being—"This is a tree"—unless the unity of the two, the being of the tree, is itself a datum of intuition. In order to see how it is possible to connect our percepts of the singular with our abstract concepts of the general, we need to have given to our intuition a datum that is the unity of the two: a datum that is both a percept and a concept. We must be able to "see" the being of the tree as directly as we see the tree as a sensible object; the "transcendental image" of Kantian philosophy must be intuited as directly as the sensible appearance and species are intuited. To see the being of physical objects is to understand how the uniting of percepts with concepts can be accomplished. *That* we can unite them is not the question; *how* we do so is the question.

In all of this, what is noteworthy is Husserl's insistence that the "how" of "reaching the transcendent" cannot be provided by more knowledge of the world and by inferences or arguments based upon that knowledge of the world but can be provided only by the givenness to intuition of the link between the cognitive act and the object of that act. This is noteworthy because it indicates that, for Husserl, cognition is not reducible to just the two aspects of perceiving and conceiving; for there is a third aspect, to which our seeing-how, or understanding, is ascribed. It is not difficult, therefore, to see in Husserl a recognition of the independence of understanding over against sensation and abstract thought. Understanding is not derivative of the other two functions but has its own objects given to it directly. Phenomenological data are, properly speaking, those givens—the data that present the "how" of the possibility that is actualized in the ordinary and scientific knowledge of the world. Natural knowledge and scientific knowledge require sensation and abstract thought, and the objects of that knowledge are given as the general in the individual or the individual in the general. In knowing individual instances as cases of general classes or laws, we gain an objective knowledge of the world. (It need not be unchanging or infallible in order to be objective, but that is a different matter.) But we do not have an *understanding* of that knowledge until we can see how it is possible, and we can see how it is possible only through the givenness to our mind of just that element which is the *connecting* of singular sense-objects with abstractly thought objects—but that is what is meant by the givenness of the "being" of things to understanding.

FIDES AS THE TRUSTING IN GOD

Understanding being is one mode of thinking, that is, one mode in which "being," as the unity or connection that is contained in everyday and scientific knowledge of the world, is presented to mind. The other mode of thinking is *fides*, or trusting God. That the *fides* of *fides quaerens intellectum* is a mode of thinking, parallel with understanding, may be far from obvious; and it is certainly the case that "belief" or "faith" can be used to mean other phenomena than this mode of thinking. When, for example, Kant distinguishes knowledge from faith by ascribing to faith subjective certainty and objective uncertainty, whereas knowledge has both subjective and objective certainty (and opinion has neither subjective nor objective certainty), this is a different conception of faith.[2] The faith that is a mode of thinking is not defined by its contrast with knowledge but by its contrast with understanding; and the distinguishing marks have to do not with subjective and objective certainty but with "being" that is the object of understanding and "God" that is the object of believing (or faith). If they are both modes of thinking, then believing must involve something comparable to the unity of singular and universal that characterizes understanding.

Several guidelines are available to enable us to see how believing and understanding are two parallel and equally basic modes of thinking. One of them is contained in the formulation "God is being," when this is understood to mean not that being is a predicate of God but that the object of faith and the object of understanding are one. Tillich's method of correlating the question of being with the symbol of God is one variation on this theme, for it implies that the ultimate concept (being) and the ultimate symbol (God) can be correlated with each other but cannot be reduced to each other. A second guideline is provided by Heidegger's elaboration of the distinction contained in the two German idioms for "there is": *es ist* ("it is") and *es gibt* ("it gives"). A third, related guideline is found in the etymological kinship of thinking with thanking. Thanking is the mode of thinking appropriate to the "giving" that is implied in *es gibt*, as understanding is the mode of thinking appropriate to the presence implied in *es ist*. These are, however, only guidelines. What needs to be done in order to make matters clearer is to show how the perceiving and conceiving that are united in understanding have a parallel

---

2. Aquinas too places faith between science and opinion, less than science and more than opinion, but not by reference to the kind of certainty: "Fides autem [inter scientiam et opinionem] medio se habet, excedit enim opinionem in hoc quod habet firmam inhaesionem, deficit a scientia in hoc quod non habet visionem" (*ST* I II 67 3c)—faith is more than opinion because it cleaves to its object but less than knowledge because it has no vision of its object.

in two elements that are united in believing and how, therefore, the *intelligibility of being*, which appears in the transcendental image, has a parallel in the *credentiality of God*, which appears in the symbol of God.

"Being," or the unity of perceived and conceived object, appears in the form of a transcendental image; "God" appears in the form of a symbol. A transcendental image is the appearance of the object of understanding (being); a symbol of God is the appearance of the object of trust (God). If a transcendental image mediates between a sensible intuition and an abstract concept, what are the moments of which a symbol of God is the mediation? In a traditional formulation, they are called *notitia* and *assensus*, which are united in *fiducia*, so that we might see a parallel between the triad percept-concept-understanding and the triad notice-assent-trust.[3] Trust unites a notice and an assent in a way analogous to the uniting of percept and concept in understanding; and a symbol of God mediates between notice and assent as a transcendental image mediates between a percept and a concept. But this will require elaboration if it is to make clear how trusting is a form of thinking. I should like to make the elaboration by considering initially Georg Picht's sketch of a way in which to think of the world as creation, rather than to think of it metaphysically in the triad of self-world-God.[4]

Modern science is, according to Picht's account, built upon an experience of the world that, going back to Aristotle, became predominant in the West with medieval scholasticism. This experience is bound to the capacity of perception, and perception is interpreted as a purely receptive capacity. To perceive is to receive in the mind what is given to it from outside it. But there are two other ways of experiencing the world. One of them, represented by Posidonius of Apameia, is based upon *sympatheia*; another, represented in the Old Testament and in early Greek thought, is tied to labor, which is not passive but a matter of exertion in which human powers are tested and to be proved.[5] The difference in the three ways of experiencing the world is that through sense perception we are opened to the

---

3. The addition of the third moment (*fiducia*) is characteristic of Protestant theology.

4. Georg Picht, *Theologie—was ist das?* (Stuttgart and Berlin: Kreuz Verlag, 1977), pp. 509ff.

5. An echo of this is found in Hegel's *Phenomenology*, which speaks of experience as the "labor of the concept (*Arbeit des Begriffes*)," Picht notes, p. 510.

world and exposed to it, through affective "sympathy" we feel it as a source of pleasure and pain, and through labor we experience its burden and gravity (p. 511). Only against the background of this third way of experiencing the world does the meaning of play become clear; for it is in play that we are freed from burdens that we bear. For that reason "we experience in play something of that hovering condition that is designated by the word 'happiness' [*Glück*]" (p. 511). In distinction from pleasure, happiness is something that delivers us from the world and its pressures instead of exposing us to them (p. 511). Such a freedom does not make a self world-less. Instead, it enables one to discover the worldliness of the world: the world is shown not as pressure but as transparency. "We speak of happiness when the world is transparent to us" (p. 511). That is why, as Picht says, happiness is a universal constitution of our makeup (*Gemüt*). If we close ourselves off to happiness, we cannot experience the creation as creation either, and we misinterpret suffering. The true interpretation of suffering arises from an anticipation (*Vorahnung*) of beatitude, not, metaphysically, as "eternal bliss" but as the bliss experienced in the constitution of happiness as our life in the midst of the world when we see the negligibility of the opposition between life and death (p. 511).

The concept of happiness, and along with it the concept of play, is associated with the concept of "thanking." Gratitude is "the response to happiness" (p. 512), and, conversely, it is only through thanking that happiness is made known to us. In the act of thanking, what is disclosed to us is the "gloria Dei," which is what we see when we experience the transparency (*Transparenz*) of the world. Picht goes on to explain the philosophical significance of these notions by reference to Schelling's ontological question, "Why is there anything at all? Why not nothing?" That significance lies in the contrast it provides to a metaphysical way of thinking. The "age of metaphysics" sought to answer the ontological question by finding an ultimate *ground* of all things in the absolute being (*das absolute Sein*) that has to be thought of as an entity (*seiend*) if it is to be that which upholds all entities. Hence, those metaphysical propositions are true which can be based on the truth of this absolute ground and which, therefore, can demonstrate what provides the sustenance (*Halt*) and inner consistency of everything that is at all. Whatever we have recognized as true on the basis of this ground, we can "posit," and the assured content of science can be designated as "positive." This metaphysical concept was taken into theology when God was identified as *summum ens* and defined as substance.

Against this background, Picht proceeds (as Schelling suggested one ought to do) to try to "get behind" being itself. When one does so, everything positive begins to quake, and the question is raised whether a perspective that prescribes basing everything on an ultimate ground, and interpreting truth accordingly as "positivity," is not mistaken. But that leads into the heart of the doctrine of creation because, in the metaphysical tradition, the creator was interpreted as the ground of, or reason for, the world.[6] And it provokes Picht to ask whether there is any other way of making a distinction between being and nothing than the metaphysical one of positing an absolute being that is the ground of being and nothing. To answer that question, he has recourse to his description of the "experience of thanking." In thanking, as well as in happiness, there is contained a certain kind of affirmation, but it is an affirmation different from the "positing" of things. The characteristic of a thankful affirmation is that it is accompanied by the experience that the thing which is affirmed can never be "posited" and, as posited, held fast. The kind of agreement contained in our receiving something with thanks is different from the kind of agreement that is contained in our positing something. "In gratitude, we experience being not as firmly grounded positivity but in the way in which it appeared in happiness: as a groundless hovering in time" (p. 513).

That also makes the relation between doubt and certainty different in thanking from what it is in positing. Doubt is the opposite of a

6. That Tillich calls God the "ground of being" does not seem to me to place him into this metaphysical tradition, as it is sometimes said. For one thing, Tillich uses "ground of being" as a "metaphor" for what is meant by being-itself as the negation of nonbeing. For another, "ground" can also mean the basis of both the identity and difference of things. The general concept of "tree" is, for example, the "ground" of the concepts "maple" and "oak" in the sense that maples and oaks are the same in that they are trees but are different in that they are different trees. The "treeness" that is the ground of their being contains that by which the two are both similar and different. When this notion of ground is extended to the phrase "ground of being," it means literally that with reference to which being and nothing, or "is" and "not," can be both similar and different. But since there is no concept which represents something common to being and nothing, as the concept of tree represents something common to maples and oaks, there cannot literally be a ground of being at all. Hence, the concept of being always terminates in a question—we cannot say what being is because there is no ground-concept to which it and nothing can be related—to which an answer can be given only through a symbol.

metaphysical certainty based on positivity, and it needs as much as possible to be excluded from metaphysical faith. By contrast, doubt plays an essential role in thanking. It only becomes possible to "thank" the unexpected marvel of creation when one has gone through doubt. Hence, Picht concludes his discussion of this theme with a suggestion: "The hermeneutics of the basic experience of thanking makes the opposition between doubt and faith disappear. To show that is the task of a postmetaphysical theology that could teach us how to say again 'Deo gratias'" (p. 514).

What Picht has provided in these remarks is a concise exposition of the difference between the being of *es ist* and the being of *es gibt*, a difference that Heidegger in his "Was ist Metaphysik?" had indicated, when he alluded to the possibility of a thinking different from the thinking based on the Greek experience of *logos*, and had developed more fully in *Time and Being*.[7] But Heidegger always denied that faith was a form of thinking,[8] and so the guideline that he provides will not take us far. Similarly, Picht follows Heidegger in seeking a mode of the thinking of being other than that of the "age of metaphysics," while, unlike Heidegger, finding suggestions for that mode in biblical thought; but he does not concern himself with the possibility of there being two basic modes of thinking contained in the *fides* and the *intellectus*. In this case, too, we have a guideline—somewhat longer than Heidegger's—but not much more.

Hence, our task will be to draw from these suggestions a comparison between the understanding of being and the believing in

7. Martin Heidegger, "Time and Being," in *On Time and Being*, translated by Joan Stambaugh (New York: Harper & Row, 1972) pp. 1–24.
8. Thus, he denied that the tale of creation in the Book of Genesis had anything to do with answering the ontological question. "[The words of the Bible] can supply no answer to our question because they are in no way related to it. Indeed, they cannot even be brought into relation with our question. From the standpoint of faith our question ['Why is there something and not nothing?'] is 'foolishness.'" But this is not quite so unambiguous as it sounds, for Heidegger goes on, in the next paragraph, to say that there is a "thinking and questioning elaboration" of the world of Christian experience and that only "epochs which no longer fully believe in the true greatness of the task of theology [namely, that thoughtful and questioning elaboration] arrive at the disastrous notion that a philosophy can help to provide a refurbished theology if not a substitute for theology, which will satisfy the needs and tastes of the time" (*An Introduction to Metaphysics*, translated by Ralph Manheim [New Haven: Yale University Press, 1959], p. 7). Still, there is nothing either here or elsewhere in Heidegger to which one might attach the hint of a view that faith and understanding are both modes of thinking.

God which will show them as two modes of thinking. Thinking never appears purely, but only in the one or the other of the two modes; it appears either as faith or as understanding but not in some third way in which faith and understanding both have their ground. Thinking as such can be abstractly defined, and in that abstract definition it means the opening of the mind to what is other than the mind and the synthesizing of the opposite elements that constitute that other. In the mode of understanding, thinking unites the singular and the universal, the percept and the concept. What does it unite when it is in the mode of believing?

If we follow the indication given by the notion of "thanking" and by the contrast between "positivity" and "happiness" that Picht makes, then it seems that the elements united in faith are the same as those united in understanding; it is only a difference of the way in which the elements are connected. Either they are connected positively by reference to a ground, or they are connected marvelously by reference to nothing but time. This is a difference, to be sure. For in the case of positivity, the thought "This is a tree, a woody perennial plant, etc." is a firm affirmation only to the extent that the connection indicated by the copula "is" can be based upon some other thing. The tree is what it is because something causes it to be so. And what causes it to be so is caused by something else, and so on, until an absolute ground or a first cause is reached. To posit means, therefore, to synthesize a reality on the basis of something else. In the case of thanking (the thanking of happiness, in contrast to the understanding of being), the connection is not based upon anything else. The thought is: "This (luckily just) is etc., though it did not and does not have to be etc." Here the reality, not based on anything else, is simply acknowledged as happening despite the possibility that it could also not have happened. This comes very close to what, in "Time and Being," Heidegger describes as the *Ereignis* connected with "there is" in the sense of *es gibt*. Thanking acknowledges the "happiness" of reality; understanding posits the ground of reality.

What this appears to mean is that the difference between the thinking of being in terms of ground (*es ist*) and the thinking of being in terms of donation (*es gibt*) are two different ways of understanding being rather than two modes of thinking. For in both cases, metaphysical as well as thankful, it is an understanding of being that is involved rather than a believing in God. In both cases it is a matter of seeing the unity of singular and general by reference to being (is, was, will be, and so on), although the character of being is interpreted differently, in the one case as positivity, in the other, as happiness. If that connection of being is interpreted as a ground or basis or reason, then being is understood metaphysically; if it is interpreted as gift or happening, then being is understood in relation to the experience of happiness. In the former case, things are "posited" when they are understood; in the latter case, they are "acknowledged with gratitude." But even in the latter case we are not yet speaking of the mode of thinking contained in the notion of *fides*. Thus, we need to look beyond Picht's account in order to determine whether we can see the three moments in the act of faith as comparable with the three moments in the act of understanding.

I am proposing the thesis that the *notitia, assensus*, and *fiducia* are a parallel to perception, conception, and understanding so that the believing in God and the understanding of being are two irreducible modes of thinking. Everything that is anything at all is a singular ("this") and a universal ("kind of thing") in one, and the one is understood as the "being" of that thing. To understand is to think of a thing *as* the kind of thing it *is*. To formulate a parallel for faith, we need to say that to believe God is to unite a singular and a universal (or a counterpart to the singular and universal of being) by reference to "God." What then suggests itself as the mode of thinking called "faith" is the unity of a particular self with the universality of selfhood as such. Or, to put it differently, in the act of faith the "notice" of the human and the "assent" of the divine are united in the "trust" that is a believing in God. The notice of the human self is, then, the parallel to a percept of a singular thing; the assent of the divine is the parallel to an abstract concept of a general kind of thing; and the trust in God is the parallel to an understanding of being. Thinking as such is directed to a pure unity of God and being that appears now as being (when the object of understanding) and now as God (when the object of faith). To understand a thing is to understand the being of the thing; to trust a person (or a thing) is to believe the God in the person (or thing). What occurs when we understand being in a thing is that we are able to synthesize the thing's perceptual singularity and its conceptual universality in its being. The being of a thing is not some object other than the thing that is perceived and conceived; it is that element in the object in which the percept and concept are united and which is made visible in a transcendental image. Similarly, what occurs when we trust God in someone (or in

something) is that we are able to unite the person's (or thing's) isolated selfhood—what it inwardly experiences when becoming aware
of the meaning of "I-here-now" (or the inward meaning of something as a unitary thing)—with the community of selfhood or, to
use other terms, the human with the divine, the I with the not-I.
When we trust anyone at all, we are trusting God, just as, when we
understand anything at all, we understand being. It is a separate
question whether we can objectify being as such and God as such to
make them direct objects of understanding and trust. If that can be
done, then our understanding of being takes place not only through
the understanding of anything at all but also through a direct understanding of being as being, so that "Being is being" is no more an
empty tautology than is "This is a tree"; and our trusting of God
takes place not only through the trusting of anyone at all but also
through a direct trusting of God as God. A discussion of this separate question need not detain us here if we restrict attention to delineating the way in which *fides* represents a mode of thinking.

To be able to understand something implies the ability to subsume
it in its individuality under itself in its generality. This is an ability
that any human being has, whether or not it is made an object of
reflection. In that sense, everyone already has an understanding of
being. To be able to trust someone implies, similarly, the ability to
place the person as an isolated self into a community of selfhood.
Again, this is an ability that any human being has because everyone
is able to trust; and, again, in this sense everyone already has a faith
in God. To trust at all is to trust God; to understand at all is to
understand being. The *notitia* of the isolated self is joined with the
assensus to a community of selfhood in the unity of God that is the
object of *fiducia*. That this is not the sense of the historical definition
of faith as consisting of knowledge, assent, and trust may be granted;
one would have to yield the argument to any historian of theology
who maintained that there is no support for contending that this is
what was meant by those who defined faith in these terms.[9] The

9. Melanchthon's definition is sufficient for illustration: "Fides est assentiri uni-
verso verbo Dei nobis proposito, et quidam promissioni gratuitae reconciliationis
donatae propter Christum Mediatorem. Estque fiducia misericordiae Dei promissae
propter Christum Mediatorem. Nam fiducia est motus in voluntate, necessario re-
spondens assensioni. Estque fides virtus apprehendens et applicans promissiones et
quietans corda" (Philipp Melanchthon, *Loci praecipui theologici von 1559 (2. Teil) und
Definitiones*, edited by Hans Engelland [Gütersloh: C. Bertelsmann, 1953], p. 371).

purpose here, however, is not one of historical theology; rather, it is that of drawing as clearly as possible the parallel between faith and understanding as two modes of thinking whose own object is as such beyond the understanding of being and the faith in God. The terminology of *notitia, assensus*, and *fiducia* is useful for this purpose even if such a usage does not reflect the historical sense of the concepts.

In summary, then, we have the following: the understanding of being is one basic mode of thinking (whether it occurs metaphysically in the form of positing objects or thankingly in the form of letting them freely be); believing, or trusting, in God is the other basic mode of thinking. They are modes of thinking because they are activities in which the mind is opened to what is other than itself, the hyperontological and hypertheological, and in which a singular and a universal aspect are united to constitute the thing or person that is the object to which thinking is directed. They are activities of which everyone who has understood or trusted anything or anyone is already capable. The mediating notions are those of the "happiness" of being (Picht, Heidegger II) and, we might add here, the "dependability" of God (as expressed, for example, in covenant theologies).

Transcending toward the Other

In the Augustinian-Anselmian formulation, faith is said to be "seeking" understanding; and this is usually interpreted to mean that what is presented in the form of faith is to be made an object of reflection and thereby to become intelligible as well. "Nil credendum nisi prius intellectum" is Abelard's variation, which puts the intelligence before the credence. Can it be applied to the relation between faith and understanding when these two are described as two modes of thinking? In what way can the trusting in God be said to "seek" an understanding of being? To be noted is that, in this case, it is being that remains the object of understanding and God the object of trust. Faith in God does not seek an understanding of that faith or that God; it seeks an understanding of being. If it sought an understanding of faith or God, it would be seeking something expressible in a proposition such as "Faith is . . . (for example, the unity of individual and communal self)" or "God is . . . (for example, that by reference to which the unity of individual and communal self takes place)."

Hence, what is involved is not a matter of reflecting on the act or the contents of faith in order to understand what they are. Rather, it is a matter of making a connection between believing-God and understanding-being so that the intelligibility of being is the object of the "quest" contained in faith just as the credentiality of God is the object of the quest contained in understanding. The act of faith (in God) is directed toward the act of understanding (of being) in a manner indicated by the idea of "seeking." What, more exactly, is the nature of that direction?

That something "seeks" something else implies an incompleteness or openness on its part. Something that is self-enclosed or self-sufficient does not seek anything else; it rests within itself. This suggests that faith in God is not self-enclosed but is directed toward something else that it "needs" or "wants" or "desires" or in some other way "looks for." But what is the openness implied in the act of trust? We said that to trust anyone (or anything) at all is to trust God in that one, just as to understand anything at all is to understand being in an entity. So the openness which is indicated by the *quaerere* of trust is not a peculiarity of the trust in God as distinct from trust in anything else; it lies in the faith, or trust, itself and as such. *Fiducia*, as such, has an openness to something else; and if that something else is the understanding of being, then it has an opening to something that is other than trust. Normally, trusting and understanding can appear to be opposites: I trust that something is so, though I do not understand how it can be so, or I trust someone even though I do not understand him or her. In these cases, trust seems to represent a kind of deficiency when compared with understanding. If we had our choice between trusting or understanding something, we might choose understanding; for, if we understand, we do not need merely to "trust" something to be so because we can see how it is so. To understand how the typewriter works may seem better than just to trust that it does work. If we understand it, we can also do something about it if it does not work. If we simply trust it to work, we cannot do anything if it does not work. So too if we understand another person, we can do something about it if that person does not fulfill a promise. If we trust the person to fulfill a promise, we cannot do anything about it if the promise is not kept.

In that way, understanding seems superior to trust. This is, however, to take "trust" in a sense different from the one meant in *fides*. The contrast between trusting a typewriter to work and understanding how it works is like the contrast between believing that something is so and knowing how it can be so. To revert to Husserl's example, we may believe on good grounds that knowledge does "reach its object" but until we see how it does so we do not understand that process. Believing-that and understanding-how are set in contrast with each other. This is not the contrast implied when we speak of believing God and understanding being or of trusting something and understanding something. For to trust someone or something is to join the individuality of that self there with the community of selfhood as such (or, in radical form, to join the human I and the divine not-I), whereas to understand something is to join the individuality of the thing as perceived with its universality as conceived. The two are not ranked against each other. This is also evident in the connotations of saying that we trust someone. For to say that someone is worthy of trust is not to say something less of him than to say that he is understandable. "You can trust his actions" does not signify a lower value than "You can understand his actions"—it only implies a different category of evaluation. The same is true if we speak of obligation. "You must trust him" and "You must understand him" do not imply a comparison between the trusting and the understanding. Trust in this sense cannot be regarded simply as a deficiency of intelligibility or as a negative quality compared to intelligibility.

That faith in God seeks the understanding of being does not, then, mean that what is merely a matter of trust is to be transformed into a matter of understanding. Rather, it means that faith in God is *interpreted by* the understanding of being. The converse is also true. *Intellectus quaerens fidem* has the sense that the understanding of being can be interpreted by the faith in God. The relation implied in the notion that the one seeks the other is hermeneutical; and if hermeneutics is a transcendence of the one toward the other, the whole matter of thinking is the transcendence of being in its intelligibility and God in its credentiality. Understanding can interpret faith because there is a parallel structure in the two, or because they are two equally original modes of thinking. The *notitia* and *assensus* united in trust are parallel to the perception and conception united in understanding as an equally irreducible mode of thinking. The relation between the two is indicated by the notion of "seeking" or "asking," and the matter sought is a transcendence.

Looked at from this point of view, Tillich's correlation of ontological questions with religious symbols appears as a form of *intellectuals quaerens fidem*. For its pattern is that the understanding of being in things is converted into an open question when the effort is made to understand being as being. We can say what a tree (or any other object) is, and how it is a tree (for example, as a physically perceptible object), but we cannot say what "being" is because there is nothing by which the term "being" can be delimited or defined. "Being is being" is true but empty. "Being is the unity of singular as perceived and universal as conceived" is a definition of the term "being" but it does not say what being is in the way that "A tree is a woody perennial plant, etc." says what a tree is. There is no concept of being comparable to the concept of a tree. This becomes clear in the fact that if we say something is a tree we say something definite about it and delimit it against other kinds of things. If it is a tree, then it is not a man. But if we say it is a being, we have not said anything that defines it; all we have said is that it is something, not further defined, and we have not distinguished it from any other thing. Of anything whatsoever we can say it is a being. To say that it is a being amounts to saying "It is . . ." without supplying the concept that defines it abstractly. In that sense "being" is an open question. If we say something is a being, we leave open what it is; and, if we say being is being, we have not said anything about anything. Thus, the question "What is being?" is an unanswerable question.

The ontological question "Why is there anything at all?" is similarly unanswerable. For there is no concept more basic than being to serve as the reason for being's being in the way that there are laws that can serve as the reason or cause of other things. "Why is *N* sniffling?" "Because *N* has a cold." "Why does *N* have a cold?" "Because a virus infected the system." "Why did a virus infect the biological system?" "Because *N* was exposed to it." "Why was *N* exposed to it?" "Because *N* decided to attend a movie theater which was crowded and in which other people already affected were coughing." "Why did *N* decide to attend the theater?" "Because *N* wanted to see the film being shown." The series can go on indefinitely, taking different branches as we move from explanation by physical causes to explanation by intentions and desires or—with other examples—to explanations by statistical generalizations instead of mechanical causation.[10] But the question "Why is there anything at all?"

---

10. See Ian Ramsey, *Religious Language: An Empirical Placing of Theological Phrases* (New York: Macmillan, 1957), pp. 44–49, for an analysis of the way in which this

is not answerable in the same way. We cannot say there is something because something caused it to be, since the something that caused it to be would already be something, and we would then have to ask why there was that something at all. Kant observed that if we answer why there is a world at all by reference to a deity who created it, that deity in turn can ask, "But where did I come from?" If it comes from some other thing, the question is still not answered; if it does not come from some other thing, but just is and always has been, then there is no answer to the question why there is anything at all. There are only answers to questions concerning why there are certain things, and those answers have to rely on some other things already there in order to give an explanation. In that sense the question "Why is there anything at all?" is unanswerable. The question of being, to put it differently, is an open question.

If, then, we cannot answer the question "What is being?" in the way in which we can answer the question "What is a tree?" or "What is truth?"; if, furthermore, we cannot answer the question "Why is being (that is, why is there anything at all)?" in the way in which we can answer why there are people with colds or why there are human as well as nonhuman beings, because every answer already makes use of the givenness of something, then the process of understanding, which is the basis of our answering other questions about being ("What is?" and "Why is?"), cannot be used in order to understand itself and its own object. What *is* it that we understand when we understand anything? The only answer is "being." There is a circular relation between the definition and what is to be defined. To understand anything is to understand being in that entity—that is what understanding means. But we cannot understand being *as being*; we cannot say "Being is such-and-such" because being is not anything but itself.[11] "Being is being" has no more intelligibility than "Tree trees tree" or "Gift gives gift" or "God gods god," and the like. This

leads to points where the last explanation has the character of a "tautology sponsoring a key word and declaring a commitment" (p. 47), such as "because I'm I," "duty is duty," "fishing is fishing," and "conscience is conscience." Ramsey's analysis does not include a discussion of the difference between the saying of being through such significant tautologies and the saying of nothing through empty tautologies.

11. We may be able to *say* being through significant tautologies, just as we can say nothing through empty tautologies. But to say being as being in this way is not yet to *understand* being as being.

is the point, therefore, at which it becomes clear how the mode of thinking that is *intellectus* "seeks" another mode of thinking as a complement.

In Tillich's method of correlation, the openness of the question of being is correlated not with an answer that provides a definition or a reason but with an answer that is a symbol. The symbol of God as creator, or the symbol of creation, "answers" the question of being by providing an image of the sheer givenness of being against the background of the possibility of not being. "There is something, rather than nothing, because God created it" has a symbolic sense rather than a conceptual sense. Since it already presupposes being (the being of God), it does not provide a reason for there being something rather than nothing at all in the way that "there is a Mona Lisa because Leonardo da Vinci painted it" provides a reason for there being a certain painting. It does not, therefore, enable us to understand why there is not nothing in the way that we can understand why there is a given thing. It does enable us, however, to *interpret* our understanding of being (in things and persons) by reference to our trusting of God (in things and persons). The symbol of God as creating the world out of nothing interprets our understanding of the world by a reference to our trusting the world. It is a concrete expression of the *fides* that is sought by *intellectus*.

Tillich's method of correlation shows how understanding seeks believing rather than how believing seeks understanding. The opposite procedure, which is also implied but not developed in Tillich's method, is the one in which the symbols of faith, which express trust, "seek" their correlate in an understanding of being. Here there may be a limitation in the pattern of question and answer that Tillich uses unless one recognizes that an answer "seeks" a question just as much as a question "seeks" an answer. That an answer "seeks" a question can mean two different things: (1) An answer does not answer if it has no question to which it is related; (2) every answer to a given question opens a new question. Both aspects are included in the notion of correlation. To receive the answer given by a symbol one has to know which question it answers; and any given symbol not only answers that question but opens up new questions as well. The symbol of God as creating the world out of nothing does not answer how the physical cosmos came into existence, whether through a big bang or through an evolution, whether by a transformation of energy into matter or by some other process. It does answer the question of the relation between being and nothing, or the question how being (namely, that which we understand when we understand anything at all) emerges out of nothing (the sheer opposite of being). It is easy to confuse the two questions "How does being emerge from nothing?" and "How did the physical universe emerge out of whatever, if anything, was prior to it?" Historically speaking, it is also true that the two questions have been treated as a single question in much of the history of theology until the beginning of the nineteenth century. But the two questions are different. Being as such is prior to energy and matter and to the distinction between physical and nonphysical or metaphysical existence. Hence, even the highly refined physics and astronomy of today, which provide a much more reliable material basis for answering the question of the origins of the universe, are not any closer to the question of the emergence of being out of nothing than was primitive cosmology.

It is probably more adequate to use a pattern other than question and answer, however, to characterize the relation between intelligence and trust. Such a pattern does indicate how the one is open to the other. But to the extent that we think of an answer or a question as having a privilege over its counterpart—Lessing said that, given a choice between the search for truth and the possession of truth, he would choose the former, and there are no doubt others who would select the latter—the equal originality of the two modes of thinking is partially distorted. Thus, the relation might be described as one in which each mode interprets the other. Each is transcendent toward the other, and each is the complement of the other; the interplay between the two is the proper matter, beyond being and God, of thinking as such. The understanding of being is interpreted by the trusting in God and, conversely, the trusting in God is interpreted by the understanding of being. Like all processes of understanding, this is an ever expanding circle.

The hermeneutical circle is one defined by the interaction between our projected understanding and our attained understanding of something. To provide a simple illustration: If we read a novel, we already project who the characters are and what the story is going to be as soon as we have read a few sentences or paragraphs into the work. The projected understanding is modified by our continued reading, with further projections and modifications, until we have reached the end of the novel and have formed an interpretation of it as a whole. Then, if we choose, we can begin again. The relation between faith and understanding is not a hermeneutical circle of that sort because it continually "jumps" from the one mode to the other mode. This is not a shifting between part and whole or between projection and correction of the sort that is involved in the reading of a novel, and in hermeneutics generally; it is, rather, the shifting back and forth between understanding and trusting. If we call this a reciprocal "interpretation," we may seem to give an edge to understanding over trusting. But such is not the intention of "interpretation." Interpretation is more than the understanding of being; it arises out of the links forged *between* the understanding of being and the believing in God.

The "seeking" in *fides quaerens intellectum* is, then, an "interpreting" process, a transcendence between the two modes of thinking. The movement between them is made possible both by the openness of each and also by the analogy of structure in them. Understanding being is open to believing God because of the fact that we cannot understand being as being; and believing God is open to understanding being because we cannot trust God as God. We can only understand things *in* their being (or the being in things) and we can only trust things *in* God (or God in things). To understand things in their being (or, what is the same, to understand being in things) is to be related to them in such a way that we can think of them in the unity of the particularity and generality. In faith, there is an analogous structure, a unity of singular and universal. The unity in this case, however, is not the unity of being but the oneness of God. The singular, moreover, is not a perceived thing but a noticed self (a noticed I), and the universal is not an abstract thought of a genus but an assent, or consent, to selfhood as such. To acknowledge the I as there in a person or thing (to "notice" a particular self) is not the same as perceiving the particularity of the sense appearance; it is, rather, to be related to a particular in the mode of trust rather than of understanding. The *notitia* of the ego is the structural parallel to the perception of the singularity of a thing. The *assensus* to the community of selfhood is the structural parallel to the abstract conceiving of the genus of a thing. To trust someone is to make a connection between the presence of the acknowledged ego and the sense of community as such, and that connection is what is meant by "God" as the object of trust. We can understand things in their being, but we cannot understand being as being. The parallel to this is that we can trust someone or something in God, but we cannot trust God as God. For God is the one by virtue of whom we trust (just as being is the one by virtue of which we understand), and the one whom we trust in trusting anyone at all, rather than the one whom we trust as such. Only in God could one trust God as God. But this is to say that, just as being cannot be the object of a definition, so God cannot be the object of an assent or consent. For the definite community of self to which we assent is not God or the kingdom of God (just as the generic concept which we define is not being). What we notice, or acknowledge, is always an ego there-now; what we assent to is a form of community of selfhood; and the unity of the two in trust is the trust of a self in God.

This is, then, the structural parallel. Just as a singular and universal are united in the understanding, so an ego and a community are united in faith. The uniting of the two is, in one mode, the understanding of being and, in the other mode, the trust in God. We understand a thing in the being that appears in it; we trust it in the God who appears in it. Between the trusting and the understanding is a hermeneutical movement, a transcending of the one in the direction of the other. The understanding of being leads toward a trusting in God, and the trust in God leads toward an understanding of being. These two *modes of thinking* are configured in the *forms of reason*.

4

The Exstantial I in Christological Reason

THE TWO MODES OF THINKING—
understanding being and believing God—are configured in forms of
reason. Theoretical reason, practical reason, and poietic reason, or
theory, practice, and poiesis, are three configurations. Alongside
them Christology implies another form of reason, an *acoluthetic* reason, specifically related to the self in its ecstatic being. That there is
a christological form of reason can hardly be taken for granted. From
Plato and Aristotle to Kant's three critiques, we are familiar with the
notions of theoretical reason, practical reason, and poietic reason,
which correspond to the three activities of knowing, doing, and
making. Even if we do not think these forms of reason to exhaust
the list, since aesthetic reason after Baumgarten does not seem to fit
into one of the three, it is not likely that we readily add to it a form
of reason called "christological." Among twentieth-century theologians, it was Paul Tillich who was most explicitly concerned about
systems, their nature, and their place in knowledge. Those who are
familiar with his system of sciences and systematic theology know
that he divided reason into the theoretical and practical forms, each
of them having two subdivisions, science and art as the subdivisions
of theory and law and community as the subdivisions of practice,
and each of them having autonomous and theonomous expressions.[1]
Science grasps the forms, art expresses the realness (*Gehalt*) of reality; law shapes society formally, community does so according to
social meaning. Tillich added myth and cult as the two other expres-

---

1. Paul Tillich, *The System of the Sciences according to Objects and Methods* [1923],
translated by Paul Wiebe (Lewisburg: Bucknell University Press, 1981); *Systematic
Theology*, 3 vols. (Chicago: University of Chicago Press, 1951–63), vol. 1, part 1.

sions of reason, whose characteristic is to use the forms of reason in order to give theoretical and practical expression to the depth-dimension of reason. Myth was aligned with science and art in theoretical reason, as cult was with law and community in practical reason.

None of these represents a form of reason that might be identified as "christological." What is true of Kant and Tillich is generally true of the encyclopedias or systems of sciences. They may identify poietic reason with aesthetic reason and subsume it under the theoretic, as Tillich does, or they may follow the predominant pattern of distinguishing three basic forms, whether called theory, practice, and art or science, ethics, and aesthetics or whether denominated in other ways. They may even expand the number, as did Ernst Cassirer, who identified five basic symbolic forms—myth, religion, language, history, and science—and, more recently, Nelson Goodman in his loose array of "ways of world making." Whether an expanded list can include a form called "christological reason" is a question that needs to be answered explicitly. In the present chapter, I propose to answer it by delineating the forms of reason as configurations of the two modes of thinking. This will require not only the distinction between thinking and reason made in the preceding chapter but also a preliminary delineation of the several forms of reason as special configurations of thinking. Historical materials will be brought in only to the extent that doing so will help to make the whole conception clear.

The unsatisfying nature of the literature on Christology, which seems unable to escape from sterile questions having to do with the most appropriate way to formulate the unity of the divine and human, may well be attributable to the absence of any fundamental questioning of the terms of the discussion. If only the adequacy or inadequacy of formulations of the christological dogmas ("two natures in one person," and the like) are the matters at issue, christological discussion is reduced to the technical or hermeneutical task of translating dogmatic content from Hellenistic philosophy into other concepts. Not since Hegel's philosophy of religion has there been an effort to include Christology in philosophical theology, or what Hegel called *Religionsphilosophie*, itself. Even in Hegel no account was taken of the meaning of Christology for an understanding of selfhood—although one could argue that this is what in effect Hegel was doing in the *Phenomenology of Spirit*. If Christology itself, however, represents a form of reason, what must be brought into view is the nature of the relation that is implied when it is reported, for example, that Jesus said "Follow me!" and there were those who "immediately" followed. How is the self of those who "immediately" follow such a summons to be compared with the everyday self that is "forgotten" in the anonymity of *das Man* or the authentic self that is an I of its own? What is the nature of the "following" on the part of those who will "immediately" follow the summons of one whose name is "I am"? And who is the "I" of the "I am" in the person who makes the summons? If there is a rationality in this following, how is its form to be compared with theory, practice, and art or technique and its validity compared with theirs? How is "following" to be compared with knowledge, moral action, and aesthetic production or appreciation? These are some of the questions to be answered by the delineation of a christological form of reason.

Forms of Reason as Phenomena

The phenomena with which we are now concerned are the forms of reason that constitute the structure of thinking. If the two modes of thinking are understanding being and believing God, the "forms of reason" are concrete configurations of understanding and believing. Hence, the forms of reason, which configure thinking into a structure, always have in them a mixture of the understanding of being and the trust in God. They are "ontological" phenomena, phenomena which appear in discourse; they are not physical objects or relations accessible apart from the language in which they appear and in which we activate or exercise the function that is referred to as the form of reason. Thus, science as a phenomenon, a form of reason, does not appear to our physical perception; scientific objects do, but science does not. It appears in the body of knowledge which we refer to as scientific knowledge, but this body of knowledge constitutes the phenomenon of science only when it is seen as the result of the form of reason which brings it into being. In this way, the forms of reason belong to the "ontological" rather than the "ontic" dimension of things.

But the ontological can be conceived more broadly or more narrowly. Broadly conceived, an ontological phenomenon is a phenomenon that appears to us only in the medium of language; it cannot be seen merely in the medium of physical or sense perception.

In the stricter sense, an ontological phenomenon is one in which the very word itself, with the meaning it carries, is the phenomenon meant. When we can separate the object itself that appears in the language from the language which conveys it, "ontological" is being used in the broader sense of the term. When we cannot separate the word in which the phenomenon appears, as the medium of it, from what is meant as the object or the phenomenon itself, ontology is taken in the narrower sense. An example of an ontological phenomenon in the broader sense is any form of reason, such as science or art or morality. An example of an ontological phenomenon in the stricter sense is the appearance or phenomenon meant by the word *God* or the word *world* or the word *I*. These phenomena are ontological in the strict sense because in each case what the word means is so intimately connected with the very word that the phenomenon appears only when the word itself is there either in written or in spoken form. Without the word *God* in English (or its equivalent in another language), there is no appearance of God; without the word *world*, there is no appearance of the world; and without the word *I*, there is no appearance of the phenomenon I. This is not to say, of course, that whenever the word appears in language, either in written or in spoken form, the phenomenon is there. Even these words can be empty.

Following the guidelines suggested in part by Husserl's understanding of phenomenon as distinct from a physical object and by Heidegger's concept of phenomenology as the discourse which lets the object appear in language as the object is on its own, we can describe the procedure by which to bring into view the forms of reason that are the configurations of the structure of thinking. The first step is to look at some language, whether it be a single word or a whole sentence or paragraph or narrative or syllogism or sorites. If we are concerned with christological reason, our first task is to identify some discourse in which that form of reason has been crystallized. The texts in the New Testament which narrate the relationship between Jesus and his first disciples by Jesus' saying to them: "Follow me!" and by their immediately following him provide one example. A narrative which conveys the form of reason called Christology is one which says in short: "The one said to the others, 'Follow me!' and the others, upon hearing the summons, immediately followed him." That compound sentence is the briefest narrative expressing christological reason. Following "immediately," rather than after pondering the matter, is important to show that the very summons which they hear coming to them from another enables the hearers to follow. Followers are ones whose own resolution is brought into being by the summons they hear in the words of the summoner. The relation is not an example of christological reason if the summons is something other than an activation of the agency, the own will, of the followers. Unless it activates their own freedom, the summons coming from another does not establish a christological relation but exercises heteronomous power. The test of a genuine christological relation is contained in the question whether disciples who follow the summons that they hear act freely. The word *immediately* in our brief narrative is important for indicating this spontaneity of following. Equally important is the word *follow*, used to describe the action taken. The person who, in the form of "I," chooses to follow the one who in another person issues the summons is the subject-agent in the christological form of reason.

This brief narrative identifies a discourse that shows the phenomenon of acoluthetic reason, reason which has the form of following. The second step, after such a discourse has been identified, is to reflect on the phenomenon itself. Can anyone who has had no personal contact with the man Jesus as did the first disciples objectively see the phenomenon of christological reason as it appears in the relation between them and him or between any other comparable followers and followed accessible to us only in the language that tells of the following?[2] The question can be approached indirectly through a different kind of example. Let us suppose that what we are dealing with is not the form of reason called christological but rather the phenomenon of anger. As an ontological phenomenon, anger is different from the psychological state that appears to us in introspection or is behavioristically described. The ontological phenomenon appears to us only when it is conveyed to us in words that express anger.[3] If we can recall a case in which immediately, sponta-

---

2. This question is different from asking whether the ordered words of a narrative may be able to embody the same person as the one embodied, in a historical past, in flesh and blood; it is different, for example, from the question implicit in Bultmann's position that Jesus was resurrected into the kerygma.

3. The example is taken from Martin Buber, "What Is Man?" in *Between Man and Man* (New York: Macmillan, 1965), pp. 125f. But one could consider too what Bultmann says about speaking of God or of love. See Rudolf Bultmann, "Welchen Sinn hat es, von Gott zu reden?" in *Glauben und Verstehen*, vol. 1 (Tübingen: J. C. B. Mohr [Paul Siebeck], 1966), pp. 26f.

neously we were angered by something, we can reflect on this emotion by recalling it after it has passed. During the anger itself we cannot do so if with our whole self we "are" angry. But afterwards we can recall it to see what it was. As described thus far, anger is an ontic phenomenon; it is a case of someone's remembering an experience of his or her own. "Memory takes the place of psychological self-experience."[4] But if we can recall the incident later only through a narrative, or some other discourse, which recounts and re-members that occurrence as a way in which we *were* ourselves at a certain time; or if there is a language which recalls that occurrence to us so vividly that we relive the being-angry upon hearing the narrative that recalls it, then what is presented to us in that narrative is also ontological and not only ontic.

In this example, there is a bridge from the occurrence to the recollection, for the person who recalls is the same as the person who experienced being angry. The example differs, in this respect, from our trying to see the phenomenon of christological reason in a narrative of disciples, who were other than ourselves, resolving to follow the Christ who summoned them. Is it necessary to have followed the summons of another, or to have been involved in a relation of following, before we are able to see the phenomenon of christological reason that appears in the narrative of following? The question does not yield to a ready answer. A partial answer is to say that, at least if we have been in a christological relation ourself, whether or not the other involved was a person named Jesus, then we are more likely to see the phenomenon in the narrative which tells of such a relation. But we cannot rule out the possibility that even someone who has never "followed" in such a way would be able to see the phenomenon through and in the narrative which conveys it. This amounts to saying that we do not need to be scientists in order to understand the phenomenon of science (theoretical reason) or artists in order to understand the phenomenon of art (poietic or aesthetic reason), and we do not need to be followers in order to understand the phenomenon of following (christological, or acoluthetic, reason). Required is only that we be able to understand a meaning in the narrative which can show the phenomenon in itself.[5] Understanding the meaning of

4. Buber, "What Is Man?" p. 125.
5. In *Death in Venice*, Thomas Mann's narrative develops the relation between Gustav Aschenbach and a mythical figure, Thanatos-Eros, who appears in several guises in the course of the novel and who summons Aschenbach to his own end. A

the narrative means being able to identify ourselves sufficiently with one or another of the persons in it so as to understand ourselves as that one. It is not a matter of our remembering who we were in a certain action or state in our past but of seeing who we become in the course of reading the narrative itself. In reading, we are, of course, aware of ourselves as readers who, though different from the characters portrayed, are capable of being one or another of them. Readers are able to participate in the phenomenon that is conveyed through the narrative and are therefore able to understand and reflect on it. This participation is something other than simple observation, just as observing the behavior of a person who is angry is different from participating in the anger. To participate in it means to be, or at least to understand oneself as capable of being, the subject or the agent of the action. If what is involved is a past action or occurrence in which we ourselves were subjects or agents, reflection is a matter of recalling who we were in those actions and reflecting on that being; and we can do this by virtue of the fact that it is recorded in language. If what is involved is nothing from our own past, the means of reflection, although they are the same, require being able to place ourselves into the narrative by understanding ourselves as ones who could be those agents. This empathetic identification with a character and the course of action or events in a narrative makes it possible to perceive the phenomena even in occurrences in which we have not been the original subject and to make them an object of reflection.

But, one might ask, what about a person whose response to a narrative of such a summons and following is the question, "How could anyone be so foolish?" Even such a response indicates the ability to participate imaginatively in the events told in the narrative and thus to reconstitute the phenomenon in order to make it an object of reflection. Only if we can neither identify ourselves with

---

reader does not need ever to have been in Munich or to have seen a man in a portico there in order to understand and to follow the course of the narrative. The power of imagination is sufficient to understand the meaning of the narrative and the phenomenon of following that it shows. The psychagogue, whose guises range from the man in the portico to the gondolier to the young Tadzio, is not a christological figure; but Aschenbach is a "follower" of this Eros-Thanatos in its several figurations because his decisions and actions are prompted by the unspoken summons he hears in their appearances.

the persons of the actions (by understanding ourselves as ones who could be such) nor distance ourselves from them by wondering how anyone could be such a person does the phenomenon not show itself; only in such a case does it elude being made an object of reflection.

The first step in our procedure, then, is to take as our starting point a discourse in which the phenomenon is deposited. For the phenomenon of acoluthetic reason, the minimal unity is a brief narrative that includes a summons to follow and a response of "immediately" following. Second, reflecting upon the phenomenon that appears in that linguistic expression is done not by a kind of external or physical observation but by understanding that one can be the agent in the narrative. If we can either recall a case in which we responded to a summons similar to the one in the narrative, or if we can identify ourselves with it imaginatively as a human possibility, we are able to get it into view as a phenomenon for reflection. The third step concerns the method of reflection.

Let us suppose now that we do have before our mind the phenomenon of following shown by a christological narrative. How do we go about the reflection? What does it mean to reflect on the phenomenon, in contrast to recalling it or holding it before the mind? In one sense, the recollection or the representation of it to mind is itself a form of reflection because what is there in and before the mind is a reflection of what occurred independently of the act of recalling it. Reflection could mean simply a reduplication in our mind of what occurred and is represented in language, analogously to the way in which a mirror reflects, or throws back, the image that is presented to it. We could think of our mind as similar to a mirror in that it reflects an image of what actually occurred. But the mind is not such a mirror. When, for example, we are watching a play in a theater and are fully absorbed by the drama of it, what is going on in our mind is not a mirror reflection of what appears on the stage; rather, it is a reenacting in us of the same actions which are going on before us on the stage. Spectators are participants to the degree that they can on their own reconstitute and be in the actions, the feelings, and the drama of the stage. To reflect on such phenomena means to take as the object of attention that reenactment which was simultaneous with the dramatic performance.

This still does not answer the question of the means by which we reflect upon the phenomena. A brief, but hardly obvious, answer is that the means of reflection are *the concepts of a systematic structure.* The means used to reflect are provided by a systematic structure of concepts that have been derived and articulated independently of the particular occurrence or experience that presents the phenomenon. That is one of the reasons why systematic articulations of conceptual structures are of phenomenological importance. A systematic derivation of concepts makes it possible to keep the phenomena distinct from and related to one another. The relation between the systematic concepts and the conceptually interpreted phenomena is similar to the relation between pure mathematics and mathematical physics. The correctness of mathematical calculations does not at all depend upon the physical phenomena; mathematics can be developed independently of empirical observation or application to empirical facts. Nonetheless, mathematical physics is possible because mathematical formulas can be used to understand the laws which regulate physical phenomena. Such a physics is a form of reflection on physical appearances. The laws of planetary motion can be expressed in mathematical equations, but the mathematics in the laws does not depend upon the correlation with physical motion; it depends only upon its own inner coherence and articulation. Similarly, systematic concepts, although they are unlike mathematical formulas both in that they are not merely formal and also in that they have their own content (the content of human activities), are like mathematical formulas in being derivable in their own terms apart from being correlated with phenomena. When so correlated, they provide a reflection upon the phenomena. Fichte's *Wissenschaftslehre* was at least half right in its intention; we can derive the system of reflecting concepts independently of world appearances. But we cannot connect the concepts to phenomena without additional means of correlation between the two, and we cannot assume that the whole network of concepts must be derived from the being of the self.

The intention of reflection with systematic concepts is to ascertain what it is that is before our mind when we recall or reconstitute an action or an occurrence. We might compare this to our physical observation of a tree. We can look at and minutely observe a tree without reflecting on the fact that it is a tree or a tree of this or that kind. When we make the judgment that the thing which we observe or contemplate "is" a tree, we are reflecting on what is presenting itself. The system of terms (tree, leaf, trunk) is provided in part by everyday language and in part by the scientific language of classification (genus, species, particular, individual). Systematic concepts allow us to say what a phenomenon is in relation to other possibilities. In the same way, it is systematic concepts that enable us to identify forms of reason. If it is said that christological reason is a form of reason in which the self as I encounters its own egoity outside itself summoning the self, then all the terms of this description—the I, the self, the ecstatic relation—can be derived and defined independently of the christological occurrence itself. When defined, they can be used in order to say what it is that makes its appearance in such a relation. The notion of the exstantial I, for example, is not derived from the material in the christological narrative itself; for the narrative has to do with the summoning of a person by another person and with the immediate response to that summons. A systematic structure of concepts, which defines the possible ways in which the self can be an I related to itself or to others, is the structure used in order to say what this form of reason is. Implicit in such a system of concepts is an answer to the question whether such a thing as an exstantial I is even conceivable. Is it even conceivable that one's following another can be an existence of one's own and on one's own? A systematic structure of concepts must relate the exstantial I to the other forms of the I.

In one sense, a systematic structure is purely formal. This is not the formality of mathematics, but it is a formality in the sense that all of its possibilities can be derived without reference to how things really are. That is so even of Fichte's system of concepts, except that his initial proposition, "I am I," also posits the self in reality. Contrary to Fichte, however, clarity does not require one and only one way of setting up a systematic structure of concepts. It requires only that there be a principle and a rule of procedure for deriving the possibilities and for recognizing when the full set of possibilities has been derived. Fichte started with "I am I" and proceeded by deducing all the concepts (identity, difference, limitation, reciprocity, causality, and the others). The derivation is complete when the next step in the deduction leads back to the starting point. The principle that we are using here is that of the self relating itself to its other. The rule of procedure is drawn from there being two terms in the relation (the self and its other) and two sources of the origination of the action (the self or its other). The systematic structure should exhibit in a formal articulation all of the possible ways in which the self can be related to its other. Simply by reference to these formal possibilities, one can answer the question whether the ecstatic I is even conceivable.

But even if it shows that the ecstatic I is formally possible, a formal system does not decide whether there has ever been an occurrence or an act in which the ecstatic I actually appeared exstantially. To answer such questions, the articulated structure of possibilities must be correlated with actual events. How to do so is a question of its own. Mathematical science does so by constructing and testing models of real occurrences. Here our concern is not with that aspect of systems but with interpreting the phenomenon appearing in the christological narrative as the form of reason involving the ecstatic I. The interpretation may itself serve as a verification, but not in the strict sense in which scientific models are verified. The summons of Jesus to his disciples could not be a summons enabling their own freedom—that is what we take to be the intention of the word *immediately*—if it were not the appearance of the I to itself, just as we could not freely attend to the voice of conscience if it were not the call of the self. A reflection upon an occurrence clarifies it by putting the phenomenon into relation with similar and different phenomena by means of the forms which define and grasp them.

The Possibility of an Exstantial I

That the self can and does project itself upon possibilities of being was made clear by Heidegger in his analysis in *Being and Time*. But does this include the possibility of an ecstasis of the self—the possibility that the other to which the self relates itself is the inwardness of the self without being a projection from that inwardness? Heidegger's concept of *Existenz* does not answer the question, for ex-sistence means only that I am who I am by projecting myself into certain possibilities. Dasein is always "ex-sistent" in that way.[6]

Let us recall the ways in which the self appears. In the first place, it appears as the phenomenon of the I in the word *I* itself. This word carries a meaning that is simultaneously a reference to something most singular and to something most universal. The word *I* gives an

---

6. Concerning Heidegger's terminology it might be noted that Dasein is "ex-sistent" (in its recollection of its having been and its running forward to its "can be" that is to come), and time, which is the meaning of Dasein's being, is "ecstatic" (in the three ecstasies of past, present, and future); the ecstasy of time and ex-sistence of the self are the correlative terms.

absolutely concrete here-and-now. The one who is the "I" is the one who in the moment of saying and at the place of saying is the one and only one meant by the term "I." Nevertheless, the same word can be said by an infinite number of persons. In that, it means something universal. The word *I* contains an internal dialectic between the singular and the universal. Whoever says the word is the one meant in the time and place of that saying; any personal subject can become the one who is the reference. In that sense, the I is the *universal singular*. It is singular because only the person who says "I" is the I meant by the term, and because this person who I am can never exchange places with another. But it is also universal because any person is capable of saying and thinking the meaning of the word and of being I in that time and place. Like the word *this*, the word *I* contains both the concrete and the universal aspects in an internal dialectic which makes it impossible to sever the concreteness from the universality. The word is a medium in which the phenomenon makes itself visible to reflection.

The phenomenon of the I has other aspects besides this unity of singularity and universality. These become visible when we notice the different connections in which the phenomenon appears. In the context of the Cartesian "I think," the I appears in its ineradicability as the agent of the whole of thinking or doubting. What remains certain even when it is called into question is the reality of the one doing the doubting or the thinking or the calling into question. But this is an insubstantial or immaterial reality. The theoretical I is not the embodied I. The Cartesian I is the self as it is transparent to itself in theoretical thought but is immaterial. In the context of the Fichtean "I am I," the self affirms itself in its real existence because it posits itself by asserting a unity of subject and predicate in itself. "A is A" is a certainty because it is a tautology; "I am I" is a certainty because it too is a tautology. But "I am I," unlike "A is A," also contains a real reference. It posits the reality of the self as one who is a self. The self affirms itself as a self. The phenomenon of the I shows itself defined by its own selfhood. The self-positing I differs from the Cartesian I in two respects. First, it is the appearance not merely of the immaterial, theoretical I, the "one who" of the thinking, but also of an I which really exists. Second, it is the appearance of the phenomenon with a definition of that phenomenon as being what it is on its own, and, as the *Wissenschaftslehre* develops it, this being of the self is the origin of the systematic network of theoretical and practical concepts. Such theoretical concepts as cause and effect and such practical concepts as freedom and duty are all derivable by a single dialectical procedure from the original proposition that I am I. The Cartesian I is pure subjectivity; the Fichtean I is pure subjectivity but also the origin for the objective grasping of the objectivity of the world. Rightly understood, Fichte's statement that the I is the creator of the world is correct. The simple proposition "I am I" contains the system of concepts by which the I is reflected and the system of concepts by which the world is established in its objectivity.

In the Cartesian and the Fichtean I, in the method of doubt and in the systematic derivation of concepts, we have the phenomena of *pure subjectivity*, of the *reality of that pure phenomenon* in existence, and of the establishment of the *objectivity of the world* (or of the worldliness of the self). A different aspect of the self is shown when the starting point is not the subject term but, rather, the activity in which the self is involved when empirically perceiving the world. The self then emerges as the zero-point of perception. If we perceive a tree with our physical senses, our initial attention may be entirely on the tree. We perceive the tree, we do not perceive ourselves as perceiving the tree. While perceiving the tree, we may change our place of viewing so as to see the object from many different sides. At any given time, we can look at it only from one side; but we can change places and put together into a single three-dimensional image the aspects that have appeared to our perception from the different locations. Though our first attention was simply upon the object, the possibility of our changing locations directs attention toward the subject. Our bodies provide a perspective upon the object, and subjectivity appears as the mobility of the body. When we then notice that it is not only our own body but also other bodies which can serve as points from which the object is viewed, we become aware that there are other points of view, not our own, upon a given object. My body is a point of view for viewing any object whatsoever, and subjectivity comes into view as an absolute point of origin, the zero-point from which everything is perceived and thought. The reality of the self that is posited in the predication of the I as an I is an embodied self; the "one who" of thinking and being a self is also a zero-point of a bodily perspective.

The self of Dasein shows another aspect of the phenomenal I. The self as I can hide in the anonymity of a generalized subject. The place toward which we look in order to discover this I-subject is everyday language, where the I expresses itself not in its singular subjectivity, not in its singularity and propriety, not as the zero-point of a perspective, but as hidden within the anonymity of a subject as such. Heidegger uses the term *verfallen* for this form of the subject, when the ego appears as a "case of" general subjectivity. If it is in the language of everyday that the self appears in its casualness, how is it possible that the self as I can lapse into being but an instance of the universal subject instead of a singular instantiation of the I? How is it possible for the self, who essentially is a singular I in its very universality, to understand itself and to express itself simply as an instance of a general? It is possible, as we know from Kierkegaard's as well as Heidegger's analysis, because the self has the character of being projective of itself. The self is not only subject and not only a world-creator; it is also a project. It casts itself forth from itself. If the self is thought of only as a subject or substance, then what follows is that the self is what underlies the material in which it appears; and then it remains a puzzle how the self can lose itself not in the material which it underlies, by identifying itself with its bodily appearance, but in the anonymity of a subject in general. Because the self is projective, it casts before itself or ahead of itself or as over against itself its own subjectivity, and it finds present to itself not only nonsubjective apparent objectivity but also a subjectivity inasmuch as the self has projected the universality of the I as such. The form of selfhood which appears in the everyday, in which the absolute singularity of the self is forgotten, is made possible by this projectivity. The generalized subject is a testimony to this projective capacity, which makes it possible for the propriety of *Jemeinigkeit* to appear in projection as the generality of *Allgemeinheit*.

Even the projected I is different from the ecstatic I, in which what appears to the ego-subject is its own selfhood in the propriety of I. In the ecstatic relation, what is presented to the ego is its own self in the form of the singular I and not in the form of anonymous subjectivity. In one respect, the I of everyday understanding (*das Man*) and the I of ecstatic understanding are similar. In both cases the self is related to its own selfhood in the universality of the I as such; it is not related as one person to another person but as self to its own egoity. The ecstatic I presented to me is the I in its authenticity as singular and absolute propriety; the I of the self-awareness most intimately my own in my own person stands outside and over against me in an ecstatic relation. In projection as well as ecstasy, the self shows its capacity for severing itself from itself, that is, its capacity for being apart from itself. The ecstatic I is an I which, identical with the I of inward awareness, is "introjected"; it has not been projected from within the egoity of the I onto a public subjectivity, but it has been introjected from without. The I that stands without is as really out-standing as the I that stands within. Its standing out of its otherness is simultaneous with the introjection of the self's ownness. Each of them, the projecting and introjecting, is equally originating subjecthood, and each of them is with equal originality the singularity and absoluteness of the I as such.

The possibility of such an ecstasis was recognized in medieval literature as *caritas*; for the theology of the Reformers it was *fides*. Petrus Aureoli gives a succinct formulation in his commentary on a distinction in Peter Lombard's *Sentences*, the textbook of medieval theology. In knowledge, he writes, the self posits itself into the phenomenal being, the *esse apparens*, that is distinguished from natural being; in doing so, it places itself before itself (*ponit se ante se*) or becomes, as it were, a proposition or a *Vorstellung*. In ecstatic love, it places itself outside itself (*ponit se extra se*) and gives itself to its beloved as an *esse datum et latum*, a being bestowed and offered (*Sentences* I, dist. 2, sect. 2).[7] Consistent with the general shift from *caritas* to *fides* that marks the Protestant theological understanding of the self, Luther formulates the ecstasis as the power of faith, when, in the commentary on Galatians, he speaks of faith as placing us outside ourselves (*fides ponit nos extra nos*). We can add to these references the text of Luke which speaks of the prodigal son as "coming to himself" (*eis heauton elthōn*, Luke 15:17) and resolving to return to his father's house, as though the self had been away from itself and had to come back to itself.

The ecstatic I is the external but proper I placed outside itself. That the self can be beside itself is, thus, not a new idea. Discipleship, as a way of the self's coming to itself by being outside itself, involves such a possibility of ecstasis. In following the "I am" who summons the follower, the self comes to itself as I. The other side of

7. Quoted in L. Oeing-Hanhoff, "Ontologie, trinitarische," *Historisches Wörterbuch der Philosophie*, vol. 6, edited by Joachim Ritter and Karlfried Gründer (Darmstadt: Wissenschaftliche Buchgesellschaft, 1984), col. 1202, where reference is made to a study of Aureoli by Theodor Kobusch, *Sein und Sprache: Historische Grundlegung einer Ontologie der Sprache* (Tübingen, 1982 Habilitation dissertation). Kobusch's study was not available to me.

this capacity for the ecstatic reception of the self is the capacity for giving oneself, as is indicated in such paradoxical formulations as this that the self can find itself only by losing itself. Not only is it possible for the self to be ecstatic in the christic following without losing its autonomy; it is also possible for the self to come to itself in another and to come to its own in that other. It can come to itself as I either through self-reception, which is the christological relation, or through self-giving, which is the relation of finding oneself in another through giving up one's own place here. It can be the self it is ecstatically in the *akolouthia* and in the *agapē*. In the christological following, the self comes to its own self here, that is to say, in the embodiment that is its own person. In the self-giving relation, the self comes to itself in the person of the other. The two possibilities are complementary. The first is that of following the summons that comes from the "I am" of a christological figure; the second is that of transposing the I in its proper selfhood from its location here to another location. The difference between losing the self as self and finding the self through giving up the self is that, in the latter case, the self does come to be its own in the other; it does not disappear as a self of its own in the self of the other. Agape-love is the relation in which the self can give itself up here in its own location and find itself in its location in another person.[8]

These are the different ways in which the phenomenon of the I appears. What is common to all of them is that language is the material of the appearance. This is the case with the self-instantiating I, that is, the I which appears when the word *I* is said or thought. This is also the case with the self-affirming or self-positing I, that is to say,

8. In the history of theology, this theme is treated under the title of exinanition and reaches its fullest formulation in nineteenth-century kenoticism, which answers the question of the subject of the exinanition (Is it God or the Eternal Son who "empties himself"?) by saying it is God who gives up deity to exist as humanity. Such a *kenosis* of God implies that God can be God as what is not God, namely, as a human being. "The difficulty of conceiving psychologically the kenotic process in the divine consciousness is," P. T. Forsyth wrote in *The Person and Place of Jesus Christ* (London: Independent Press, 1909), "certainly an impediment, but it is not an obstacle. 'It is out of reason' is the complaint. 'We cannot think together the perfect God and the growing man in one person.' No, we cannot think them together. But also we cannot realise them apart" (p. 305). The same concept of exinanition can be applied to the being of the self expressed in "I am." The self can be itself as the "I" in this-person-here-now that "I" am; it can be itself also in another, that is, in the other-there. Both ways of being are proper to the self as I; both are authentic, or *eigentlich*, possibilities.

the self that posits itself as real in the judgment "I am I." It is the language of the proposition or of the judgment in which the self appears. This is the case, thirdly, with the self as the zero-point of perception when a connection is made with the body and the real existence of the self-positing I. For this connection can be made only to the extent that the body too is a form of language, that is to say, a material texture which is capable of bearing a meaning. The body is capable of being not merely something brutely there but a material texture that signifies something. What it signifies emerges in the process of our becoming aware of a zero-point that is the origin of the location of the body. Fourthly, this is the case with the hidden I, as it is, finally, with the exstantial I. The I that is hidden in the anonymity of the general subject is one that appears in the use of everyday language. The exstantial I is the I which appears in the language that summons to following and also in the donative language that expresses the giving of the self to another and which comes to itself in giving itself away.

Systematic Reflection of the Phenomenal Self

A systematic grasp of a phenomenon provides the means for defining what it is. The object before us, the christological form of reason, is phenomenological, not empirical or logical. A tree is a physical object; a judgment is a logical (mental), or psychical, object; truth is a reflective object, a transcendence; thinking, as the object of thinking, and judging, as the object of judging, are reflexive objects. Thus, the mental activity called "judgment" ("*A* is *a*") is one of which we can be directly aware when we make a judgment (and if it is a judgment about a judgment, rather than about something else, then the judgment about which one makes a judgment is a reflexive object as well as a logical one); and we know the difference between a "judgment" and a "question" ("Is *A* *a*?") on the basis of our awareness of what we are doing or what is going on when we judge and ask. We never see "judging" by empirical observation (as we can a tree); we can be aware of it as we perform the action. But such mental activities can be made phenomenological objects in the medium of language. Just as a word makes it possible, when I understand the sense of the word, to constitute the object it means (a tree, for example) as an ideal object, such sentences as "This is a tree" and "The leaf is green" make it possible to constitute an object called "judgment." To say that a judgment is the subsumption of a subject under a predicate or the inclusion of a subject in a predicate or the ascription of a predicate to a subject is to provide various descriptions or definitions of the phenomenal object of which we are directly aware when we make judgments. All of these descriptions or definitions are reflections of the act which use a system of logical concepts (subject, predicate, subsuming, and the like).

Moreover, we can also define a judgment (or other mental acts) by the way in which the act relates the one judging to that about which the judgment is being made. How does judging that what one sees is a tree relate the observer to the tree? The phenomenal object in this case is not just the mental act (characterized as subsuming, including, ascribing, or in similar ways) but also a form of reason, that is, a definite way in which the self is related to its other through an activity. The judgment "This is a tree" can be taken, accordingly, not only as an example or case of judging but also as the enactment of *theoretical reason*, a form of relating the agent to the object of the act. The definition of such forms of reason uses a system of concepts to distinguish and interconnect the forms.

Our present concern is with the form of reason contained in christological assertions or narratives. The assertion "Jesus is the Christ" can be treated as an example of a judgment, representing the same kind of object and form of reason as "That is a tree." But, if it expresses a distinct form of reason, called christological or acoluthetic, it raises other questions. What relation between the self (as the one who makes the judgment or tells the tale) and its other (the one about whom the judgment is made or the tale told) is formed when the words are said and their meaning understood? What constitutes *christological reason*? The process of uncovering the form of reason in the sentences and narratives is a phenomenological reduction. The words of the statement or narrative are analyzed in a process that leads back to the relation erected between subject and object in them.

What such a phenomenological reduction amounts to can be made clearer by initially listing the different ways in which a statement or an assertion can be analyzed. "The leaf is green," for example, can be analyzed *grammatically* as a statement composed of a subject and a predicate joined by a copula, in which the subject is modified by a definite article, the predicate is adjectival, and the copula is the third person singular of the present tense of the verb "to be." Again, it can be analyzed from the point of view of its *meaning and truth*. The meaning, or sense, refers to what is understood when the words are heard or read. If it should happen that the sequence of sounds in the spoken words "the leaf is green" coincides with a sequence of sounds in a language other than English, the same sounds may have quite different meanings; but in both cases the term "meaning" designates what is understood in hearing the words. (It is not easy to find a complete sentence with an acoustic or optic equivalent in another language, but Umberto Eco gives an example of one which can be read as either Latin or Italian with quite different senses: "I vitelli dei romani sono belli," which means either "Go, Vitellius, at the sound of war of the Roman god" or "The calves of the Romans are beautiful."⁹) The truth of the assertion has to do with the question whether what is asserted is indeed so, or whether the way in which the thing meant is shown in the words of the assertion is the same as the way in which it shows itself from itself; a true assertion shows in its words a thing as it is on its own. The meaning and truth of assertions are different, but we cannot determine truth without understanding meaning.

Again, an assertion can be analyzed with a view to determining its *use* or *function*. "The leaf is green" is not being used in the present context in order to tell the reader anything about a leaf but in order to illustrate what is meant by a phenomenological analysis. In other contexts, it can serve such other purposes as giving information about a leaf, translating into English a sentence from another language, and showing a child learning to speak what the color green looks like.

None of those reductions—grammatical, semantic, functional—is phenomenological; for a phenomenological analysis is intended to uncover the form of relation between self and other that appears in the making of the assertion. The same reduction can be done upon a piece of music or a work of art as well as a linguistic expression; it is phenomenological if the intention is to uncover the form of reason that appears in the work. Reason is the structure, the self-to-other relation, contained in thinking; but that structure appears in different forms. We cannot just think. We can only think in some way—in theoretical, practical, aesthetic, poetic, or other rational forms. The

9. *A Theory of Semiotics* (Bloomington: Indiana University Press, Midland ed., 1979), p. 140.

form contained in the thought "The leaf is green" is theoretic: the self involved is an observing subject in relation to its other as an observed and formally grasped object. Theoretical reason, so defined, is one form of the structure of understanding, and understanding is one of the two modes of thinking. To uncover that form of the self-other relation in the linguistic work "The leaf is green" is to reduce it phenomenologically. Doing so presents the phenomenal object that appears in and with the linguistic work.

Like other assertions or linguistic works, the statement "Jesus is the Christ" or the narrative of following can be analyzed from various points of view. If it is viewed as a rational phenomenon, the intention is to analyze the form of reason that appears in it. The words represent a possible assertion or possible tale, something that *can* be said by someone, without regard to the number of those who have actually said it or to the understanding they had of it. A linguistic work has to be possible in this sense; it must represent something that someone *could* say or think and something that has been said or thought at least once. If a christological assertion or narrative, an acoluthetic form of assertion, did not make any sense, it could not embody a form of reason; whatever the phenomenal object might be, it would not be a form of reason. If the sentence or narrative made sense but no one ever actually thought it or said it of anyone or anything, it would not represent a real phenomenon. "John is a George Babbitt" is a possible assertion, but it remains an abstract possibility as long as no one has ever said of someone named "John" that he is a George Babbitt. If it has once actually been said or thought, then a real phenomenon can appear in it. A phenomenological reduction will need to distinguish the several forms of reason that might be the phenomenal objects in a given linguistic work.

Such a reduction should not be confused with reductionism, which is the view that the thing traced back to something else is less "real" than that to which it is traced. It is reductionism when, for example, one says that a feeling of pain is nothing but a certain neurological state. It may well be that, corresponding to every distinct pain, there is a distinct neurological state, so that every sensation of pain has a corresponding neurological state and every description of a pain can be translated into the description of a neurological state and thus reduced to such a state. But from this it does not follow that pain is nothing but a neurological state, since the experience of a pain is as real in its being felt as is the neurological state in its being instrumentally observed. The reduction of a work to a form of reason is not reductionist in that sense. Its intention is to define the phenomenon that appears in the linguistic work. It is a way of answering the question "What phenomenon makes its appearance in a work?" The form of reason that is the phenomenal object in such judgments as "The leaf is green" is a theoretic one.[10]

How many forms of reason are there? The answer can vary, for the determination of the number of possible forms is a function of the system used. A system, in this minimal sense, consists of a principle according to which the possibilities are derived and related to each other. In a strict system, such as Fichte's *Wissenschaftslehre*, there is one principle and one method of procedure by which all the concepts are derived from the principle; and the systematic derivation is complete when the procedure has led to a point where the next step in the derivation brings one back to the beginning.

Schleiermacher, whose dogmatics may be the most systematic of any organically conceived theological system, and Tillich, whose *Systematic Theology* is among the most systematic of contemporary theologies, provide clear illustrations of such a procedure. In *The Christian Faith*, Schleiermacher defined religion by reference to the threefold division of knowing, feeling, and doing. The principle Schleiermacher used in order to identify knowing, feeling, and doing as the three forms of reason is that of the life process as one in which the self remains within itself or goes out from itself. "Life," Schleiermacher wrote, "is to be conceived as an alternation between an abiding-in-self (*Insichbleiben*) and a passing-beyond-self (*Aussichheraustreten*) on the part of the subject" (§3.3). The basic structure is that of the self relating itself, or being related, to the world. The structure appears as the self-positing and non-self-positing elements in self-consciousness—one is conscious of positing oneself but also of not having posited oneself in just this way (§4.1). The three possibilities implicit in this structure are (1) that the self remains entirely within itself, taking the world contents into itself; (2) that the self goes out from itself, emptying itself into the world contents; (3) that there is a reciprocity between the two. The three reflect the basic logical principles of identity, difference, and limitation. According to

---

10. Forms of reason can also be called *habitūs*, in the Aristotelian sense of ἕξεις, that is, ways in which the self "has" itself and its object in the relation, rather than in the ordinary sense of "habits" as repeated actions.

these possibilities, Schleiermacher construed feeling as a relation in which the self remains entirely within itself; for, "not only in its duration as a result of stimulation" but "even as the process of being stimulated," it is not something done by the subject but something taking place in the subject, and it thus "belongs altogether to the realm of receptivity" and is "entirely an abiding-in-self" (§3.3). Doing (*Handeln*) is the opposite of feeling, because the self goes out from itself. Knowing is intermediate. As a possession of knowledge, it is, like feeling, immanent; and, as the act of acquiring knowledge, it is transcendent, like doing. Since these three—feeling, doing, knowing—exhaust the possibilities, and since, on further scrutiny, it turns out that religion can be recognized as different from any of them, one must ask where religion belongs. Is it a form of reason at all? To answer the question, Schleiermacher first determined that one of the three forms of reason—feeling—is both a form of reason of its own and also the accompaniment of all forms of reason. Feeling is distinct from knowing and doing when it is regarded as one of the ways in which the self is related to its world. But as "immediate" feeling, it also "accompanies" knowing and doing. In every knowing and doing, as well as in every objective feeling, there is also an immediate, accompanying feeling. It is with that aspect of feeling that Schleiermacher identifies religion. Religion as the "feeling of absolute dependence [*schlechthinniges Abhängigkeitsgefühl*]," or the feeling of dependence pure and simple, is not one of the forms of reason but an accompaniment of every form of reason. It is shown indirectly in knowledge and doing as the feeling that accompanies them.[11]

On Schleiermacher's analysis, then, there are three possible forms of reason and, with them, a substratum (if one may call it that) of immediate feeling that accompanies all the forms. The unity of the subject's immanence and transcendence, or the unity of knowing,

11. As the literature on and responses to Schleiermacher make plain, the picture is somewhat confused because Schleiermacher seems to use the term "feeling" to refer to a form of consciousness—knowing, doing, feeling—as well as to both of the forms of self-consciousness—receptivity, spontaneity. The feeling of dependence and the feeling of freedom are the two forms of self-consciousness. Thus, the "feeling of dependence" can be combined with "gloomy" as well as "joyful" feelings (§4.2). The feeling of joy, along with similar feelings, is a form of consciousness, whereas the feeling of dependence or of freedom is a form of self-consciousness. The latter has to do with how one feels one's self in the world; the former has to do with how one feels the world.

feeling, and doing, is "the essence of the subject itself" which manifests itself in those forms and is "their common foundation" (§3.3). What connects knowing, doing, and feeling is not a superordinate fourth entity but the field of immediate or pure feeling. To this field belong such feelings as joy and sorrow. Thus, the feeling of joy can accompany a knowing (as when one makes a discovery or comes to recognize something one had not recognized before), a doing (when a Kantian moralist does something that is right just because it is right and regardless of self-interest), and a feeling (a feeling of pain can be accompanied by joy if it occurs in a limb that has been paralyzed—the pain is an indication of its life). In all those cases the pure feeling is not a function different from the knowing, doing, and empirical feeling but an accompaniment to them. An "objective" self-consciousness, such as the judgment of self-approval (instead of the feeling of joy), does not accompany a knowing or doing but is a knowing or doing of its own. Similarly, the immediate feeling of worldliness (the feeling of the reciprocity of dependence and freedom) differs from the feeling of something in the world. Finally, then, Schleiermacher can distinguish religious feeling from other immediate feelings (such as joy or reciprocity) as "unqualified [or unconditional, absolute, *schlechthinnig*] dependence." The feeling of reciprocity that accompanies knowing, doing, and feelings is the feeling of the world; the feeling of absolute dependence is the feeling of God. But neither the world nor God is an objective term in a relation. Each is, rather, a qualification of immediate feeling that appears in all of the terms of the relations of knowing, doing, and feeling.

The purpose for citing Schleiermacher here is not to assess his definition of religion but to show how the classification of the forms of reason is determined by a systematic principle. If, as in Schleiermacher's case, the systematic principle is contained in the question whether the self is immanent or transcendent in a given relation, then there are only three distinct forms: immanence, transcendence, and interchange. (If one is at home, one has only three choices concerning where to be: one can stay at home, one can leave home, or one can leave and come back. There is no fourth choice, unless standing on the threshold is considered to be a neither-leaving-nor-staying distinct from any of the other three. But, strictly speaking, a threshold is like a boundary: one is never on it but always on one or the other side of it.) Immanence, transcendence, and interchange are the phenomena that appear in affection, action, and knowledge. If what we otherwise, apart from the systematic divisions, recognize as religion does not permit us to equate it with any one of those three, then it cannot be a form of reason. If it is not a form of reason of its own, then it has to be placed into the region in which the forms of reason are connected with each other, the region named as the "foundation" of the forms. There would be no other place for it in the systematic arrangement. The matter may be somewhat unclear in Schleiermacher because the "feeling of absolute dependence" (which is the same as the feeling of the nonabsoluteness of freedom) seems to be different from other feelings. There can, for example, be a state that is identifiable as the feeling of joy. But there cannot be *a* state that is identifiable as the feeling of absolute dependence, since the feeling of absolute dependence belongs to that unity of knowing, doing, and feeling which is called their "common foundation" or the "essence of the subject itself" (§3.3). "A feeling of absolute dependence . . . cannot exist in a single moment. . . . But the self-consciousness which accompanies all our activity, and therefore, since that is never zero, accompanies our whole existence, and negatives absolute freedom, is itself precisely a consciousness of absolute dependence. . . . Without any feeling of freedom a feeling of absolute dependence would not be possible" (§4.3). Even so, one can see that in Schleiermacher's systematization the common foundation is manifest in a feeling that accompanies activities and passivities but not in the doing or knowing itself. Besides other feelings, which rank alongside knowings and doings, there is the feeling of absolute dependence, which expresses the essence of the subject itself and the common foundation of the three forms. There are particular feelings (like anger and gratitude), there are feelings of the whole (like joy and sorrow), there are existential feelings (dependence and freedom), and there is absolute feeling (the absoluteness of dependence and the nonabsoluteness of freedom). But there is no similar gradation in knowing or doing: we cannot say there are particular, existential, and absolute knowings or doings. The essence of the subject or the common foundation of the forms of consciousness is, thus, not manifested in knowledge or doing but in feeling.

Schleiermacher's systematic delineation has no form of reason distinctively identifiable as acoluthetic. There are the forms of theoretical reason (knowing), of practical reason (doing), and of affective reason (feeling); but those three exhaust the possibilities in a system whose principle is the immanence and transcendence of the subject in the life process itself. Within that system, then, an answer to the question of the phenomenon that appears in the christological assertion or narrative is confined to the three basic forms of reason and to absolute feeling. If the assertion is not theoretical, practical, or aesthetic, then it must be a religious expression, that is, a reflection in theoretical reason of the feeling of absolute dependence. In his actual interpretation, Schleiermacher follows the line indicated by this last possibility: christological statements are not theoretical judgments about an entity but theoretical reflections of religious feeling.

Schleiermacher's system of science, morality, and feeling is but one example of a systematic definition of phenomena. A second example—cited here, again, only for the purpose of illustrating how an implicit or explicit system determines the definition of the phenomena—can be drawn from Tillich's systematics. This system is more elaborate than Schleiermacher's in allowing for a few more possibilities. Like Schleiermacher's, however, it is a system, systematically derived. There is a principle in it, and a rule of procedure, which together determine the figures that appear in the system and indicate when the systematic derivation has been completed. Schleiermacher's is the principle contained in the conception of the life process as composed of two moments of the immanence and transcendence of the subject. Tillich's is the principle contained in the self-world ontological structure that is implicit in the being of the entity (human being) which can ask the question of the meaning of being, "Why is there anything at all?" The question implies an asker and an asked-about, or the two elements of subject and object (self and world). Self-related-to-world, or, epistemologically, subject-in-relation-to-object, are two ways of designating the basic structure implied in the asking of any question at all.

Tillich divides reason into its theoretical and practical forms, depending on whether the mind is "grasping" (theoretical) or "shaping" (practical) reality. This division reflects somewhat Schleiermacher's conception in the *Dialektik*, with its distinction between *darstellende* and *symbolisierende* reason, and it has obvious affinities to Kant's distinction between theoretical and practical reason. But it is not a conception that Tillich simply borrowed from anyone else; it was worked out in the course of a number of different systematic expositions, the last of which was his *Systematic Theology*. Theoretical reason, in this system, comprises science and art; practical reason comprises law and community. Noteworthy in Tillich is that art is considered to be a subdivision of theoretical reason, that is, a form of receiving or grasping reality, rather than a subdivision of practical reason (as a shaping of reality) or a third division coordinate with theory and practice. Tillich's principle of division is, then, the distinction between grasping (or receiving) and shaping.

A second principle—the principle that every thing has not only a form and a content but also a *Gehalt* (which means substance, import, realness, depth-content)—is used to distinguish the two subdivisions. Within theoretical reason, art differs from science because it uses forms in order to express the import (*Gehalt*) of the real whereas science uses forms in order to grasp the forms of the real. What does not play into Tillich's account at all is the distinction *in form* between cognition and art—the fact that the forms of mathematical physics are, for example, different from the forms of painting and music. That is not a limitation in the system as such but only in Tillich's explication of it. The only systematic distinction that he made between science and art was based on the difference of the two intentions. Forms can grasp the formed content of things, forms can also express the real *Gehalt* of things. If the forms involved are theoretical ones, they constitute science when they grasp the forms of things (and forms always are forms with content) and they constitute art when they express the real *Gehalt* of things. It is this same principle which distinguishes between law and community in practical reason. Practical reason shapes human being individually and socially. If the shaping is done according to law, it is a shaping in which the form itself is determinative; if the shaping is done according to community, the forms of social interaction have the intention of expressing a communal *Gehalt*. In both cases the forms are the same. But in the one case, the intention lies in the forms themselves, in the other case the intention lies in what is expressed through the forms.

In Tillich's system, there are, accordingly, four possible forms of reason, two theoretical and two practical: science and art, law and community. In them the self relates itself to its other or, in Tillich's words, the mind is related to reality. In earlier sketches, Tillich had made provision for two other possibilities, which he called metaphysics and ethics. Metaphysics is to theoretical reason what ethics is to practical reason—the rational unity of the formal and the expressive. Metaphysics is a unity of science and art; it uses theoretical forms both in order to grasp the forms of reality, as science does, and also in order to express the realness of the real, as does art. Ethics, similarly, unites law and community; its forms are those which shape society, as does law, and that express communal identity, as does community. In the *Systematic Theology*, the place of metaphysics and ethics is taken by myth and ritual. They are forms of reason whose intention is to break the forms of reason in order to express a content or grasp a reality that exceeds every rational form. In myth and in ritual there is a unity of the forms of reason, for myth is both science and art, and ritual is both law and community; but the intention of myth and ritual is fulfilled only when the rational unity is fractured by a real depth that breaks into them and seeks to create new forms. Do myth and ritual in the later system simply displace metaphysics and ethics in the earlier sketches? Not necessarily; for the same principle which was used to distinguish between science and art or law and community can also be used to distinguish the theoretical unity that is metaphysics from the theoretical unity that is myth and the practical unity that is ethics from the practical unity that is ritual. Metaphysics and ethics see the unity of reason from the standpoint of its unity of form (the form that embraces science, art, law, and community), whereas myth and ritual see the unity of reason from the standpoint of the unconditional that, at a given time, manifests itself by breaking into the rational forms. Myth and ritual are the "ecstatic" counterparts to the theoretical and practical unities of reason.

What constitutes Tillich's system is, then, the set of possibilities derived from the basic structure that is implied in our being able to ask any question at all—the structure of the self relating itself to what is not itself or, in Tillich's terms, the self-world ontological and the subject-object epistemological structure. The distinct ways in which the self can be related to its other are derived from the principle that this relation is either a grasping or a shaping of reality (the two corresponding to the realms of nature and society) and the principle that the grasping or shaping can intend either the forms (with the content that the forms form) or the import, the depth, of the other. The rule according to which one proceeds in order to make explicit the possible ways in which the self can be related to its other is that the self is either formed or forming (grasping or shaping) and that the intention is either the form or the real import of the other. If this rule of procedure is followed, the system is complete when all of its possibilities have been made explicit. The criterion for recognizing whether all possibilities have been explicated is that following the rule of procedure any further only duplicates possibilities already made explicit. Schleiermacher's principle that the self is either immanent or transcendent yields at most three distinct formal possibilities (the self can remain within itself, it can go out from itself, or it can in some way do both, if not simultaneously, then sequentially) because any fourth possibility is a duplication of one of those three. Whether we take remaining within or going out as the first possibility, the complete account turns out to contain the same number of possibilities. The only thinkable fourth possibility is one which marks the boundaries of the sphere determined by the difference between immanence and transcendence in the self, the possibility of a movement that is at once a remaining within and a proceeding without. Such a movement no longer fits into the possibilities definable by reference to the *difference* between remaining within and proceeding without.

Systems can be evaluated in their own systematic terms according to such considerations as whether the rule of procedure was consistently followed in deriving the possibilities from the principle and whether it was followed to its end so as to have exhausted all the possibilities. They can also be evaluated by comparison with other systems. Is subsuming art under theoretical reason less refined systematically than seeing art as neither practical nor theoretical but poietic? Finally, they can be evaluated by the extent to which the systematic divisions fit with what we otherwise know or may suspect nonsystematically. Do we understand a work of poetry differently from a work of science or a work of morality? It is on this last account that the two illustrations—Schleiermacher's and Tillich's basic systems—seem to be deficient for our purposes here. Neither system makes room for the possibility of a distinct form of reason that is neither theoretical nor practical nor aesthetic (or poietic) but acoluthetic, a form of reason, in other words, that involves the self in the full range of its existing possibilities.

In explicating the systematic concepts needed to reflect on and define acoluthetic reason, or to define "following" as a form of reason, I shall use a looser system, deriving the forms of reason implicit in the structure of self-in-relation-to-other from a set of four questions:

1. Do the *terms* of the relation (namely, the subject and the object) have the character of *personal* being or of the being of *things*? This is a question of the being of the two terms involved in the relation.

2. Is the *self* (the first term of the relation) *mindful* or *forgetful* of itself in the relation? This question intends to take account of the phenomenological recognition that the self can be itself in two ways, those of mindfulness and of forgetfulness. Egotism and altruism are the psychological manifestations of these two possibilities.

3. Does the *other* of the relation have the form of an I, a thou, or an it? On the self-side of the relation, personal being has to be in the form of an I, whether as mindful or as forgetful of itself. On the other side of the relation, personal being can have the form of an I, a thou, or an it (he, she) and nonpersonal being (the being of a thing) has the form of an it.

4. Is the *form of relation* one of objectifying and objectified (theoretical distance), one of demand and respect (moral recognition), one of appeal and self-identification (self-recovery), or one of following and authority (self-donation)? The first of these three is involved when the other in the relation has the being of a thing. In the remaining three forms, the other has the being of a person.

These four questions represent a *system* of possibilities but not in a strictly formal sense and not in such a way as to indicate that the system is derived by a single procedure of derivation or that it is a complete system. Instead, it takes as given a three-element basic structure (self, other, relation between) and applies to the extreme terms a double possibility and to the relation a quadruple possibility. The mode of being of the other is either the being of a person or the being of a thing. The mode of being a person is as I or as thou or as he (she, it). The mode of presence of the self is either mindfulness or forgetfulness. The mode of interaction between self and other in the relation is one of four: objectifying an object, respecting a demand, hearkening to an appeal, and being enabled by an authority. That there are only two modes of being the other (nature; person) and only two modes of having a self (mindful and forgetful) or that there are four modes of relation between the self and its other is not shown in the systematic derivation itself. The tenability of that part of the system will have to be made apparent indirectly through its capacity for making clear certain forms of reason that are recognized and exercised independently of the systematic description. The looser systematic account of the possibilities does set up the framework within which the various choices are made; but it does not indicate whether the four forms of reason that are treated are a complete list of the possibilities even within this systematic frame. It will, however, be sufficient for a characterization of christological reason as a distinct form over against science, art, and morality.

5

Forms of Reason:
Theoretical, Practical, Aesthetic, Acoluthetic

ACOLUTHETIC, OR CHRISTOLOGI-
cal, reason is that form of reason in which the I of selfhood is exstantial; the inwardness of self is confronted with itself outwardly. It
is not the relation to a thou or an it (he, she) but to the I. The mark
of this relation is that it involves an ecstatic possibility of the ego.

Christological and Ethical Reason

The relation of respect, which defines the ethical, appears to have a
close kinship with the christological, if the features of acoluthetic
reason involve a relation of the I within to the I without. For ethical
reason, too, is a relation of the self to its other in which both the self
and its other are subjects. The same will be true of the aesthetic. In
this regard, the ethical and aesthetic differ from the theoretic, in
which the self is subject but its other is object. How do we then
distinguish the christological from the ethical, the "following" from
the "respecting" of the other?

In ethical reason, what is presented to me is a subjectivity other
than my own; in christological reason, what is presented is a subjectivity that is my own. This is a relation not of respect, as in moral or
ethical reason, but of ecstasis; the "I" of which one is otherwise
aware only inwardly and as different from the world and everything
in it is now presented not as "you" or an it but as *ego extra me*. The
ethical relation is constituted by respect because the I which is there
in the person of the other is not my own. The christological relation,
by contrast, is constituted by *akolouthia*, following, because the ego
there is the same as (not analogous to) the I here. Despite the differ-

ence in place between the other and one's own person, one recognizes the other not as "you" but as "I" and the other's being as "my" being, externalized and appearing in "my" world.

In other relations, whether theoretical or practical, what comes into view and is objectifiably knowable is never I as such, since I am always the one for whom any world is world. In christological reason, however, that absolute origin comes into view, so that the I which in inward experience is always the point *from* which every activity proceeds and to which all appears is now present and therefore in the world (for me). The "authority" (in the sense of *exousia*, or "being out") that is exercised by a Christ-figure depends upon such an identity of the "I"; without it, authority is opposed to one's own freedom, one's own will, and is authoritarian.[1] If Jesus was the Christ for his disciples, and if he is the Christ for followers today, then his person so affected and affects them that they recognize in him their own being. He is for each of them the inwardness of the self's subjectivity as they each on their own know it, but he is that outside them, and his *exousia* lies in the way that their freedom and his voice exactly coincide, the one the externalization of the other. He is not for them a "thou," as he would be in an ethical relation, but "I"; he is their "I am," and their following him is their coming to themselves.

This account of the christological relation provides a basis for distinguishing between valid and invalid followings. Every form of reason is subject to its own measure of validity. Theoretical reason involves the values of true and false; practical reason, the good and evil or the right and wrong; aesthetic reason, the beautiful and the ugly or the sublime and lowly or the deep and the superficial. Christological reason involves the autonomous and heteronomous or the authoritative and the authoritarian. There is christological authority only when the other in the relation is identical with the I of the self and is recognized as such. The ecstasis of the one and the *exousia* of the other in the relation coincide. "The tree is tall" is a statement of theoretical reason, which, as to its validity, can be true or false. It is true if what it says shows the tree as the tree shows itself from its own place. "Do this!" as an unconditional imperative, is a statement

---

1. *Exousia* is a noun form of ἔξεστιν (literally, "it is out"), which is Greek for "it is permitted." The word *exontic*, which is used here, is formed from the present participle of the same word and is parallel to *deontic* from δεῖ (it is obligatory).

of practical reason, which can be right or wrong (good or bad). It is right, or deontic, if it enacts freedom, if the doing of it is an act of freedom. "What beauty!" as an exclamation of losing oneself in the object (the painting, the poem, the music) is a statement of aesthetic reason, which can be sublime or lowly, expressive or superficial. The work is sublime if one can give oneself to it, or be elevated into it, without losing one's being a self. "Follow me!" as a summons, not a moral imperative, is a statement of acoluthetic reason, which can be authoritative (exontic) or authoritarian. It is exontic, or authoritative, if the power in the summons is the same as one's own "can be." In the gospel narratives, Jesus' "Follow me!" is exontic as identical with the disciples' will—"immediately they followed him." The acknowledgement given in ethical reason to another person is a respect "elicited (or demanded)" by the person of the other, although it is given on no other basis than that of our being able to do so because we are ourselves free persons. The following that is given to the other as Christ is "enabled," or made possible by the other; it is a free response enabled by the word of summoning.

Like other forms, acoluthetic reason is not realized purely. It has the same symptoms of imperfection as the other forms. Theories fall short of being purely true, moral actions purely free or deontic, and aesthetic contemplation purely sublime. Following falls similarly short of being purely exstantial and exontic. But acoluthetic reason raises the further question whether this very form of reason is, like religion, a symptom of the imperfect. In the heavenly city of the Book of Revelation there are no temples. Religion is gone because God is all in all. Can there be a "following" in such a city? Is the exstantial I a possibility of subjectivity as such, or does it indicate a deficiency, a disease of reason? Provisionally, the answer can be given in both ways by indicating how this form of reason may belong to rationality as such and how it may also be a symptom of falling short.

If christological reason is understood as an essential possibility, belonging to the perfection of finitude, it implies that the relation between self and world is one in which the world can be a mirror of subjectivity not only through the analogies it provides (the "you," "he," "she," and "it" in "my" world) but also through an identity (the "I" exstantial in "my" world); it also implies that the self has the capacity not only to objectify things in the world and to respond to other subjects in the world but also to be "in" the world while being the one to whom every world must be a world to be a world at all.

And, finally, it implies that the christological relation does not have the intention of dispensing with itself. It is not established with a view to enabling the self to come to itself on its own and be its own self within itself alone. Instead, the freedom of the self as I is constituted within and without, immanently and exstantially, so that the plenitude of the I as I includes its ecstasis as well as its being in place.

If, however, this form of reason is thought of only in soteriological terms, that is, as indicating a disease or corruption of reason, then it arises from and as a remedy for the misuse of freedom. The self can then be restored only by having its freedom given to it from without, through the enabling power of the *ego extra me*. Once the restoration is complete, the relation is no longer necessary, neither for personal being nor for being a self in a world. In this case, the intention of the christological relation is to do away with itself. The Christ, who at the start is there in another over against "me" although identical with "my" being, is at the end no longer there because he has returned to the state of inwardness.

Whether christological reason is of the first or the second kind, essential or estranged, cannot be decided just on the basis of possibilities. It may not be decidable even as a historical question of the Christian tradition either. The New Testament's account of the ascension of Jesus in view of his disciples can, for example, be understood in either of these two ways. With the ascension, Jesus ceases to be present among the disciples as one person among others; instead, he becomes a spiritual presence, with no special place, no special here or there, but capable of being identified with any place and time. (If, before his death, he was with all of his disciples except Judas at a table, there were twelve distinct individuals there; after his death, if he was at the same table with the same group, there were only eleven distinct individuals sitting there.) This can be interpreted to mean that the disciples subsequently are in the world in such a way that they have over against them the things and persons of the world—in theoretic, practical, ethical relations—but neither the world nor anyone in it is presented to them as the exstantial I. Having come to themselves through the following, they are able on their own to be the ones they are. This same ascension can, however, be interpreted to mean not that the Christ is no longer there for them in the world but rather that, henceforth, anything and anyone in the world can be for them the exstantial power that Jesus was. The christological relation, in this case, is not eliminated; rather, being spiritualized, it is universalized. Not only the man Jesus, but anyone, can then be the exstantial I; any other can not only elicit respect as a free human being but also enable the will as a Christ. Such a universalization of the man Jesus is already made in the New Testament; for, as the tale of the Last Judgment makes clear, to clothe the naked, to visit the imprisoned, to feed the hungry, and all such caritative works, *are* actions in which the self is related to the Christ. "As you did it to one of the least of these my brethren, you did it to me" (Matthew 25 : 40) comes in reply to the question, "When did we see you?" But this identification is anonymous, and it is restricted in such accounts to the neighbor who is in need, so that there is a mixture of the ethical and the christological in a peculiar way. By enabling the disabled, the disciples are for them the figure of the Christ while the needy in turn are the Christ anonymously for the disciples. The question whether christological reason is a symptom of falling short or an essential possibility can thus be answered in either way, if one has in view the biblical and the Christian theological tradition.

The intention in the present context is to see "following" as an essential possibility of selfhood, that is, as a rational form of its own, and not only as a symptom of the corruption of reason. There are several reasons for this intention. One is that the self's ecstatic capacity is not a deficiency, just as ethical respect for the other person and artistic empathy are not deficiencies. Moreover, there are "good" and "bad" cases of following as there are of judgment, practice, and artistic creation or appreciation. To those reasons a third might be added, although it is more elusive: the attestations of ecstatic states, of being "beside" oneself, are as double-valued as are attestations of other acts of reason. All of these would indicate that it is not the exstantiality as such that is the deficiency connected with *akolouthia*.

The marks which distinguish christological from ethical reason are, then, these: In christological as well as ethical reason, the relation is that of personal being to personal being; both *terms* of the relation are personal being (a unity of ego with a here-now). But in an ethical relation the subjectivity of the other appears as "you" or "he (she, it)," and in a christological relation it appears exstantially as "I." Moreover, the character of the ethical and acoluthetic relations is different. The subjectivity of the other as you or him (her, it) elicits from me respect for its freedom, a respect for that in it which is analogous to that of which I am aware within as my subjectivity (what I understand when I understand the meaning of the word *I*). The exstantial subject does not elicit respect; rather, its authority, its *exousia*, enables one to be the self that one is as one's own.

Christological and Aesthetic (Artistic) Reason

Like the ethical, aesthetic reason is defined by a relation in which both the self and its other are subjects. In this case, the relation seems to be even more like the christological than is the ethical. This is suggested not only by the Platonic connection between poetry and ecstasy, in which being outside oneself is characteristic of the moment of inspiration, but also by an analysis of an aesthetic phenomenon. For in aesthetic experience there is an identification of the self with its own "I" presented to it in another place. It is an identification of the self with an I-there.

As an example of the aesthetic in this sense, we can consider what happens while watching the performance of a play that completely engages our attention. As the play is performed, we lose awareness of ourselves as spectators and become identified with the persons of the play or with the agents of the action that is unfolding on the stage. It is possible then that we are so completely identified with one of the *dramatis personae* as to become oblivious of the "I" here. Such an occurrence is an aesthetic way of being outside oneself "here"; I am oblivious of "I" here because of being completely absorbed in the subject there, the person of the drama, and a return to the self here takes place with the end of the play. As the aesthetic world can break away from the everyday world and displace it (sometimes making it disappointing, or at other times a relief, by comparison), so too the aesthetic "I" can break away from the ordinary position here and can be posited as being there in the artwork. The ecstasis of the occurrence lies in this dislocation or translocation of the subjectivity of the self.

This is obviously not an adequate description of everything that we would normally call aesthetic experience. But it describes a recognizable event. If one admires a still life or is entranced by the *Mona Lisa*, there is a kind of self-forgetting and self-transporting implicit in the relation to the painting. One finds oneself transported into the time and place of the painting itself and forgetful of oneself as one who is contemplating it from the outside. To that extent there is an oblivion of the self here. The identification does not have to be made with a particular figure in the painting; it can be with the whole scene. In these cases there is an identification of oneself with the scene of the painting. One is, as it were, translocated from here to there and identified with a place there.

How does this being transported differ from the ecstasis in christological reason? It differs in that the aesthetic self is oblivious of itself as one "here." In the christological relation, it is true, the self is presented with the being of the "I" outside its own person. But the I as it is aware of itself within, instead of forgetting its own being-here over against the ecstatic self, is made all the more conscious of it. The *exousia* of the Christ is the very thing that recalls the self of the disciples to its own place, enabling it to be itself on its own "here." Instead of letting the self forget its being "I" here, it enables the self to come to itself. The aesthetic identification allows the self to find itself in another without the need to return to itself here; the christological identification presents the self to itself outside itself and also returns itself to its being an I of its own here. One way in which this is expressed christologically is through the theme of the necessary but freely chosen death of the Christ, which removes his external presence and, in so doing, returns the self of a disciple to its own. The authority that is initially exercised exstantially becomes thereby a freedom exercised within; the self is brought to its own self as "I" by the death of the one who is recognized as the Christ. This description of aesthetic reason is not intended to make it sound pathological. Losing oneself by becoming identified with an imaginary person or world does not necessarily connote a pathological state, for there is in the notion of the self's capacity to inhabit worlds other than that of everyday concern nothing that is inherently pathological. Obliviousness of self-here and disappointment in, or relief in, the everyday world are thus intended to be descriptive and not evaluative terms.

Like the ethical and the christological, but unlike the theoretical, the aesthetic relation is that of subject to subject though not necessarily in the same world. Like the christological, but unlike the ethical and the theoretical, the aesthetic relation is exstantial, a relation to the "I" without. Unlike the christological, but like the theoretical, the aesthetic relation involves an oblivion of the "I" here. That is one set of comparisons. Another set has to do with the character of the relating. If the ethical relation to the other as "you" is one of "respect" which is "elicited" by the other person, the theoretic relation is one of "positing" the other as an "object"; the aesthetic relation is one of "identification," made possible by the "appeal" of the "I" of the *dramatis persona* or the scene of the artwork; and the christological relation is one of "following" made possible by the "authority" (*exousia*) of the Christ-figure.

All of these relations are presented as human *possibilities*. They are all possible ways for the self to be related to its other in a world.

None of them, as systematically described, contains any information as to how many times or in what materially specific ways these forms of reason are actualized. Moreover, since they are systematically defined possibilities—derived from the formally possible combinations of self, other, and the relation between them in a certain system—examples of them can be (and need to be) given only by approximation; but approximations are all that one needs to understand them as real possibilities. We do not need ever to have been purely in a condition of aesthetic self-forgetfulness in order to understand the nature of that relation; approximation to it is sufficient (as when, say, beholding Matisse's *Pianist and Checker Players*, we find ourselves just for a moment in that room listening to the silent piano playing and oblivious of ourselves in our empirical surroundings). Furthermore, a given act of reason does not need to be purely one or another of the possible forms. The christological, while dominating in a relation, can simultaneously have ethical and aesthetic as well as theoretical dimensions. Of course, to the extent that, in christological and ethical reason, the self is mindful of itself here, it cannot also be forgetful of itself in one and the same respect. But in any particular act, the mindfulness and oblivion of the self can be mixed.

In summary, then, we can compare christological with aesthetic, ethical, and theoretical reason in this way:

1. The *terms* (the two relata, self and other) of the relation are either personal being or objective (natural) being. In theoretical reason, one term is personal being and the other is objective being. In aesthetic, ethical, and christological reason both terms are personal being.

2. The *self* is either mindful of itself or forgetful of itself as I-here. In theoretical and aesthetic reason, it is forgetful; in christological and ethical reason it is mindful.

3. The *other* is in the first, the second, or the third person. In theoretical reason, it is third-person objective being ("it"). In ethical reason, it is second- or third-person personal being ("you" or

"he [she, it]"). In aesthetic and christological reason it is first-person personal being (exstantial "I").

4. The *form* of relation is that of positing (placing there, over against the self) and objectifying (in the theoretical, I posit it as an object); of appeal and self-identification (in the aesthetic, I identify myself with the one that appeals to me); of eliciting and respect (in the ethical, I respect the other as a freedom analogous to my own); and of following and enablement by authority (in the christological, I am enabled to be the self that I am here by following the *exousia* of the I there).

Christological reason is, then, that form of reason in which the inward I is related to the exstantial I through the authority (*exousia*) that enables the following.

Between Possibility and Actuality

The reference to a pathological possibility in the aesthetic relation calls attention to a distinction, applicable to all forms of reason, between what they are as such and how they are actualized. The connection between what they are and how they are is "nonrational" in the sense that giving an account of what something is does not tell us whether there is anything of that sort or how a thing of that sort is what it is. *What* they are is their *quiddity*; *how* they are what they are is their *essence*; and *that* they are what they are as they are is their *existence*. But there is a gap between the *what* and the *that*. From the definition of what a tree is we cannot determine whether there is any such thing in the physical world or how an individual tree will appear as the tree it is. There is always a gap between the definition of a thing and the ascertainment whether and how it exists. Since it is, however, "I" who both define what something is and ascertain whether there is a thing of that kind in the world and how it is, one connection is provided by this subjectivity. It is I who can both conceive an object as possible and perceive whether there is such an object and how it is as that object. There is always, then, at least that much of a bond between the possible and the actual; and it cannot surprise us that the modern thought inspired by the Cartesian method saw the substantial self, the I of "I think," as the basis of all knowable reality. But even this ego cannot eliminate the nonrationality of the transition from the possible to the actual. The only exception lies in those realities which are susceptible of an ontological proof. Proofs for the existence of God which, like Anselm's, are based only on the meaning of the name of God and not upon real conditions in the world are one example. Tillich provided a second example in his theses on Christology of 1911, in which it is argued that the existence of the Christ is implied in the being of the Christ.[2] From the meaning of the symbol "Jesus as the Christ" it is possible, Tillich argued, to say with certainty that the Christ was actually some historical person, even if he was not Jesus of Nazareth, for there is something in the very being of the symbol which makes a connection of its own between the meaning of the symbol and the real existence of the one symbolized. If there are such meanings, they provide a second connection between possibility and actuality besides the one given in the subjectivity of the I as the one who can both conceive the possibility and ascertain the reality.

The systematic definition of acoluthetic reason is intended to indicate the way in which this form of reason is a human possibility. When called christological, it is named in a Christian vocabulary, but it does not necessarily depend upon the material of the Christian tradition for its actualization. It is a universal possibility, systematically derived, according to the different ways in which the self can be in relation to its other and illustrated by approximations. The first disciples of Jesus who responded to his "Follow me!" by leaving everything and following him provide one such example. In modern times, Albert Schweitzer is another example if we take as explaining why he left the security of his university professorship in order to start a medical mission in Africa the words with which he concluded his study of the historical Jesus: "He comes to us unknown and without a name. . . . He says the same word [as he said to the first disciples]: 'Follow me!' and sets us the tasks that he must solve in our time. He commands. And to those, wise and unwise, who obey, he will reveal himself . . . , and they will experience as an ineffable mystery who he is."[3]

Of itself, this form of reason need not be theological.[4] It is so, however, in the Christian theological tradition, in which there is an

2. For an evaluation of this argument, and pertinent literature, see my *Inscriptions and Reflections* (Charlottesville: University Press of Virginia, 1989), pp. 183–96.

3. *Geschichte der Leben-Jesu-Forschung* (Tübingen: J. C. B. Mohr [Paul Siebeck], UTB, 1984, repr. of 7th ed.), p. 630.

4. Forms of reason are configurations of understanding being and trusting God. If a form is not only the rational form it is but ontological or theological as well, it is so because one or all of its terms also show "being" or "God." To say that the chris-

identity between the "I am" of Jesus and the voice that spoke to Moses from the burning bush (Exodus 3:13f.), and in which the eternal Logos, who was with God in the beginning and who was God, became flesh as Jesus. In this tradition, there is, therefore, a closer kinship of the theological to the christological than to the ethical or the aesthetic. Being enabled to come to one's own "I am" through the *ego eimi* of Jesus is directly interpreted in theological terms more than are the ethical or aesthetic relations. "It is clear," Bultmann writes in opposition to a philosophical view of authentic selfhood, "that . . . the New Testament . . . affirms the total incapacity of man to release himself from his fallen state. That deliverance can come only by an act of God."[5] That the christological is more closely associated with the theological does not deny that both ethics and aesthetics may have a theological dimension as well; it is only to say that the theological tradition of Western Christianity has maintained a fusion of the christological with the theological while it has not done so with the other relations. "Secular" science, art, and ethics have been granted as possibilities; "secular" selfhood has not. Bultmann, against Heidegger, stands clearly in this tradition. It has been granted that there can be genuine works of art that have no direct theological reference; it has also been granted, although perhaps more reluctantly in Protestant than in Catholic circles, that there can be genuinely moral acts without a direct theological reference—the moral virtues can exist without the theological ones; but that the christological following can, similarly, be actual without overt theological reference is an idea that finds no place in the systems of Christian theology. True, there are Enlightenment theologies in which the relation of the disciples to Jesus is interpreted in nonmythical terms as an ethical and historical one which, as such, need not be directly theological. Locke's *Reasonableness of Christianity* is one example. There are also Idealist theologies in which Jesus

---

tological relation is also theological is, thus, to say not only that it is a configuration of the trusting in God which, as a mode of thinking, is configured in every form of reason but also that, unlike other forms of reason, it is at one and the same time a direct expression of that trusting. If following the Christ is a trusting God, and following the "I am" is understanding the meaning of being, in this sense, then acoluthetic reason is theological and ontological in an exemplary way.

5. *Kerygma and Myth*, edited and translated by Werner Bartsch (New York: Harper Torchbooks, 1961), p. 24.

is an aesthetic figure, a singular representation of the universally human; and, as D. F. Strauss put it, the "mode in which Idea realises itself" is that it is "not wont to lavish all its fulness on one exemplar and be niggardly toward all others: . . . it rather *loves to distribute its riches among a multiplicity of exemplars which reciprocally complete each other.*"[6] But these are not the same as understanding the possibility of a christological relation distinct from the ethical and the aesthetic.

Reflection and the Forms of Reason

Is a systematic definition of reason an exercise of reason, and, if so, of what form? How is the second-order self related to the first-order subject? A brief account of these concerns should be given before we proceed.

The first-order subject is the self as it is actually engaged in acts of theoretic, practical, aesthetic, and acoluthetic reason. In analyzing and systematically defining the forms of reason, however, the self is not directly related to its other; it is related to its own relations. This second-order relation is a form of reason, since it does involve the relation of a self to an other, even though the other in this case is its own relations to its other, and it does involve questions of validity (systems can be more or less adequate, clear or unclear, and the like). We can relate ourselves not only to other persons and things, as we understand, act upon, react to, and respond to them, but also to our own activities of relating. In purely reflexive form, we can perceive our perceiving, think of our thinking, will our willing, and intend our intending, in abstraction from any other object. But intermediate between the direct and the reflexive is a reflectively theoretic relation in which the object of our understanding is not only theoretic reason but the other forms as well. Thus, we have the following possibilities:

1. The first-order subject is the self as it is engaged in acts of theoretical, practical, aesthetic, acoluthetic reason. The other to which it is related is a thing, a person, an artwork, the external I.
2. The first-order subject can, in addition, be related to its own psychic states, as it introspects its feelings or recognizes its own

---

6. D. F. Strauss, *The Life of Jesus Critically Examined*, translated by George Eliot, edited by Peter Hodgson (Philadelphia: Fortress Press, 1972), pp. 779f.

acts (for example, what a judgment is in contrast to what an emotion is).

3. The first-order subject can also be related to transcendencies, such as truth and beauty, where "transcendency" means a bridging of meaning and reality. Truth, for example, is not a direct object but a crossing over of meaning and reality (a *trans-cendens* in that sense) that appears, for example, when what is said is the same as what is so.

4. The second-order subject is the self as it is related to its own relations (its theorizing, practicing, making, and following). Since the definition of the forms of reason is itself a theoretical act, the phenomenological analysis is an exercise of theoretical reason but of a second order. Its object is reason in all its forms.

Whether the standpoint of reflection can be practical and aesthetic as well as theoretic—whether one can practice the practicing, theorizing, aesthetic contemplation, and following, or follow the following, and so on, is a matter that need not be decided here, although there is nothing to be said in advance against the notion that the aesthetic, acoluthetic, and moral acts can be of an aesthetic, acoluthetic, and moral act (that, for example, we can be ethical about ethics). What does need to be discussed is the question of the compatibility of reflection and christological reason with each other. It could be objected that reflective reason must by its very character miss the substance of Christology. This is especially the case when the christological assertion is understood in a strong confessional and exclusive sense. For in such a case it can be held that christological reason involves the self totally, so that the self cannot reflect on its own relations; the "following" that characterizes the relation of the disciple to the Christ is all-determining and makes impossible the withdrawal necessary if one is to reflect on it. To reflect on it is, in other words, tantamount to disrupting the immediacy of the relation, thereby destroying it, just because the acoluthetic relation is one that absorbs all others and determines how they are shaped. A confessional Christology might be possible, so the argument would go; a phenomenological Christology is not. It is not clear that anyone has ever made the objection quite so strongly. If it were actually asserted, however, the objection might be answered by the observation that the objection itself is already the result of reflection on the christological relation. One cannot assert that christological reason must exclude reflection without, in the very assertion, making it an object of reflection.

However that may be, the christological tradition in Christian theology contains both a more absolute (and exclusive) as well as a more
universal (and relative) strand.[7] The absolutist tendency is to conceive of salvation, that is, the rescue and healing of the human race,
as brought about exclusively by the person identified in the New
Testament as Jesus. He alone is the Christ, the Messiah. Through no
other one can the same be accomplished. Such a position can be
supported by quotations from the New Testament, if one wishes to
do so. "There is salvation in no one else, for there is no other name
under heaven given among men whereby we must be saved," Peter
said to the rulers and elders, according to Luke's account in Acts
4 : 12. A radical exclusivism implies that there is no neutral position
from which one can view christological assertions and their counterparts; one cannot reflect on them but only, as it were, confess one's
own confessions. Indeed, any purportedly neutral position is not
neutral at all but a denial of the confessional relation that is required.
To believe that one can occupy a reflective position is to have missed
the meaning of the original confession. That Jesus is the Christ can
be confessed or rejected but not be discussed or analyzed or viewed
from some point which is neither that of confession nor that of denial. This would represent the strongest form of exclusivism.

The universalist tendency—also supportable by biblical passages
(for example, by Jesus' reference to the "many mansions" in his Father's house)—can be described thus: The significance of Jesus is
relative to a tradition. His figure may have universal significance if
the principle or truth embedded in it is abstracted from the material
of the tradition, but the universality is not tied to the specific tradition nor to the historical person. What is important about Jesus is
not the particulars of his person but the fact that he is *logos*, a manifestation of the human in the divine and the divine in the human.
But there are other manifestations of the same Logos. What matters
is not who makes manifest the truth of the divine-human unity but
rather that it is made manifest.

The universalist interpretation, whether by reference to an eternal
Logos or through some other means, provides no difficulty for a
phenomenological approach, with the one exception that it may con-

7. See Carl Braaten, "The Uniqueness and Universality of Jesus Christ," in *Christian Dogmatics*, edited by Carl E. Braaten and Robert W. Jenson (Philadelphia: Fortress Press, 1984), vol. 1, pp. 557–59.

flict with an element in the phenomenon itself, the experience that the concrete material involved (the historical person of Jesus as the universal Logos) is not indifferent to its concreteness. But this exception does not provide a liability for the phenomenological method itself or the possibility of reflection as such.

Besides the two tendencies thus schematically described, there is a third possibility. If Christian absolutism says there is only one Jesus and only in him is there salvation, so that it is not the principle which he incarnates, not even the religious principle of divine grace, which is important, but the person himself; and if Christian universalism asserts, to the contrary, that Jesus embodies a universal principle abstractable from his person, so that some may come to know the truth through Jesus as Christ and others the same truth by other ways and still others, like William James's once-born or those to whom Jesus referred as needing no physician, have always already known it; then a third possibility is to hold the view that the same person who appeared under the name of Jesus and was recognized as the Christ by his disciples appears under other names as well, so that the universal is to be found, not indeed in an abstract principle or a general truth, but in the identity between the subject who now is here under one name and now there under another name. It is not, then, that there are many names for the universal Logos but that there are many sounds and appearances for the one name, or many names for and appearances of an identical personal agent. In effect, this is to assert that the name of Jesus, though a proper name (and therefore normally not translated into other languages or linguistic figures), is translatable because the same name appears in other figures in other languages, one and the same proper name appearing in different linguistic figures and meanings. These possibilities will provide a basis for discussion of the theological aspect of Christology.[8]

8. Chapter 8.

6

Explication of Acoluthetic Reason

The Topoi *of the Self: Everyday, Owned, Disowned, Ecstatic* [1]

WHO IS THE "I" OF "I AM THIS-
one-here"? What are the *topoi*, the times and places, of "I" who am
when I think? One obvious answer is that it is this individual person,
the entity that in each case I am, or the subject that is identical in all
the changes. This obvious answer can be misleading. In some ways
it is an inevitable starting point. For the one who is meant as the
subject of "I am here" is the entity who says or thinks the "I." Yet it
is misleading because a reference to the entity is not enough to disclose the I as the self of that entity and because it is possible that the
self who is the subject of everyday human existence is not properly
I. We cannot, therefore, answer the question, "Who is this one
here?" by biographical or autobiographical information. We cannot
answer it ontically by reference to a *kind* of entity alone, and we
cannot answer it by reference to the formal givenness of the I in
reflection, the I of "I think." The I that is transparent to itself, and
posits itself, in reflection is not the full answer to the question of
who is meant as the subject of "I am this-one-here," the "who" of
Dasein. The reflective I is a formal indicator but not the full disclosure. The ontic datum is the fact that some personal entity is always
meant by the word *I*; the person who says or thinks the word is the
one to whom it refers. But the reference is only formal. It says nothing about the ontological constitution, about what the *being* of that
kind of being is, or about the connection of the formal indication
with any material content; and it does not take into account that in

---

1. "Ecstatic" and "exstantial," the latter with its allusion to "substance" and "substantial," are both used here, with no intended difference in the reference.

everyday existence the self as I may be precisely that which is lost or hidden. Hence, for the ontological constitution in that ontic datum, the notion of substantiality and its possible exstantiality can serve as a guideline. In his account, Heidegger gives a second reason why we cannot start with the formal givenness of the I (*SuZ*, §25). Not only may the self be lost or hidden in everyday existence; there is also no isolated self without the world and others. The world may be overlooked, and the self may be lost, but an isolated self does not exist anywhere and cannot therefore be used as a key to understanding who it is that is the subject or substance or—we may add—the exstance of "I am this one here."

For purposes of clarity, we should recall here some terminology. In the discussion of the meaning of being, we mentioned that, as the connection between particular and general (individual and universal), "being" is the "substance" of a thing in contrast to its abstract nature (its concept) or its concrete presence (its percept). The same is true of personal being, with the exception that in personal being the universal concept appears logically and grammatically as the subject-term and the concrete as the predicate-term ("I am this-one-here" in contrast to "this-here is a tree"). The "substance" of an objective thing and the "understanding" of a person are their "being" in which abstract and concrete are actually united. This substance can be interpreted in different ways. A traditional interpretation has it that the being of human being is spirit: spirit synthesizes soul and body, the I as such (soul) and a concrete place and time (body). A Kierkegaardian interpretation is that the self (the substance of human being) is not a synthesis but an active relation that relates the self to itself. A Heideggerian interpretation is that this substance is ec-sistence (ex-sistence): the self stands outside itself (in anonymity and in worldliness) and comes to itself, so that the substance of human being is, in effect, the coming-to-itself of the self. These are three different interpretations of the substance of the human being that is expressed in the proposition "I am this-one-here" or "I am here-now." That Heidegger's is similar to Kierkegaard's in the way it is opposed to the conception of human being as a spiritual unity of soul and body is plain. But there is a difference between Kierkegaard's articulation of the self as the activity in which the self relates itself to itself and Heidegger's articulation of the self's coming to itself from itself; and this difference has bearing especially on christological, or acoluthetic, reason.

The "who" of existence is not the same as the substance of human being. The peculiarity of human being is that the universal is not the *all-gemein*, the common-to-all, but the *je-mein*, the always-mine. Asking who is meant by the "I" of "I am here" is, therefore, parallel to asking what is meant by the "thing" (in the sense of "something") of "this is a thing." How do we uncover that element which is the *Jemeinigkeit* of human existence, the universal that is ever and again joined with the "here" in the substance or understanding of human being?

Discovering who is the subject of "I am here" refers us to some kind of language. But the question is whether it is the instantiating word *I* to which we take immediate recourse or some other language. Here the kind of existential analysis provided in Heidegger's *Being and Time* offers a useful guideline. For, if it is true that the self has different "time-places," different *loci* or *topoi*, then finding the "who" of personal being is a matter of investigating the different ways of speaking or writing in which the self comes to expression, or in which the self *is* there. Heidegger, as we know, sought to make clear the difference between the existence of objective things and the existence of the self by using a distinct terminology for each—*existentia* for things like trees and stones, *Existenz* for Dasein, and *Fall* for being a case (*casus*, falling) of a thing, *Verfallen* for being a case of Dasein. That there is something of which we can say that it is a tree is what is meant by the tree's existence; it is the *that* of the tree's being in contrast to the *what*. That there is one who can say, "I am here," is what is meant by one's *Existenz*. If one term covers both cases, then the distinction between the existence of a personal being (Dasein) and of an objective being (*Vorhandenheit*) is not made clear. An individual person is a "falling" of the "I," and in that sense ex-sistent, as an individual object is a "case" of a thing and in that sense existent.

What languages serve to show the "who" of human existence, the one who is the subject of personal being? If the "I" of "I think," the I in the language of reflection, is the proper language—in the sense that the very word *I* is here used to refer to what is meant—of that subject, there are nonetheless improper languages as well. By a "proper" language is meant one in which the very word *I* itself appears in a signifying way. The proper language of the subject of Dasein, human existence, is the language of personal pronouns. The improper language is that of dailiness (to use a word from Virginia

Woolf) or the language of *Alltäglichkeit* (to use the Heideggerian word). Where (at what *topos*) do we find the expressedness, the instantiation, of the I in the language of everyday?

In the language of everyday, the subject of human existence (the "I") does appear; but it appears as forgetful of its egoity. The I does not speak *eigentlich* in it.[2] Its place, or *topos*, is that of the speaking of death in a way that disguises death's characteristic as pure possibility and its characteristic as the possibility most my own. "Everyone has to die sometime (*man stirbt auch einmal*)" is the everyday locution in which a recognition of human finitude is expressed. The I appears, but not in the instantiating provided by the very thought of the meaning of the word *I*; it appears as anyone and everyone. Yet this is an appearance of the self as I, even though in its self-forgetfulness. What brings the egoity to mind? What brings the I out of *das Man*, what transforms the anonymous being of existence into the propriety of existence? In Heidegger's analysis it is the call of conscience, which is the I calling to the anonymous self to come to itself as, in the parable, the prodigal son, upon "coming to himself" (Luke 15:17), resolved to acknowledge his having wasted his own. In the language of everyday, the self has itself only as "a case of" (as *verfallen*) existence in the world. When it comes into its own as its own, as an I, then what is expressed as pure possibility (the possibility of not having any possibility of being in the world) shows the I-ness of the self. The language of my-ending, summarized in the prospect "I can die," is one language in which I appear properly. But there are other ways of speaking which also disclose the I in its egoity. One of them, as Ricoeur pointed out in his analysis of Heidegger's question of the "who" of "I am," is the asking of the question of the meaning of being.[3] To ask that question is to pose something

---

2. The German word *eigentlich* means, of course, both "real(ly)" (as in "Eigentlich liegen die Dinge etwas anders": "Really [actually] things are a bit different") and "proper(ly)" (in the sense of belonging to one's or its own). *Eigentliche Existenz*, usually translated as "authentic existence," is the mode of existence in which the I appears as I. There is a linguistic connection between "authenticity" and "authority" by way of the Latin *auctoritas*; for the Greek church fathers' αὐθεντία is in Latin the noun *auctoritas*, with *authenticus* as the adjective form. The faint auditory connection of the *ei* of *eigentlich* with the English word *I* is fortunate but not significant.

3. Paul Ricoeur, "Existence and Hermeneutics," in *The Conflict in Interpretations* (Evanston: Northwestern University Press, 1974), pp. 3–24.

in language that refers backward to an origin (the one who asks), which in turn refers forward to the question of being itself. Ricoeur sees in this the connection between Heidegger I and Heidegger II—namely, that backward and forward relation between the question of the meaning of being and the question of the subject of existence. This is to say that the asking of the question of the meaning of being and the appearance of the I in its egoity are simultaneous. I am I, or I am as I, in the midst of asking the question "What is the meaning of being, what does it mean to be at all?" But even here the way in which the I appears is such that it still has to be uncovered through the backward relation between the question and the one who, as I, is asking the question. We cannot ascertain who is asking simply by introspecting ourselves as askers of the question. Rather, we can see who I am only through a process of *interpretation*, a hermeneutical process, in which we put into concepts what we understand in the words of the question.

The authentic and the everyday *topoi* of the self are familiar from existentialist analyses, which have dealt in many ways with the everyday and the authentic, with the casual and the proper, or the unowned (inauthentic) and the owned (authentic), appearances of the I. Some of them, as in Kierkegaard and Sartre, also reveal a third *topos*—the place at which it is in conflict with itself (the hamartetic self). Beyond the everyday, the real, and the hamartetic, and omitted in existential analyses, is a fourth *topos*, the exstantial I. It is important that, before taking up the fourth *topos*, we distinguish the hamartetic from the everyday; the former is a disowning I, the latter a self-forgetting I, lost in the generality of *das Man* and coming to itself in the call of conscience. The hamartetic is not an unowned but a disowned I. Its dialectic is that of an unending end rather than of the self's coming to itself in the end.

The hamartetic self (*hamartetikos* from *hamartia*: missing the mark, or missing what is intended) differs from the lost self in a significant way, so significant that one cannot, as Bultmann seemed on occasion to do, adopt Heidegger's notion of the casualness, the *Verfallen*, of the self as equivalent to sin nor even as the ontological-existential region within which the theological concept of sin can appear, as Heidegger suggested in *Phenomenology and Theology*. The Augustinian-Christian view of sin as radical self-assertion or egocentrism, of the self as curved in upon itself, and the notion of the self as having forgotten itself in the anonymity of everyone and any-one are far from the same. The point of contact, which Bultmann rightly noticed, between Heidegger's concept of inauthentic exis-tence and the concept of sin lies in the idea of making the world available or a guarantor of the self's security. The mode of existence in which one tries to secure oneself in the world, by denying the constitutional openness of being-there in the world, is opposed to the mode in which the openness or insecurity is courageously ac-cepted. But this point of contact does not eliminate a significant dif-ference between the notion of inauthenticity, as meaning that the self is not owned, and the notion of sin, as meaning that the self asserts its ownership inordinately. This latter is the *hamartia* of miss-ing the self by a disowning. The self-missing I is different from the self-forgetting I.

How does this hamartetic self appear? If it is in the language of everyday talk that one can see who is the subject of everyday living (and see that it is one in whom the self is an unowned I), to what discourse do we look in order to uncover the disowning self—the self whose state of despair Kierkegaard analyzed under the title of "the sickness unto death"? The self can lose itself, Kierkegaard showed, not only by failing to be on its own, as in its daily lostness, but also by asserting itself as I. It can disown its own by trying on its own to be what it cannot be—entirely within the world or en-tirely out of the world. This is the dialectic of selfhood that gets submerged in the Heideggerian analysis of the everyday. The I of the self can be lost because it forgets itself in the "everyone and anyone"; but it can also be lost because it misses the mark when, called out of the crowd, it disowns what it seeks to own as only its own. The voice of conscience calls the self to own itself as answerable for the "not" of being in the world. Who is the one calling? It is the I of the self, calling, as it were, from out of the world. The one who is "here" can listen to it as the voice of another—one can will to hear what is said *to* oneself. Even in everyday existence, we can listen to each other talk. Talk means, indeed, an interchange between one and another. That we can hear what is told to us is what provides the condition for the possibility of listening to the voice of conscience. But whom do we hear when we so listen? No one else than the "I" who is forgotten and unowned in the anonymity of the everyday. This "I" is not the individuality of my person, nor is it the voice of the other person; it is the I as such that is in the coming here and now but still concealed from view because still unowned. If two people listen to the call of conscience, and if, for both, the one from whom the call comes is the "I" to be owned, it is the same "I" who calls, not two different I's. The universality of the I that is the voice of conscience was at one time formulated in terms of natural law as the law of conscience. The *lex naturalis* is the law of the being of any human being whomsoever. But the conception of "natural law" grasps in the form of an object—a law of nature—what is not an objectivity. The I of the call of conscience is no more the individuality of the person than is the I of the *ego cogito*. The I who am there in the midst of doubt, as well as in the call of conscience, is but the subjectivity meant and shown by the word *I* in its universality.

We have discussed, so far, the *topoi* of the self indicated by the terms "everyday," "own," and "hamartetic." The everyday self is the self in which the I on its own is hidden in the "self" of the "oneself." The authentic self is the self in which the I has been brought out of its anonymity into its own by answering for the "not." The hamartetic self is the self which, though it has come out as an I of its own, cannot appropriate its own being as a self of its own; it cannot accept its being culpable for nothing (and therefore answerable for everything). This self is different from the everyday self just because it has come to itself on its own. But it is different from the conscientious self on its own because it tries to undo its having come into its own. The everyday self does not own a self to disown; its being on its own is still sheltered in its being with the generalized subject that is everyone and anyone, and even its having-to-die is sheltered in the nature of things in general—everyone dies sometime. The hamartetic self, by contrast, is the self for which the "I can end" has come into its own as the possibility most the self's own (when the self is itself as I) and for which the whole endeavor is to turn the possibility into an actuality, to transform what is purely a possibility for the self into its own actuality, to make of the "I can always" an "I do now." The hamartetic self is on its own but unable to be on its own, unable to be as the pure "I can" never turned into an "I do." What is still hidden from this self on its own is its own impossibility. The possibility most purely its own has already manifested itself and brought to light the egoity of the self. At no time is the self an I of its own more than when it bespeaks its "I can die." It is still on its own when it tries to transform the "I can" into an "I do." But then its being on its own has the form of pure nonactualizability, pure impossibility, of a disowning owning that can never end.

The I of the purely possible end and of the purely impossible end is, unlike the everyday self, entirely interior. The call of conscience is heard voicelessly within one's own being; it is not a voice that comes from without. Whatever another person may say to me, or a thing "speak" to me, the content is in any case not the call of conscience because it comes to me from without. It may be the call of a thou, it may be the eliciting of respect for the other person as another person; but it is not the call of conscience. Even if another person says, "For the sake of your own freedom, you should . . . "(or "You just should because you can"), those words are not the content of the call of conscience. They can indeed become the occasion for hearing that voiceless call; but, as words with meaning and content, they are the speech of another to me and not the address that calls to the self to come to itself as I. The same is true of the language of confession. It is only an interior language. If a person confesses something to another, the words are not the content of confession but an imparting of information from one to another person. Confession itself is done by the silent voice of the I; it avows the I who have been. Conscience calls to answer for; it is the voice of the I who can be. Penitence is the voice of the I who have been "not."

That would be the end of the topology of the self if it were not for another possibility. If there is an exstantial I, an I without, then this I is different from the I that calls voicelessly as conscience as well as from the I that avows voicelessly as penitence. The I that really is the *ego extra me* is the one whose summons is external and voiced. It comes from a person other than my own person or from a thing other than my own embodiment. The one who so speaks to me that the command of the voice speaking from outside is at one and the same time the activation of the freedom of the self of which I am inwardly aware in my own person as I is the exstantial self. The place of the exstantial I is outside my own person; its summons is not the call of conscience within. Yet it is exstantial, rather than thou-like or silent. It speaks, and what it says in the form of "Follow me!" is a meaning which enables the self to be on its own in the midst of its own impossibility. Its own impossibility is its self-disowning. In heeding the call to follow which comes from the exstantial I, I *do* do what otherwise I only *can* do: come to an end of my own. Hence, the exstantial I is the place of the self that is designated as its possibility of being a self of its own in the midst of its own impossibility. Its own impossibility appears, phenomenally, in the language of the will to end oneself. The instability of the state of despair is that the self cannot abide its own possibility as being purely a possibility. It cannot abide the thought that it becomes most its own in facing what is for it always and purely a possibility, never capable of actualization. The state of despair is the unending experiment with turning the possibility into an actuality. The result of the experiment is always the same—"it cannot be done." Its being a self on its own as I manifests itself as a possibility that can never be actualized. "I," as I, always "can" but never actually "do" end.

The exstantial I is exterior, its summons comes from without, and yet it is identical with one's interiority. What is presented in the voice of another person is identical with the meaning of what I am aware of in my own person as the I of its own in its own self. This relation is the basis of the self's being *given* the possibility of being a self of its own on its own. That is, in sum, the possibility of turning the pure *I can* of the proper self into an *I can and do*. On my own, as exposed in my own being as a self amidst the impropriety of the everyone and anyone, I can always but never do come to an end. On my own, as being my own self in response to the summons to follow that is at once the enablement of my own self in its egoity, I have always already been able to come to an end in fact. The language of the self of everyday, in which the self on its own is hiddenly expressed, is the language of actuality: "everyone dies sometime but for the time being not I"; the language of the self on its own, no longer hidden in the everyone and anyone, is the language of pure possibility: "I alone only can always come to an end"; and, finally, the language of the hamartetic self is that of pure impossibility: "I alone always never do come to my end." But the language of the self given itself, through the mediation of the exstantial I, is the language of the new possibility that has already been enacted: "I have always already come to an end." "You have died," Paul writes to the Colossians (Colossians 3:3), who themselves can read his letter.

The places, or *topoi*, of the self are indicated by ways of speaking that manifest the self. There are, in the preceding sketch, four such places, indicated in four distinct ways of bespeaking the self: hidden in the "everyone and anyone" of everyday and manifest only as a not-yet I; on its own, answering for its being nothing in the world; on its own, incapable of appropriating the possibility most its own; and, finally, external to itself. This last is the ecstatic, or christological, self. The Christ-figure is the other whose "I am" is both most removed from and most interior to the "I am" of the self owning itself.

The *topoi* are the places where the I is. In the everyday, it is unowned; in the call of conscience, it is owned; in its *hamartia*, it is disowning; and in the summons to follow, it is ecstatic. What procedure do we follow in order to uncover where the I is? The starting point is a discourse in which the self manifests itself. For the hermeneutics of existence, as in Heidegger's *Being and Time*, this is the language of everyday, which means language as it is used to communicate, without there being any reflection on the meaning of language as language. The end is spoken of in such daily talk as: "Everyone has to die sometime. It can happen to anyone; and it does happen to everyone. One has to die sometime; it's only a question of when." This talk indicates how the self is understood and why it is hidden in the "everyone" or "anyone." In the talk no distinction is made between the self in the first person and the self in the third person. What is implied in "one has to die sometime, it's only a question of when" is "I too have to die when my time comes." What does not appear in the talk is the phenomenon of the end as something that I *can* do (not must do), but never *do* do, and as something that is such a possibility only with reference to the self in the first person. "I" always can but never do end.

If the hermeneutical starting point is in the language of everyday or in some other discourse, the next step is to formalize what appears in the particularities of that language. Such a formalization of the language is comparable to finding the genus or generality in specific concepts. It is a matter of finding the general form of talk that is in the particular talk. Talk of the end, in the everyday, is formalized when we say that to die means for Dasein the coming to an end of its possibilities. Death as the possibility of having no possibility of being-there is the formalized concept of the way death, as it appears in everyday talk, is understood. No one, in everyday talk, actually says, "I have the possibility of having no possibility of being in the world." Instead, what is said is: "Everyone dies sometime. It can happen to anyone at any time, and it does happen to everyone at some time." That end is connected actually with some time and possibly with any time, and it is connected with everyone actually and anyone possibly. Thus, the formalized concept of the understanding of death in the everyday is that death is the end which is an actuality for everyone at some time and a possibility for anyone at any time. This concept of the end of Dasein is the existential concept that interprets how death is expounded, or laid out and understood, in the talk of everyday—it interprets how death is understood before the question is explicitly put, "What is death?"

We have started with the understanding contained in everyday talk; we have formalized this understanding in the existential concept which interprets the initial understanding. The next, third step is to fill the formalized, existential concept with the meaning of being-there. We do this when, for example, we understand death as the possibility that is most our own, which is to say, the mode of being that for the I appears always as a "can" but never as a "do." This can occur, however, only after the self has been called out of the "everyone and anyone" into its own egoity. The calling is done either by methodical reflection (as in Descartes's method of doubt) or by conscience. Methodical reflection does not appear in everyday talk. Hence, as far as daily discourse is concerned, the uncovering of the self as I occurs not through methodical reflection but through the call of conscience. The language in which we speak of conscience is the talk that shows what is hidden in the talk of death, namely, the I in the "anyone and everyone" or, to put it differently, the self as I that is forgotten in the "one" of anyone and everyone. There are other ways of speaking besides talk, which constitutes the objectivity of everyday. We can speak in avowal or confession, through which the I appears as answerable for a negativity. We can also speak in poetry, in which being becomes apparent as happening and happiness. This third step in the procedure is, then, to show where the self is in a given way of speaking by explicating the understanding of the self that it expresses.

The method for identifying the *topoi* where "I" am is, then, as the preceding paragraphs illustrate by reference to the self of everyday, to start with the language that says where the self is (whether it be the language of everyday, or of poetry, or some other discourse), then to formalize the understanding expressed in the language, and, third, to show, or explicate, the meaning of being in that understanding. Thus, one place of the self is that of being hidden in the "anyone and everyone" but appearing as the recipient of the call of conscience. Another place is the self on its own as I, appropriating the possibility that, as a possibility, is most its own, namely, the "I can die." This second *topos* is the self as answerable for and to nothing, in the full ambiguity of the concept "answerable for and to nothing." The condition which Kierkegaard analyzed as the state of pure despair is another place. Its dynamics are those of the pure impossibility of the I, just as the dynamics of the state of death (I can die) are those of the I's pure possibility. I always can but never do come to an end. That is the self's pure possibility, appearing with the form of self that is the first person singular. I never can, but always try to, put an end to the self as I. That is the language of pure temptation—a trial to end that can never end.

The self called to its own by conscience appears as what it is: the I on its own as subject of its being-there. But can it appear in its authenticity, its *Eigentlichkeit* or ownness, as misappropriated or disowned? The concept of the hamartetic self is the concept of a self that has come to its own but as disowning its own. Can we make a clear distinction between the I that is forgotten in the "anyone and everyone" and the I that, now fully brought to light, is its own self in disowning itself? These questions lead us not in the direction of Heidegger's *Daseinsanalyse* but in the direction of Kierkegaard's analysis of the constitution of despair.[4] The despairing self is the I which has come out of its anonymity but which, now unhidden and exposed, can only misappropriate itself. The hamartetic self is the I in contradiction with its own egoity. It is not the casual I as a "case of" selfhood in general; it is not the self of everyday *Verfallen*. It is,

4. In "The Death of the Heart," a column in *The Washington Post Magazine* of 26 April 1987, p. 7, Richard Cohen offered a remarkable interpretation of Menachem Begin's self-imposed seclusion, into which he had retreated after the failure of the war in Lebanon in 1982. The interpretation depicts exactly the hamartetic I, which has come out of its anonymity into its own as I but cannot be reconciled with itself. "Once a terrorist, always a realist" (so Cohen describes him), Begin had used violence before, and with success: after the bombing of the King David Hotel, the British had one more reason to pull out of Palestine; allowing the settlement of the West Bank defied world opinion, but after the protests had died, the buildings were there, the deed done. No such success followed the Lebanon war: "the dead rebuked." Then, Cohen concludes, Begin did what was probably unique among world leaders, many of whom would take "responsibility for everything but hold themselves accountable for nothing": he "closed the door to his apartment, and over the traffic in the street you can now hear the unsaid word 'I'. *I* was wrong. *I* am responsible. No one else. . . . For his wife, for the dead of Lebanon, he seems to be a man in grief. . . . Behind his door, he awaits the final accounting."

rather, the self on its own against itself. The utterly duplicitous self is the I which can do nothing else than try to disown itself but which can never succeed in that effort because it always owns its own disowning. Its state is an unending end, a "sickness unto death" to which death never comes. The self in which "I" am "my" own "I" by disowning "me" is the self that can never possibly either "win" or "lose" but can only exist in a conflict without cessation and without fulfillment. It is a radicalization of the Sisyphus.

In what kind of language does this self speak? The self-forgetting self bespeaks its impropriety in everyday talk; the self coming to its own speaks the language of responsibility, which answers for the "not." The I comes out on "my" own as I in connection with the possibility that is most its own and can never be transferred, as a pure possibility, to another. Only in the first person singular is it true that come-to-an-end is what I always purely "can" do without ever actually doing it. In reflective form, "I can die" gives voice to the possibility in which the I is purely on its own unhidden in the "one" of "oneself" and unconnected with any actual fact. But the reflective form is not the form in which it appears initially. Initially, it appears in the call of conscience, which calls to the self to become an I that is nothing in the world. It is the call to be what I *can* be: there in the world as nothing in the world. The self can be called because the self can listen as well as talk. It can therefore hear itself called to itself by the calling of the voice of conscience, which the self only as I can hear alone. It is brought to itself as I by the I that calls in a voice which, initially, it can hear as the voice *of* . . . coming to it, without knowing from whom it comes. Only when it appropriates itself as I does it recognize that the voice calling to it was the same as the I which comes to its own through the voice. The soundless voice of "you should . . . ," "you owe . . . ," "you ought . . . ," is the voice of the I as it comes to its own. If the structure of the self as possibility is shown in my-death ("I can come-to-an-end"), the structure of the hamartetic self ("I" against "me") is shown in the language which expresses sheer division. There seems to be a division already in the possibility of my-end: I can always end but, since I never do end, I in some sense also cannot *qua I* end except as the auditor of the conscience that is the actuality most my own. But the hamartetic self is the pure division of "I" against "me." It speaks the language that disavows the fault that is its own—not the language of *Verfallen* but the language of past failure, the language of the I who have always already failed.[5] For the exstantial, or ecstatic, self the language is a summons to follow, as in the brief narrative: "He said, 'Follow me!' and immediately they followed."

The Christological Figure as the Exstantial I

Our conception of the christological figure depends on our ability to distinguish the I as such from the personal embodiment in which the self appears. This I comes into our awareness as the zero-origin of all of our actions and as the point of view from which the world is seen but which as such never appears in the world and is never an object to which we are related. This characterization applies to the normal or nonecstatic forms of reason. In the ecstatic form, however, this pure subjectivity takes on objective form different from an ethical relation. "Christological figure" refers to the other term in this ecstatic relation. How is this figure to be delineated? How is the figure expressed in the words *I am* to be characterized when it is the objectival term in a rational relation?

As such a term, the christological figure is, in the first place, the one to which a subject as I is related. In the nonecstatic forms of reason, the I in its own quality as pure subjectivity is something of which I am aware within myself. In the ecstatic form of reason, the infinitely recessive origin, the zero-point or blind spot of the "I who," not only appears in the world but appears as the other term of the rational relation. The christological figure, even though the object-term in the relation, is also the "I" of my own here-and-now. A relation to this figure is much more intimate than is a relation to another person in ethical or even in aesthetic reason. Thus, the acoluthetic form of reason is the one in which the I in its most intimate selfhood is related to its own intimacy outside. But this is not a narcissistic relation. Narcissus, as the Boeotian myth tells us, was the young man who fell in love with his own image upon seeing his reflection in the water and could not tear himself away from it. Thus, he perished in longing for the self which he could not attain. The christological figure does not involve such a narcissistic relation. To

---

5. Ricoeur seems to me to be wrong in thinking that this language has to be symbolic, as he does in *Fallible Man*, or that we can reflect on fault only by means of symbols and not directly. Rather, there is not only everyday talk, but also the voice of conscience, the avowal of fault (which, like conscience, can only be silent), and the summons to follow. All are equally nonsymbolic language.

encounter the one whose being is simply expressed in the statement "I am" is not the same as to encounter one who is a mirror reflection of one's individual person. It is a real figure; it is what it is on its own independently of one's encounter with it. Even if it is true, as the definition of the figure implies, that what is encountered in the christological figure is the self as we are normally aware of it within ourself only, it is also true that this figure is an entity on its own and not simply a surface mirroring of ourselves to ourselves. It is the appearance of the I of "I am" in another person different from my own. It is possible to be related to the other in an ethical form of reason; but if that other person also is or becomes christological, then there is not only an analogy between the two I's but an identity between the I-there and the I-here. In that sense the relation is ecstatic—the I in its inwardness not only is within but also appears exstantially.

This is to say that one way of distinguishing between a christological figure and a narcissistic reflection is to call attention to the fact that the christological figure is always in a person other than my own. But the christological figure is also one whom I recognize to be not merely another person, equally personal in its own being, but also the appearance of egoity as such in my world. In this way too the christological figure is not a narcissistic reflection. It is the I as such and not simply the particular personhood of the other person or, still less, of my own person. Though being really another person than the one I am and though remaining really different from me in my own person, the figure is able to show that universality of subjectivity of which otherwise one is aware only inwardly but which is not identical with one's own person.

If the christological figure is not narcissistic, it is also not a representative of some cause that persons might have in common. It is not the appearance of a communal subjectivity. The christological figure is different from a charismatic leader, a leader who might represent in his own person a cause that is common to many persons. Such leaders play an important role in society and in political affairs. That role can be positive at critical junctures; for a charismatic leader, embodying a cause larger than his own, is capable of forging a social bond, and by reference to that larger cause the diversity of individuals is forged into a community. With the christological figure, however, it is not a matter of representing a common or overarching cause. Rather, the Christ-figure represents the freedom that is most intimate and singular. The figure is nothing more and nothing less than the intimacy of the I as such externalized and placed there, over against me as this-one-here. A charismatic leader can inspire to action by appealing to the cause which is common. A christological figure summons to following simply by the capacity to activate the freedom of a subject's action. The one who summons to follow does not say, "Follow me in order that we can bring about a new order of society." He does not say, "Follow me for the sake of the cause I represent." He says, rather, simply: "Follow me!" No cause is involved, no common concern.

The voice that thus summons seems closely related to conscience. What is the difference between the call of conscience to become answerable for our own finitude and the summons of the Christ to follow? The one calls to become answerable. The other summons to follow. What is the difference between becoming answerable and becoming a follower? In both cases, it is in heeding the voice that one comes to oneself. Both voices are heard inwardly, both can be audible from without. But there is a difference. Although the call of conscience can be embodied in the actual voice of another person, it need not be so embodied, for it is authentically the silent voice of the self coming to itself. The christological voice, by contrast, must be external; it comes from another even though what is heard in the summons is, likewise, the power of inward subjectivity. The major difference, however, lies in the content of the summons. In following, the followers follow the freedom of subjectivity that confronts them in the person of the one who summons. They come to themselves by being able to follow the one who is the exstantial I, and they are summoned to be beyond their own end. Whether such following is a necessary stage in the self's coming to its own self depends upon the context in which the christological figure appears. For the everyday self, lost in the anonymity of *das Man*, the christological figure is simultaneously the call of conscience and the call of freedom. When it appears to the self lost in the everyday, it not only calls the self out of its anonymity by making it hear its own conscience but also calls the self to come to itself by following the path of the other. The summons makes the self both responsible as a self and also a follower of the self. For the authentic I, the I that has already come out of the anonymity of the everyday, the exstantial I in the christological figure provides the occasion for the exinanition, a movement outward that is a self-giving or a self-emptying of the authentic self. For the hamartetic I, being itself in its impossible ending, the exstantial I makes it possible to be beyond the end.

The Modification of the Ratio

That reason can be acoluthetic at all implies that the I can be exstantial. It implies that subjectivity in one person is capable of encountering not only an analogy of its own inwardness in the person of the other, but also the identity of its own I in the other. But, like other forms, acoluthetic reason can be modified in a condition of existential self-contradiction, a condition in which reason is contrarational and which can be interpreted either in its own destructiveness or in its signifying a meaning beyond itself. This difference in interpretation is the basis for connecting the voiceless call of conscience with the summons from the voice of the exstantial I. Conscience calls to become culpable; and the voice summons to follow, but in a following that appropriates the self from which the call of conscience estranges the self. The culpability of the self for nothing appears in fact when we are held responsible for something that we did not do or neglect to do and over which we had no control in the first place. We are held to answer for our being here-and-now, even though that *da* is, for each of us, never a matter of our having chosen it but of its having been given to us to take over. There is an answerability not just for the way in which we are ourselves here-in-the-world but also, and fundamentally, for the fact that we are here-now at all. To be held responsible for just that condition, in which one had no say whatsoever, and to recognize that responsibility, a responsibility, strictly, for nothing that we have done or failed to do, is to exist in the contradiction between the egoity of the self and the worldly location in which it finds itself. The contradiction does not emerge until it becomes clear that the self can enact its own selfhood only by setting itself with all its resources *against* its being in the world as answerable for the world. The language of that contradiction is the language of metaphysical rebellion, the unconditional refusal to accept responsibility for the facticity of being in the world.

The nature of this self-conflict, however, is such that it appears not only in the extreme form of metaphysical rebellion but also in modifications of the several forms of reason. The particular modification with which we are concerned is the contrarationality that in traditional language is called the state of sin. It should be recalled that

this is not the *Verfallen*, or being-a-case-of, of which Heidegger
speaks in connection with everyday existence. For *Verfallen* means
the condition in which the self as I is submerged in anyone and
everyone in the form of being-a-case-of; I exist as an individual case
of a self in general, and the possibility most my own appears as a
case of something that is always happening anyway. Being-a-case-of
is not the same as being in radical self-conflict. In sin the I has indeed
come into its own, but it is on its own in such a way as to be incapable of appropriating its own self. It can, indeed, resolve to accept
the responsibility for being just here where it is and to accept it in
such a way as to treat it as the result of its own freedom. In that
sense, I *can* be what I actually *do* be. Such an appropriation works
retrospectively. I can take over as my own the destiny which is mine,
that of having come into being just here now as the person I am; I
can assume as my own act the whole of what has befallen me; I can
exist as one who is solely responsible even for those events and things
about which I had no say and over which I had and have no control.
But there is a limit to this appropriation. I cannot appropriate as my
own deed my own coming-to-an-end. That is the difference between
my coming into being and my coming to an end. Coming into being
as this person here and as no other can be appropriated, in response
to the call of conscience to answer for the negative; one's coming
into being is, after all, something which has already occurred and is
in fact so. But coming to an end—"my" end—is different, for I do
never come to an end as "I." Hence, although I can freely accept and
adopt the destiny that is my own, in response to the call of conscience, and in that sense can be what I actually am as an "I," I *do*
not ever do what I always *can* do. The possibility always mine is the
actuality never mine.

The sheer contradiction between the possibility and actuality of
the I on its own, which determines the dynamics of the state of despair in Kierkegaard's analysis, is also reflected in other relations of
the self to the world. We can therefore analyze the contrarational
state from the four points of view involved in the forms of reason:
the object to which the self is related; the relation between self and
the other; the self in its relation to the other; and the self within
itself. The overarching rational structure is contained in this formulation: " 'I' am here now related to entities for 'me.'" The contrarational modification can appear upon the object or in the relation

between the subject and the object or in the subject or, finally, in the I (that is, between the "I" and the "for me").

CONTRARATIONAL OBJECT

To understand the nature of a contrarational object we can conduct an experiment of the imagination. We imagine viewing an object in such a way that we could never bring together our percept and our concept of it. When we look at this object, our eyes can see it only as a tree but our mind can conceive of it only as (let us say) a lion. (This is not like Wittgenstein's duck-rabbit, a figure so drawn that it looks now like a duck and now like a rabbit.) The purpose of the experiment is to envisage how a contrarational state would appear at the objectival pole of a theoretical relation if it ever appeared purely as such. Normally we can understand the being of an object because we can synthesize the perceived particulars with the abstractly conceived genus in the same object. To be in a contrarational state would mean to be incapable of performing that synthesis. We might be able to perceive something in its singular this-here-ness but would not be able to fuse it with a concept that grasps the universal in it. We could not understand what it *is* because (in this experiment) we imagine our being able to perceive the object as such and such (as a tree) but we imagine that at the selfsame time and with respect to the selfsame object we are able to conceive of it only as something else (as a lion). We would simultaneously be aware of the irreconcilability between the object as perceived and as conceived and would, nonetheless, be unable to resolve the conflict between them. To our seeing, hearing, touching, it would always appear as one thing; to our thought about it, it would always appear as a different thing.

The situation thus imagined is not entirely different from what happened in a familiar example from intellectual history: the astrophysical and everyday points of view on celestial objects. To an everyday point of view, it seems obvious and incontrovertible that the sun rises in the morning and sets in the evening and that the sun moves around the earth. That this is so can be confirmed by anyone standing at any place on the earth and using the normal sensory apparatus to see what is going on. To an astrophysical view, the unmoving point of the everyday is the moving one. What seems to be obvious to the naked sensation is seen, not only interpreted, differently from an astrophysical point of view. There is a contradiction not only between empirical facts and their interpretation but between the point of view for everyday experience and the point of view for astrophysical experience. Everyday talk and astrophysical theory do not give different interpretations of the same data; they provide different vantages from which to view what really is so. They see things differently. Without the possibility of placing ourselves at a viewing position other than our physical position on the earth—the possibility that mathematized astronomy provided in early modernity—we are not able to "see" the movement of the earth and sun in any way other than as the sun's moving across the sky while the earth remains fixed.

The historical conflict of the new science with the old philosophy and theology at the beginning of the modern age was woven of many strands. Part of it was a philosophical conflict between rational and sense-empirical orientations. Part of it was a conflict between ecclesiastical authority and scientific autonomy. But what is important in the present context is that it was also a conflict arising out of the new possibility, offered by astronomical science, of occupying a perceiving standpoint different from the standpoint of one's physical location. Today the idea of such a possibility presents no difficulty; space exploration has even made it possible to relocate ourselves physically. But when the possibility of occupying a different standpoint, one located elsewhere than on the earth on which we with our bodies are located, was first offered, there was no obvious reason why common sense should let itself be taken in. That the perceiving-thinking human being would see himself, in his viewing-thinking, as standing *not* on the earth, where he patently and physically is, but off the earth at some point where the motions of the sun, the earth, and other celestial bodies appeared different from what they are to everyday senses needed time to be appropriated.

The emergence of modern astronomy provides a partial historical illustration of the condition we are describing by way of an experiment in the imagination. We can imagine how contrarationality appears in an object as our not being able to reconcile with each other the way in which we sensibly perceive and the way in which we conceptually grasp a reality. This is close to the situation in which our sensible apprehension of the movement of celestial bodies cannot be brought together with our mathematical grasp of the same movement when both of them provide ways of seeing the reality of the world. But with the astrophysical and the everyday views of the heavens, we have to deal not with how things are perceived with our senses and how things are conceived with our thoughts but with two different standpoints from which to view them. The astrophysical view implies that if we are able to place ourselves physically at some point other than on the earth, we have a different perceptual view of the very same bodies that appear to us while standing on earth. From the different physical location, the discrepancy between the everyday view and the astrophysical one disappears. The possibility of occupying two different positions from which to perceive does not, of course, settle the question whether either of them offers a view closer to the truth of things. The contradiction appears in an object, strictly speaking, not just as two points of view that we might take upon it but as the inability to understand the being of the object because we cannot bring together the particularity of the object as perceived and the generality of the object as conceived from any point of view. But *if* we cannot reconcile the everyday perception with the astrophysical conception of the solar system, that inability is an approximating example as well as an expression of the contrarational in forms of reason. Any such conflict has both destructive and significative potential. It can destroy the capacity to be related to the object in the objectivity of its being what it is on its own; but it can also be a sign pointing to some meaning beyond it, and in the case of this historical example, the new meaning was a new understanding of what the celestial system is.

CONTRARATIONAL RELATION

The number of ways in which the self relates itself to things in the world is unlimited. The forms of reason, as we have analyzed them, are basic configurations of the relation. The basic structure implicit in them is that of the I, to which everything appears and which itself is not in the world, and the world, in which everything appears but which does not itself appear. The I and the world are, in Kantian language, infinite ideas but not single subjects or objects. We can, accordingly, portray a contrarational state by imagining the relation between these two structural elements as an insoluble conflict. For that purpose, the four polarities that Tillich used to define the ontological structure will serve as well as any others. The first polarity is that of self and world as constituting the basic ontological struc-

ture. The remaining three are the elements constituting the basic
structure: freedom and destiny, dynamics and form, and individualization and participation. The "and" of all these polarities contains
two opposing possibilities of relation.

In a polar relation as such, the two opposite terms are realized
reciprocally rather than inversely. When self and world are polar opposites, then the self is in the world in such a way that the more I
am I, the more the world is world, or the more the self is centered
as a self, the more the world is a whole in itself. The ego that lacks a
center also lacks a world over against it. Polar opposites are, thus,
not analytical opposites. In an analytical opposition, an increase in
the one term brings with it a decrease in the other. The more circular
a figure is, the less it is a square; the more independent something is
of external factors, the less dependent it is on those factors; and so
on. But self and world, as polar opposites, increase or decrease in
being what they are concomitantly rather than inversely. For the self
that is perfectly centered as an ego, the world is perfectly whole as a
cosmos. If we imagine the I as somehow completely expressed in a
here-now (which would simultaneously have to be an everywhere-
everytime), then this I would simultaneously be the full realization
of the world in the world.

How do we imagine, then, the contrarational state in respect to
such polar concepts? We do so by turning the polarity into a contradiction. The self strives to realize itself not in conjunction with the
worldliness of the world but in exclusion of it; in the process both
the self and the world are lost concomitantly. The self is lost, for
example, in situations of moral conflict in which worldly causality
and the self's freedom cannot be reconciled—in which, therefore,
freedom defeats itself by pitting the self in its freedom against the
self in its worldly, causal connections. The self loses its center, its
capacity to mediate between the opposing aspects of its being in the
world. It cannot see things from a unitary perspective or act as a
single responsible agent. The world is lost concomitantly; instead of
being a meaningful whole, it is a chaos of destructive forces.

To imagine the contrarational state by reference to the self-world
polarity, we must form an image of a relation between the two poles
of such a kind that the activity of being-in-the-world splits the self
from itself and, simultaneously, the world from its own wholeness.
This same pattern is repeated in the relation of the elements that
constitute the ontological structure. Freedom and destiny are pitted
against each other instead of sustaining each other. The freedom of

the I in the "I am here" is in conflict with the destiny of the "here." We can imagine a person living in the twentieth century who is so at odds with this century as to spend all efforts in trying to be in another century. Essentially freedom and destiny are not in conflict with each other, and the fullest freedom is the freedom which always chooses what exactly coincides with what destiny grants. We can imagine such a possibility even when we do not know any such person. The *aut Caesar aut nullus* (to use an example Kierkegaard cites) on the part of one who is not Caesar is an expression of such an existential conflict—if I cannot be Caesar, then I am no one; and, since I cannot be Caesar, I cannot be anyone else either. Freedom (one cannot be Caesar) and destiny (there is no one else that one can choose freely to be) are perpetually at odds.

Similar considerations apply to the polarities of dynamics and form and of individualization and participation. Dynamics is the power to transcend any given form; form is the necessity of being something definite. The dynamics drive the self to become other than what it currently is. In a polar relation, the capacity to transcend any given form is matched by the capacity to create new forms for the dynamism. In a state of existential contradiction, the dynamic transcendence of given forms is not matched with the appearance of new forms to contain the dynamics or the new forms are without material dynamics. So too with the third set of polar elements. The normal condition of being in the world is one in which everything individual also participates in a universal. A subject participates through perception, imagination, conception, action, and poiesis in a whole world and does so without ceasing to be an individual subject. The more individualized the self, the greater is the extent of participation; a self-conscious being (such as human being) is more individualized than a conscious being (such as an animal) and participates in a correspondingly larger world. When existential conflict appears in this relation, the self loses itself as a whole (and becomes, as Tillich put it, restricted to a cognitive self) and, with it, loses the wholeness of the world (which is restricted to a mathematically knowable object).

THE CONTRARATIONAL IN THE SELF

We can form a conception of the contrarational state of the forms of reason not only by reference to the way in which the conflict appears in an object and in the relation of being-in but also by reference to the self in itself. In Kierkegaard's analysis, "sickness unto death" is a state in which the self is radically and insolubly in conflict with itself. The aim of the will, in such a state, is to do away with the self, and all of the activity of the self is directed toward self-annihilation. But, although that is the direction of the will, the effort cannot succeed. Hence, the state is one that is always "unto" death. The state would not be one of despair if it were possible for the self to succeed in doing away with itself. For then there would be an outcome. But because it can neither desist from the effort nor succeed in the effort, the self is pitted radically against itself, and despair is a sickness for which not even death can be a cure—it is the sickness that is always only "unto" death. It is the state in which the self is perpetually owning its disowning and disowning its owning.

The rule of analysis that we are using here in order to provide a description of the splitting of the self within itself is that the contrarational is an existential conflict, instead of a polar tension, of the ontological elements. The conflict extends so far as to involve the self within itself. It appears not only in the object (as a conflict that we can imagine in a case of not being able to bring together the percept and the concept of an object), nor only in the relation between the self and the world (the other of the self), but also within the self itself as a disowning owning, or in Kierkegaard's ontic terms, the self not willing to be itself and the self defiantly willing to be itself. The christological relation, or the form of thinking that is acoluthetic reason, provides a scene of conflict, in which the interior I appears exstantially. The summons of the other lies in its being the appeal of the I as such (of just the "I am" and not of any particular person); but the I is externalized in the person of another. To heed the voice is to "follow" the christological figure. Does acoluthetic reason have a contrarational expression? Is the externalization of the I to itself perhaps something that *ought not to be so* even though it is so?

For a portrait of the possibility that the exstantial I is rational, and not only contrarational, we might consider the role of the tree placed "in the middle of the garden" for Adam and Eve and representing the unconditional prohibition "Do not eat!" The tree is in the middle of the garden; it is at the center of the world, the center also occupied by the I as such. If the tree standing in the center of the garden and expressing the limit of being in the garden through its "Do not eat!" is an image of the exstantial I, then Adam and Eve can follow the command as long as the command itself is their own resolution. If they ask neither why there is a command nor whether they ought to obey it but, instead, spontaneously do what it stands for them to do, then it has the power in them of their own deciding. It is in external form the same agency of which they are inwardly aware in the meaning of "I." The freedom, however, is spontaneous until the serpent presents another possibility. The serpent's role is to raise the possibility of reflecting on the command. Indeed, to ask the question, "Has God really said?" is to disrupt the relation between the tree and Adam and Eve. At the very moment when they can understand the question, they have already lost the spontaneity of their freedom toward the center of the garden. The "Do not eat!" can be the voice of their freedom only as long as they do not hear it as a command given to them but as a description given of them; the command *is* their resolution. To reflect on it is to have lost it as the voice of the freedom to be finitely. "Reflection is sin," as Barth wrote in his Romans commentary.

But the Kantian categorical imperative is also the voice of freedom. The moral imperative, understood in Kantian terms, is based upon nothing else than the power of freedom in the command itself. It is moral just to the degree that it is unconditional; it sets no conditions and gives no reasons; it appeals only to the freedom to do it as a realization of freedom. A moral act is an act performed simply out of the will to do what one should do because one can do it, when the "because" indicates not a reason for doing it but the source of the action, and the inner sense that accompanies a moral deed is the sense of freedom. Freedom can, as Kant's contemporary critics observed, be inhibited by attachment to the "sensible consciousness," which is motivated by pleasure and pain rather than by freedom, but such inhibition does not change the character of the moral imperative itself. In itself it has no other basis than that of the freedom to respond and to carry out what it commands. What, then, is the difference between the moral imperative, as so conceived, and the imperative connected with the tree in the middle of the garden or the "Follow!" of acoluthetic reason? What is the difference between the moral and the christological?

They are similar forms of reason in that both of them are based on nothing other than the relation of the self to its own freedom. Moral respect for another person has no basis other than the recognition that the other person, as an I in its own embodiment there, is as free as I am free in my own being here. It is mutual recognition, reciprocal *Anerkennung*. This differs, however, from the christological relation in two ways. First, in becoming aware of the moral imperative, we respond to it for no other reason than that we recognize we can do what we should do. What is presented in the moral imperative is the freedom of human being, having multiple locations in the here-and-now of the self. In becoming aware of a christological summons, we become aware of the concrete unity of I and the here-now which is a unique embodiment. The content of the christological summons is not human freedom, in contrast to bondage to sensible consciousness or to the *Verfallen* in the generalized "one." Rather, "Follow me!" differs from the moral imperative because, though equally unconditional, the christological summons contains a unity of my being I and my being here-now, whereas the moral contains a unity of should and can (I should do because I can do and can do because I should do). There is no ought in the christological following.

Second, in the relation between two persons, the characteristic of moral respect is that the one acknowledges the other's being as free as I am in my own person. That is the intention contained in formulating the moral relation as one in which we treat a human subject, whether in our own person or in the person of another, always as an end in itself and never as a means to an end. In the christological relation, however, the other person is not one who, like me in my own person, is free but rather one who *is* I, one who is who I am exstantially. The moral relation of self to self is constituted when I recognize that what I am aware of within myself in understanding the meaning of "I" is analogous to what the other person is aware of within his or her own person when similarly understanding the meaning of "I." The christological relation is constituted when I recognize that what I am aware of within myself is presented to me outside myself. The I appearing *to* me in the form of the other person is identical with the I of which I am inwardly aware. This is not a relation of analogy (what I am to myself in my own person, the other is to the other self in his or her own person) but a relation of identity. This is also the relation expressed by the tree of life in the center of the garden for Adam and Eve.

There do not seem to be in the literature any analyses of this christological relation, and its contrarational possibility, comparable to Kierkegaard's analysis of the radical split that marks the state of despair. Kierkegaard's is an analysis of the conflict of the self within itself but not of the disruption between the self within and the self presented from without. The contrarational ethical relation is one in which I cannot acknowledge the freedom of the other; it reaches the state of despair when all of my activity must be directed toward disrespecting the freedom of the other and when the result of that activity is always to reestablish the respect in the disrespect. The contrarational existential relation is one in which I cannot synthesize the two elements that constitute the being of myself as this one here; all efforts are directed toward doing away with myself, and the result of those efforts is only to make me all the more the self that I cannot and will not be. This existential disruption is what Kierkegaard analyzes in *The Sickness unto Death*. The contrarational christological relation would have to be described as one in which the exstantial I is an externalization which *should not be* but which *in fact is* (or, conversely, which should be but in fact is not). If it has a desperate form, then that form is one in which all of the following given to the acoluthetic summons is directed toward overcoming the externalization but in which the externalization, far from being overcome, is more and more intensified.

Such analyses being absent from the literature, let us try to imagine what a contrarational form (not necessarily a desperate form) of christological reason might be. First, we can picture the integral form of it to be like a mirroring in which what is mirrored is not my own appearance but the "I" of my own being. In the theoretic, practical, and poietic relations, we are in the world in such a way that the I is the blind spot, the point of view from which all is seen, the one to whom all things appear but who never appears as such. In christological reason it occurs that this very "I" is reflected to me. Thus, we can imagine the christological form of reason to be one in which the very thing that can never appear does appear. What is seen in that mirror is not (as in the ethical relation) a freedom that is analogous to mine but rather the very freedom of which I am aware within. What is otherwise the most private, the most intimate, the nonexternalizable aspect of my being is mirrored back in the embodiment of the other person. What is meant by the Christ is the one who serves as such a mirror. The Christ-figure differs, therefore, from other human beings by being the one who reflects the very inwardness of the self. If there were no such things as mirrors, we could never see the eyes with which we see. If there were no Christ-figure in the world, the "I" of the here-and-now would be a point of view from which everything is viewed and understood but could not itself be seen or understood. The contrarational form of the ecstatic relation is one in which the figure that mirrors our own being ourselves as I is one against which we oppose ourselves instead of "following" it. How are we to imagine that possibility? If the I of which we are intimately aware is shown *to* us in another person (or, for that matter, in a thing), then how can there be an estrangement between the two, the self and its own selfhood? The answer is that we may oppose ourselves to following just as we may not like what we see in a mirror.

In a few statements, then, we can summarize how the contrarational modification of the several forms of reason can appear in the object, in the relation to the object, and in the subject.

First, if the theoretical relation is a form of reason in which I am a subject over against the other as an object, the contrarational can appear in any of these ways: (1) the distance between subject and object is not maintained, so that I do not let the thing show itself but interfere with its self-showing; (2) the thing cannot be synthesized into an object, for how I perceive it and how I conceive it remain at odds with each other; (3) the subject is split within itself, so that I as one who perceives the object am opposed to myself as the one who conceives the object (I, as I am in my everyday world, am opposed to myself as I am in my *Weltanschauung*, for example).

Second, if the moral relation is one in which I respect the other as being, in the other's own there-then, the same as what I am in my here-now (but analogously, since we can never exchange places), then the contrarational modification of that relation occurs when (1) respect is replaced by a will to dominate, or (2) the other self cannot be acknowledged as a self, or (3) I lose my own self as a deciding and acting center. When I cannot translate the "should," heard in a moral imperative, into a "do" by virtue of a "can," there is a split in the moral subject. When domination replaces respect as the relation between persons, there is a split in the moral relation of a subject to its other subject. When the other cannot be acknowledged as a person but is treated as a thing, a means to an end, there is a split manifested in the other of the moral relation. I am always myself in relation to the other as itself (himself, herself). The contrarational modification of moral reason can be manifest in the I-myself, in the relation to the other, or in the other itself.

Third, if the aesthetic relation is one in which I am transported from my here-now to myself as there-then, then the contrarational modification can appear (1) when the movement cannot be accomplished because as a spectator I cannot participate in the being of the *dramatis persona* or the scene of the artwork, (2) when the other, the *dramatis persona*, is not another embodiment of the I who am embodied here-now, and (3) when I, who am myself here-now, cannot return from the other embodiment here-and-now, from the *dramatis persona* with which I have identified myself by being transported to it and forgetting myself here-now.

Fourth, if the acoluthetic, or christological, relation is one in which the self as I is related to the exstantial I as I, then the disrupted relation is one in which (1) the externalization is itself something that should not be, (2) the relation between the inward and outward forms of the I is not one of enablement but of disablement, or (3) the I does not come to itself through the I-without but remains unreconciled with itself. To these three we can add a fourth one, which is dependent upon the universality of the exstantial I. If the exstantial self is centered at one place, in one other person, and cannot be identified with other places—if, in other words, the "I there" is not also an "I possible everywhere"—that likewise is a sign of the contrarational.

Freedom and Truth

Both in the biblical account of christological following and also in philosophical history (from Plato and Aristotle to Hegel and Heidegger) there is an explicit connection between freedom and truth. According to the Gospel of John, Jesus said to those who believed in him, "If you continue in my word, you are truly my disciples, and you will know the truth and the truth will make you free" (John 8:31f.). How are freedom and truth associated? The question can be treated from three angles of vision. The first has to do with the connection between faith, or the mode of thinking called "believing," and the content of the "I am" in bringing wholeness or salvation. The second has to do with the way in which freedom and truth are intertwined in the concept or the phenomenon of truth itself. The third has to do with the characteristic of the Christ-figure as one who elicits a free response.

It is particularly in the Gospel of John that the connection between the saying "I am" and believing is made explicit. The passages in this Gospel, however, are not isolated examples; they have ante-

cedents in the tradition of the Torah.[6] In the statement of Jesus to
his believers a threefold connection is made. Continuing in the word
leads to knowing the truth and to becoming free. What does it mean
to continue (*menein*) in a word, and how does such continuing bring
freedom? The Greek word that is translated as "continue" means to
dwell in, to abide in, to remain continuously in. But how does one
dwell in someone's word? We can dwell in a house, we can inhabit a
land, we can remain in a certain spot. Does continuing or remaining
or dwelling in someone's word mean something more than remembering what the person said and living by the saying? Is there some
aspect of dwelling or abiding that can illuminate the meaning of the
relation to Jesus by way of his sayings? Usually, the Johannine verse
is interpreted to mean that Jesus calls upon his disciples to remember
the words which he spoke to them and to let their thought and work
be shaped by what those words say. The words are to guide the spirit
and the behavior of the disciples. Their function is comparable in
kind to the advice given by Polonius to Laertes: "This above all: To
thine own self be true." Does dwelling in a word amount to heeding
the advice given through the words? If I advise someone never to tell
a lie, and if that person, on occasions when tempted to do so, recalls
the advice and decides to follow it, then he can be said to have continued in the word. This is certainly a possible interpretation of the
idiom of dwelling in a saying or a word.

Perhaps, however, something more is intended than heeding advice given. But what other sense might there be in the notion of
dwelling in language? Where would the disciples of Jesus be dwelling if they did not dwell in the word of Jesus? And is it possible to
dwell in the word if that word of Jesus is the saying "I am"? If one
is to dwell in the saying "I am," then dwelling cannot amount to the
heeding of advice because none is given to be followed. This is true
even when the I-am sayings have a predicate. "I am the resurrection"
or "I am the vine" or "I am the way, the truth, and the light"—none
of these contains advice or counsel that one would be able to heed.

6. See Hans Klein, "Vorgeschichte und Verständnis der johanneischen Ich-bin-
Worte," *Kerygma und Dogma* 33, no. 2 (1987): 120–36. Boy Hinrichs, *"Ich bin":
Die Konsistenz des Johannes-Evangeliums in der Konzentration auf das Wort Jesu* (Stuttgart: Katholisches Bibelwerk, 1988), endeavors to show how the literary structure of
the Gospel of John is built upon the saying "I am." The argument is undoubtedly
forced, but the very effort indicates the central importance of the saying in the Gospel.
See Nikolaus Walter's review of the book in *Theologische Literaturzeitung* 115, no. 5
(1990): 346f.

Dwelling or abiding in such sayings must, therefore, refer to a form of relation other than heeding counsel. To dwell or to abide means to find one's home. The question has to do with the place of one's abode. Where would the disciples dwell if not in Jesus' word? The choices are, as the Gospel of John seems to make clear, two: to dwell in the world and to dwell in the word. To dwell in the world is to exist in such a way that one understands oneself by reference to the cares that are laid upon one by the world itself; it means having to take care of tasks, having to care about what one does and how one does it, having to care for others as well as for one's own being, and having to be concerned with being in the world at all in prospect of one's not being. Dwelling in the world amounts to living in those cares, and living in those cares amounts to understanding oneself as defined by the things or the matters with which one has to be concerned. The other possibility is to dwell in the word. If dwelling in the world means to understand oneself by reference to the cares of existence, then dwelling in the word means to understand oneself by reference to the meaning contained in the sayings.

Let us assume that the only word we have is the saying "I am." Let us then ask what it means to understand oneself by reference to the meaning in that saying. The meaning is the sheer positing of the being of the self as an I. To say "I am" is to affirm oneself as a free and underivative subject of one's own. We recall that at the end of the Cartesian method of doubt the I emerges ineradicably in its egoity. But dwelling is more than practicing a method or following a path, and dwelling in the "I am" includes more than a methodical practice of doubting the meaning or reality of the I of "I think." To dwell in the saying is, rather, to continue to understand oneself by reference to the I of the saying "I am" and to understand one's being by reference to the "am" of the same saying. Understanding ourselves by reference to the relation of care differs from understanding ourselves by reference to the meaning of the saying "I am." In the first case, we are worldly beings caught up in the process of coming to be and passing away that defines worldly existence; the self as ego is lost in the cares of the world. In the second case, our being is that of coming to be ourselves in the I that is on its own. The very materiality of the written or spoken "I am," as we read or hear the words, makes it a possible place of dwelling.

The same considerations apply to the "I am" statements involving the use of predicates. To dwell in the saying "I am the resurrection and the life" is to understand the being of ourselves according to the meaning that is contained in those words. Autonomy in worldly existence is being able to take over as one's own deed the end. It is appropriating as our own act or deed that which befalls us. But this authentic existence is not a dwelling in the word of Jesus to his disciples, in which one becomes a self not just by reference to appropriating death as one's own freely executed past deed but also by appropriating the meaning contained in the saying "I am the resurrection and the life." Dwelling in the word differs from dwelling in the world in the same way that understanding oneself by reference to meaning in language differs from understanding oneself by reference to cares. The sense of the phrase "continue in my word" is, then, according to the reading being offered here, that the alternative is to dwell within the world of concern or to dwell within the word "I am." In Isaiah 43:10, Jahweh says: "Believe that I am," and: "I am Jahweh, beside me there is no savior." This passage, one of the antecedents of the "I am" passages in the Gospel of John, also makes a connection between believing in the one whose word is "I am" and attaining salvation or freedom. Knowing the truth is understanding that to be human is to exist as an autonomous I having the destiny of one's own death and simultaneously as an autonomous I having as one's own gift the being that is the meaning of the saying "I am the resurrection and the life." The wholeness of the self is its being "there" and its being "given." To know the truth is to come into one's own in the double sense of appropriating one's own having to end and of appropriating the resurrection presented as a gift from the external, or exstantial, I. Knowing the truth means being in that mode of existence in which one as an authentic I both is answerable for having to die and is recipient of the gift of being beyond death. Kierkegaard's knight of infinite resignation, capable of giving up everything, can be in the world as one whose being has already ended in the world. But the knight of faith is one who, unlike the knight of infinite resignation, gets back what he has given up. That Abraham would be willing to give up his son Isaac expresses the power of infinite resignation; what makes him a knight of faith is that Abraham also believes he can be given back what he will have given up. So the question at issue between the existentialism of Heidegger's *Being and Time* and the existentialism of Bultmann's theology is not whether it is possible to become authentic as an I without the donation of a power beyond what is already available to any human self; it is, rather, the question of the way the authentic self can be—not only as an I whose most proper deed is that of my-own-end but also as an I who can appropriate the gift of being be-yond death. By accepting as my own deed the necessity or the fate of death, I do indeed exist in the world freely as an I on its own in its absolute and universal singularity. But beyond this possibility is that of being beyond death. The mode of existence called not know-ing the truth is existence defined by one's concerns in the world, which terminates in the end of the possibility of being in the world at all; knowing the truth is being authentically in the world as one who is already dead to the cares of the world and alive to the pos-sibility beyond the possibility of having no possibility of being in the world. "Knowing the truth" is a mode of existence, not simply an intellectual cognition of a state of affairs. It is called "free." Authentic existence is free because the self has emerged from enclosure in the anonymity of the generalized human self. It is achieved by the deed of accepting one's own existence in its totality, appropriating as one's own free choice the possibility of one's own coming to an end. It is free because the self appropriates what appears as a necessity im-posed upon human existence as a free existential choice. To that ex-tent authenticity is itself liberation from bondage to the concerns of being-in-the-world. A further liberation frees the self from the au-thenticity of the finite I in its finitude. This is to say that there is a difference between being in the world, authentically, as one who has already come to an end—that is, one who has appropriated the pos-sibility that can never be one's own actuality—and being in the world as one who both has already come to an end and also exists in the promise of resurrection. To dwell in the word of resurrection while in the world is to be in the world differently from being there as one who is dead to the world. To be in the world as one who dwells in the word "I am" is to be in the world freely, that is, as a self which is a self on its own as I. To be in the world in the mode of existence of one who dwells in the word "I am the resurrection and the life" is to be in the world both authentically as an I of its own and also ecstatically beyond the deed most one's own.

The preceding paragraphs give the general connection of abiding in the word with knowing truth and with becoming free. A second consideration is involved. The connection between truth and free-dom is made not only in biblical language or the Gospel of John but also in the philosophical tradition. Heidegger makes it explicit in *Das Wesen der Wahrheit*, in which he discusses what is meant by truth in the sense of *alētheia* and how this essence of truth fits with the traditional definition of truth as the agreement between understanding and reality. In one sense truth does mean the agreement between a proposition and reality. If one says that there is a gold coin on the table, the truth of the assertion does involve a correspondence between the content of the proposition and the state of affairs, for the assertion that there is a gold coin on the table is true if there is indeed a gold coin on the table. Correspondence does not have to be understood, of course, as a likeness between a mental image and a real appearance. The likeness theory of the correspondence is but a particular, and limited, version of correspondence. In his essay, Heidegger was not primarily concerned with formulating a better theory of truth but with probing beneath the surface of the theory. At the surface, we may indeed mean by truth an agreement of some sort between what is said and what is so. There is no similarity in appearance, however, between the words in the proposition "There is a gold coin on the table" and the appearance of the real gold coin on the table; the coin does not look at all like the words. How then can we account for the fact that we recognize whether there is or is not an agreement between what is said and what is so? Even if there is (in some cases at least) a similarity between a mental picture formed upon understanding a statement and a real appearance presented upon looking at the object meant, this does not answer how it is possible for us to form a mental picture on the basis of understanding the words in the first place. What is the connection between understanding the meaning of words and the formation of mental pictures, and what is the connection between the capacity to understand the meaning of words and the ascertainment of what is so in the world? This is the question of the *essence* of truth, or of the way in which truth is what it is, as the condition of the possibility of our seeing whether words reveal truth.

Heidegger uses the term "freedom" to indicate the possibility of making the connection between language and reality. Freedom designates what is between the understanding and the reality. It designates that which is between the subject and the object or one subject and another subject. It designates it in such a way as to indicate that what is between intelligible language and experienced reality is an open region. To be free means to be in the open between meaning and reality.

We can put the matter differently. Being appears in the proposition as meaning (borne by the "is" of "there is a gold coin on the table"); the meaning is what is said. Being appears in the object as reality (borne by the "is" of the gold coin on the table); the reality is what is so. What is between meaning (being in the proposition) and reality (being in the object) is neither meaning nor reality but freedom (an opening)—the opening of thought to reality and of reality to thought. Truth is connected with freedom because it too appears between meaning and reality; it appears as the language that can both say the meaning and show the reality; it appears as the opening of what is said and what is shown. The same words in which we understand the meaning of the proposition, even when we are not in the room, can be used to show the gold coin on the table when we are in the room. It is the same words which both say the meaning and show the reality. Between the words that say and the words that show is nothing but the opening between meaning and reality.

We would not be able to recognize whether what is said is the same as what is so if we were not existing as that open region between subject and object or meaning and reality. Between the understanding of meaning that appears in language and the ascertainment of reality as it appears to our senses there is no third thing, only the openness of freedom. To be free, in this account, means to be in the open or to be exposed. It is primarily understood in the positive sense of an openness in our own being. The primary mode of existence is to be in such a way that one is already from the start already exposed to and involved with the reality of the world. Meaning and reality are exposed to each other, and the openness of the one to the other is what is meant by freedom. To be in the truth is to be free, or in the region between the two. Freedom is the related to truth, then, in the sense that if human existence were not this open region between the meant and the real, there would be no way of connecting two such dissimilar things as the appearance of meaning in a proposition and the appearance of reality in an observed object.

Can we say that language, which is between thoughts and things, is the embodiment of freedom? To do so would conform with the path we have traced here. The mode of being that is human being is a being in the open, and that open region is the unfilled space between the purely subjective and the purely objective, or the purely ideal and the purely real. It is an open space, but it is continually being given a shape. The shape given it is the configuration of language; and the essence of truth, or the way in which truth is what it is, is the configuration of a language that is both meaning and reality. The openness of the opening between the ideal and the real takes on a texture that includes the ideal as well as the real elements; that is the texture of language. Language is openness in the sense that it fuses the noetic and the real, the intellectual and the sensible, but the fusion has no fixity; it is openness because it is continually creating the unity of meaning and reality, of subject and object, that configures the openness of being there in the midst of nothing. Human existence is word-bearing; it is signifying existence. Being free is being in the open, and the way of being in the open is to be as a sign, that is to say, it is to have a linguistic mode of being. When existing in the world, the subjectivity of the self is merged with the objectivity of the world in the concerns or cares by which the self understands itself. When authentic, it is disengaged from the world; between it and the world is the open region. When the open region is filled by linguistic configurations of it, these take the place of the cares or concerns that, prior to authentic selfhood, linked the self with its worldly objects. The authentic self is, therefore, no longer involved with the world. The question is whether this freedom from the world is the last chapter of the story or whether a new mode of being in the world as an authentic self is possible. The end result of our meditation on the Johannine passage is that dwelling in the word of "I am the resurrection" is an existence in the world without being defined by one's worldly cares. The mode of being which is a continuing in the word of resurrection is free in the sense that it is a being in the open between the subject and the object and a continual filling of that opening with the language of "I am the resurrection and the life." To live in the word "I am to die" is to be free in one way, for it is a living or abiding in a word rather than an abiding in the world; it is a mode of existence in which the self-understanding is defined not by its cares in and for the world but by the meaning that is contained in the language in which it bespeaks itself. But it does not reestablish an essential connection to being in the world at all. It can come out of the world, but it cannot return to the world to be in the world beyond the event and deed that are one's own death.

There is still a third way in which freedom and truth are connected. The first had to do with the saying of Jesus to his disciples as contained in the Gospel of John. The second had to do with the essence of truth in Heidegger's essay under that title, when truth means coming into the open, or coming out of concealment, and freedom means being in the open. The third connection is provided by the nature of acoluthetic reason. In this form of reason, the relation between myself as an I and the figure that is the exstantial I is a free relation in the sense that the response which is elicited by the exstantial I is not compelled. If the christological figure summons by saying "Follow me!" there is nothing in this summons that compels a recognition of the ecstatic presence of the I. The summons "Follow me!" can elicit a yes and a no. An affirmative response is given by those who, as it were, leave their nets and immediately follow. A negative response is given by those who do not change their course of action at all. It is in the nature of the acoluthetic summons that both responses are equally legitimate. If compulsion were exercised, the summons could not be the enabling of a self's own freedom. If there were something in the christological figure which imposed itself upon one's own decisions and actions, so as to compel them, then these decisions or actions would no longer be one's own; there would then be a contradiction between being authentically, as an I of my own, and being a follower of one who summons. The one who summons to follow freely is capable of enabling one's own free action despite the fact that the acoluthetic figure appears as external. The response is free; a yes or a no can be given, and the exstantial I can elicit either the one or the other response. The Christ-figure does not say: "Follow me because I am your true self" but simply: "Follow me." To know the truth by continuing in the "I am" of one who summons to freedom is to become free to be in the wholeness of one's own selfhood; it is to come into one's own wholly by giving a response.

What it means on the part of the exstantial I to be open to both affirmative and negative responses, and thus to be the whole truth, might be made more clear by the central figure in Pirandello's 1917 play "It *Is* So! (If You Think So) (*Così è, se vi pare!*)," which has to do with the possibility that appearance is reality or that, at least in certain circumstances, what one is is no more and no less than what one is taken to be.[7] "I am really what you take me to be; though . . . that does not prevent me from also being really what your husband, my sister, [and others] take me to be—because they also are absolutely right!" says Laudisi; it is not the case that "people [have] to be this, or that, and nothing else" (pp. 70, 71). A person is just what

7. Luigi Pirandello, *Naked Masks: Five Plays by Luigi Pirandello*, edited by Eric Bentley (New York: E. P. Dutton & Co., 1952).

he or she is taken to be by others; and, if the others have conflicting responses, they are all true. This possibility provides the theme of the drama as it finally centers in the *dramatis persona* of Mrs. Ponza. The townspeople are understandably puzzled when they learn of the strange living arrangements adopted by the Ponzas and Mrs. Frola when the family moves to the town where Ponza has become secretary of the prefecture. For his mother-in-law (Mrs. Frola), Mr. Ponza has rented a fashionable apartment in the residential district; for his wife he has rented an apartment at the top floor of a dirty tenement at the outskirts of town, one with an interior court "so dark at noontime you can hardly see your hand before your face" (p. 64). The explanation for this arrangement that the neighbors pry out of them is that either it is done for the health of Mr. Ponza, who, according to Mrs. Frola's explanation, is so deeply devoted to his wife that no one can be allowed to enter their closed world, or it is done for the health of Mrs. Frola, who, according to Mr. Ponza, went mad at the death of her daughter and recovered a fragile hold on her sanity only because by a remarkable chance she came to think that the present Mrs. Ponza, a second wife, is her daughter, Mr. Ponza's first wife. In the one case, Mrs. Ponza is in reality Mrs. Frola's daughter; in the other case, she is someone else. But all three members of this circle willingly live with this arrangement. Moreover, the explanations of Mrs. Frola and Mr. Ponza make sense not only of the arrangement but also of each other's understanding of the arrangement. In Ponza's explanation, Mrs. Frola only believes that he does not want her to see Mrs. Ponza, but her believing this is what makes it possible for them to live so that she is never given the chance to see Mrs. Ponza closely enough to recognize that she is not the daughter Mrs. Frola believes her to be. In Mrs. Frola's explanation, Mr. Ponza will not allow her to see her daughter because Ponza has "a sort of disease," an excess of love for his wife, her daughter.

But the curiosity of the neighbors is strong enough to impel them to discover the truth behind the conflicting appearances, and they can equip themselves with an array of rationalizations for having to know. They seek the answer despite repeated pleas from Ponza and his mother-in-law that this is an arrangement they have willingly adopted for the health of all three and that prying into it threatens to destroy the sanity it has made possible. Finally, after all other resources fail, it is decided that Mrs. Ponza must herself answer who she really is. She appears, and to the initial relief of all she declares:

"The truth? Simply this: I am the daughter of Signora Frola." But the relief is quickly displaced by consternation when she continues: " . . . and the second wife of Signor Ponza." "No, no, Madam," the prefect objects; "for yourself you must be either one or the other." This is met with Mrs. Ponza's final answer, "No! I am she whom you believe me to be" (p. 138). With that and Laudisi's declaration, "There you have the truth" and his question, "Are you satisfied?" the play ends.

One could hardly ask for a portrayal more dramatic than this one of a savior figure who will be who she is only in the others and not for herself. For Mrs. Frola, she is a daughter; for Mr. Ponza, she is his second wife; for everyone else she is the one they take her to be. Her healing role depends upon her being able to be nothing for herself but only the one she is in the others. Yet what prevents Pirandello's portrait from being a real possibility is that in biological fact she is or is not the daughter of Mrs. Frola and in juridical fact she is either the first or the second wife of Mr. Ponza. Moreover, she knows which of the two she is, and she is, therefore, for herself in her theoretical knowledge one or the other. Which of the two she is may be forgotten by everyone, herself included, and there may be no documentary or other evidence to permit others outside the circle of the three to conclude whether she is the one or the other— Pirandello is at some pains to account for the absence of such evidence by reference to a disaster that wiped out the town from which they came. *For herself* she is, as the prefect declares, one or the other as long as she knows who she is. As a savior-figure, she can indeed be to Mr. Ponza the one he takes her to be and to Mrs. Frola the one she takes her to be. She can be in truth what each of them takes her to be. But she also exists on her own apart from what she is in them, where there is no escaping the alternative—either she is or she is not biologically the daughter of Mrs. Frola. Pirandello's play, even so, creates in Mrs. Ponza an aesthetic figure which can show how the christological figure, the "I am" for whom there are no such biological predicates, is one whose being is completely open to either the yes or the no in the response to the acoluthetic summons. That is to say, Pirandello's experiment with the notion that the truth lies in, and not beyond, the appearance has as one of its results the creation of a dramatic figure who shows how the being of the exstantial I can be defined by the contradictory predicates implied in the responses to "Follow me!"

7

Textuality: The Inscription of the Self

THE PHENOMENON OF TEXTUAL-
ity, along with the difference between the incarnation and the inscription of the self that it brings to view, requires special treatment.
In our discussion thus far it has been left out of consideration. We
have considered the self in the framework of an existentialist conception of Dasein. According to this conception, human being is defined not by reference to a genus and specific difference, as is done
in the traditional definition of man as a "rational animal," but by
reference to a time and place, a *da*, or a chronotope (a time-place
unity). The being of this human self is care in the sense that its way
of be-ing in the world is one of taking care of, caring about, caring
for; and the meaning of care is temporality in the sense that time
indicates the for-the-sake-of-what caring is done. The self is there,
but not really so, when it is oblivious of its propriety hidden in the
anonymity of anyone and everyone; it is there really, or authentically,
when it comes into its own as "I," and it does this when it understands itself by the possibility which delimits it uniquely as I. *Sein
zum Tode* enters the definition of Dasein in the same manner as delimiting concepts enter definitions of anything. When we define an
entity, we do so not only by reference to what it is (through its genus
and specific differences) but also by reference to what it is not. Thus,
to be a rational animal is to be what is not a nonrational animal—not
a stone, not a tree, not an angel, and so on. But if human being is
definable only by saying "where" the entity is, and not by saying
"what" it is, then the delimitation is provided not by another genus
or species but by a negation of the time-place indicated by the
"where." If, furthermore, the way in which the self is anyone at all is

through understanding itself by projecting who it can be, then what delimits its being anyone at all is the possibility, the "can be," of not being anyone anywhere at all. This is the possibility, or the "can be," that Heidegger formulated in the phrase *Sein zum Tode*. The negative delimiting of human being is done, then, not by all nonanimal and nonrational entities, as it is in the classical definition of *animal rationale* (the Latin for the Greek that means, more literally, "living thing that has the capacity to talk"), but the "can not be anywhere at all" that is the meaning of *Sein zum Tode*.

If it is said that the meaning of Dasein is temporality, this includes more than what is initially suggested by the notion that what we are always concerned about is to have time. To some extent that is certainly true because to have time is the same as having the possibility of being there at all. But temporality comes into the picture in another way, even in Heidegger, when one takes account of the fact that time is not something in which the self is but the temporalizing that is the being of the self. " 'Spirit' does not first of all fall into time," Heidegger wrote against Hegel, whose concept of time Heidegger judged to be the apex of the popular conception, "but *exists* *as* the original *timing* of temporality. This is what times world-time, in whose horizon 'history' can 'appear' as intratemporal. 'Spirit' does not fall *into* time; rather, factic existence, as being-a-case-of [*verfallend*], 'falls' *out* of original, real [*eigentlich*] temporality [into the temporality of anonymous subjectivity]" (*SuZ*, §82; p. 436). The reflection on time that makes a connection between temporality and the self goes back to Augustine.[1] For in book 11 of his confessions, the end result of the meditation on time is the recognition that the experience of time is possible only because the soul is capable of being distended between the past that it remembers and the future that it anticipates in the present moment. Because the soul is thus distended, it is the source of the measurement of time, the basis of the experience of time. One of the ways in which Augustine sought to make this clear was to consider what takes place in the recitation of a memorized psalm. When we are in the course of reciting a

1. See Paul Ricoeur's exposition and analysis in *Time and Narrative*, vol. 1 (Chicago: University of Chicago Press, 1984 [French edition 1983]), chap. 1, and the literature there cited. Unlike Heidegger of *Being and Time*, Ricoeur sees the unity of cosmic and psychological time not in Dasein's timing as such but in historical consciousness which makes use of the poetic mimesis of events.

memorized verse, we are extended or distended between that part of the verse which we have already recited and can remember as past and that part of the verse which still remains to be recited in the present moment.

> I am about to recite a song that I know. Before I begin, my expectation is extended [*tenditur*] over the whole; when, however, I have begun, my memory too extends over [*tenditur*] as much of it as I have already taken from my expectation into the past, and the life of this action of mine is also stretched [*distenditur*] into memory because of what I have already recited and into expectation because of what I am to recite; what still remains present is my attention, through which what was future is transported [*traicitur*] so that it becomes past [*praeteritum*]. The more this goes on, the more memory is expanded and expectation shortened until the whole expectation is used up [*consumatur*] when the whole action is finished and has passed into memory. And what happens with the whole song happens with each of its parts, with each of its syllables; happens also with the longer action of which this song is a part; happens with the whole human life, whose parts are all the human actions; and happens in the whole history [*saeculum*] of the human race, whose parts are all the human lives.[2]

This provides a picture of the passage of time. The passage of time is like the passing of what is as yet unrecited through the present reciting into that portion of the verse which has already been recited. An application of this experience of time, as based upon the distension of the soul, to cosmic time, or to the whole of history, depends in Augustine upon thinking of God as related to the whole of history

---

2. "Dicturus sum canticum, quod novi: antequam incipiam, in totum expectatio mea tenditur, cum autem coepero, quantum ex illa in praeteritum decerpsero, tenditur et memoria mea, atque distenditur vita huius actionis meae in memoriam propter quod dixi et in expectationem propter quod dicturus sum: praesens tamen adest attentio mea, per quam traicitur quod erat futurum ut fiat praeteritum. Quod quanto magis agitur et agitur, tanto breviata expectatione prolongatur memoria, donec tota expectatio consumatur, cum tota illa actio finita transierit in memoriam. Et quod in toto cantico, hoc in singulis particulis eius fit atque in singulis syllabis eius, hoc in actione longiore, cuius forte particula est illud canticum, hoc in tota vita hominis, cuius partes sunt omnes actiones hominis, hoc in tot saeculo filiorum hominum, cuius partes sunt omnes vitae hominum" (*Confessiones*, book 11, 28:38)

as the reciter of a psalm is related to the whole recitation.[3] Time is, in any case, connected with the self. There would be no experience of time if the soul were not such that, in its present attention, it could be stretched between what has already gone (the *praeterita*) and what is yet to come and is anticipated. In Heidegger, the relation to time is somewhat different, although it is still the case that it is the self which does the timing so that time is not something *in* which one is or *into* which one falls. The self is the temporalizing of reality. The self is in some way the original timing of itself and all things. Over against Augustine, Heidegger sees the relation between the future and the past not by comparison to the passage from the as yet unrecited into the already recited but rather as a movement in which the self comes to itself; that is the *Zu-kunft*, the future in the sense of advent or coming-to. Here the original temporalizing is not the soul's being distended, in its present attention, between what it has already done in the recitation and what it has yet to recite but rather its being stretched between the self that it was when it was hidden in the anonymity of the general subject and the self that is coming into its own in the call of conscience. We can experience time because what is meant by the past is the self that has already been and what is meant by the future is the self that is coming to itself. The self comes to itself, and the self goes away from itself. The fact that the self is capable of experiencing itself in this threefold fashion (as coming to and going away from itself in the now) is what provides the basis for the experience of time.

In neither the Augustinian nor the Heideggerian account of this stretching of the self between the "was" and the "will be" is there, however, an indication of a kind of temporality which would include not only the future and the past of the self but also the presence of the self to itself in the form of an exstantial I. Hence, we must raise the question whether, in the relation between the self as it is here in its own self and the self as it is presented to itself exstantially in the form of the outward I, the self is still involved in temporality. That temporality does comprise the self whose being is care, the self who is concerned about having time and being both past and future in the present, is clear. But is temporality also the meaning of

---

3. "Why do I tell you all these things? Not so that you might learn anything from me," Augustine declares at the beginning of book 11(1:1).

the being of the self indicated by the possibility of acoluthetic reason? Is the following on the part of the I also a form in which the temporalizing of being takes place? This is the question which we still need to answer in connection with the exstantial I, or the christological "I am."

The Modes of Being There

We can approach the question by considering the three modes of being there as we find them in Heidegger's existentialist analysis. The one mode of being there, the being of Dasein, is the mode designated care; its meaning is temporality. A second mode, which appears in the later Heidegger, is the being of a work of art. If the being of Dasein is a being in which the self is there, the being of a work of art is a being in which the world is there; it is a particular "worlding" of the world as such. The being of a work of art, which is thus different from a self, is configured in the play of the fourfold. A work of art is a configuration of the interplay, the *Spiegelspiel*, of mortals and immortals and of the earth and sky, just as a self is a configuration of caring. If we can define the being of Dasein as the stretching of the self between the remembered past and the anticipated future in the present attention or as the coming to itself and going away from itself in the present moment, we can conceive of the being of an artwork as a playing together of divinities and mortals, sky and earth. Dasein cares; an artwork plays. Just as there is no human being, no self, where there is no stretching that is a temporalizing of future and past in the present, so also there is no work of art that does not involve an interplay of mortals and immortals and of earth and sky. If any human being is, then, the existence of the self, any work of art is a "worlding" of the world. The structure of the self is the structure contained in the notion of care and of time as its condition or meaning. The structure of a work of art is the fourfold interplay, whose meaning is the meaning of the being of the world.

There is a third type of being, distinct from these two, which we can recognize as the being proper to poetic words. If the being of the self is Dasein, and if the being of an artwork is the interplay found in the concrete worlding of a world, the being of a poetic word is a being that can be circumscribed as the self-announcement of the meaning of being as being. We may recall that Heidegger's question, unanswered in *Being and Time*, was that of passing from the meaning of the being of Dasein to the meaning of being as being. "*How is a disclosing understanding of* Sein *possible at all by reference to Dasein* [*daseinsmäßig*]? . . . In existential-ontological terms, the totality of Dasein is based on temporality. Accordingly, an original mode of timing on the part of ecstatic temporality must itself make possible an ecstatic projection of being at all. How is this mode of timing to be interpreted? Is there a way that leads from original *time* to the meaning of *being*? Does *time* itself reveal itself as the horizon of *being*?"[4] The impasse met here was that of finding no way by which to move from temporality as the meaning of care to time as the horizon of being as such. In the later Heidegger, it is the poetic word which serves as the temporal self-annunciation of being as being, or the horizontal timing of being as being. It is in such a word that we find the meaning of being as being, about which the ontological question asks, just as it is in temporality that we find the meaning of the being of Dasein and as it is in the fourfold interplay that we find the meaning of the "worlding" of a work of art.

This is, admittedly, to make Heidegger more systematic than the Heideggerian works themselves appear to be. For it amounts to saying that the three modes of being which Heidegger works out—the being of Dasein, the being of an artwork, and the being of poetic words—are interrelated in the way that self, world, and being-itself are interrelated. It is a way of saying that, if we regard self and world as the polar elements of the ontological structure, then the meaning of the self ontologically is contained in temporality, the meaning of the world ontologically is contained in a work of art, and the meaning of being as such, the meaning of the being of which the self and world constitute the structure, is contained in the poetic words which serve as the self-announcement of being.

4. *SuZ*, §83, p. 457, italics in text. These are the last sentences of the book. "If entities *are*, then be-ing must 'be around' [Wenn Seiendes *ist*, muß das Seyn wesen]," Heidegger wrote in his explorations that began in the mid-1930s. "But *are* entities? On what other basis can thinking decide, if not on the basis of the truth of being? Hence, being can no longer be thought of on the basis of entities, it must be thought up from its own basis [Aber *ist* Seiendes? Woraus anders entscheidet hier das Denken, wenn nicht aus der Wahrheit des Seyns. Dieses kann daher nicht mehr vom Seienden her gedacht, es muß aus ihm selbst erdacht werden]" (*Beiträge zur Philosophie* [Frankfurt am Main: Vittorio Klostermann, 1989], p. 7).

In this scheme, more systematic than Heidegger's, we can find three distinct modes of being there: the being of the self, which is care and whose meaning is temporality; the being of the world, which is a "worlding" of world and whose meaning is the play of mortals and immortals and of earth and sky; and the being of being as such, which is the appearance of being in the meaning of poetic words whose own meaning signifies something other than all entities. These modes, along with the auxiliary modes of being at hand as a tool, being before us as an object, and being-there-too as a fellow human being, we can, for our present purposes, take as a full account of the modes of being, and the meaning of these modes, to be found in a Heideggerian existentialist analysis and interpretation. What is significant is that none of these modes opens a path toward an understanding of the possibility of a mode of being for the exstantial I. The "stretching" between the I-here and the I-there, as it is formed in acoluthetic reason, is neither a temporalizing of Dasein nor an interplay of form in a work of art nor yet a word that is concretely the meaning of being. If we are to give an account of the being of the exstantial I, we must, as the preceding chapters have shown, go beyond this existentialist analysis.

We must also call attention to an important variation in the way another self can be "there too with" us (*auch mit da*). This is a being-there-too not in the manner of another self whose materiality is that of a flesh-and-blood body but in the manner of a self whose materiality is that of a text. In Heidegger's account, there is, alongside Dasein, as the being that I most on my own am or can be, a Dasein that is the being there of other human beings, the being which Heidegger calls "being there too" (*Auch-mit-Dasein*). If we are thinking primarily in terms of the authenticity of the self, we are thinking of the self whose uniqueness is identified by the pronoun in the first person singular. The other self comes into the picture as one who is there too. And if care identifies this being, then being there as "we" is made possible by reference to a common concern. Dasein in the form of "we" is still Dasein; it is still a mode of being that is defined by care, whose meaning is temporality. But there can be a meeting of the self and the other self, or a common meeting of selves among themselves, to the extent that there is a common concern; and, although the meaning of this common concern is still temporality, it differs from the caring about being that is characteristic of the self as I because it embraces more than an I alone. In the real "we" is recognized a society of the I that is individualized in a particular human person. In one sense it is true that the concern of the self in the form "we" is, like the concern of the self in the form "I," that of being at all. The possibility of having no possibility of being in the world is what delimits the self in the form of "we" as much as it does of the self in the form of "I." Yet there is a difference. Only of the I in the first person singular can it be said that this self always "can" but never "does" die. The same is not true of the self in the form of "we." (This is one way, perhaps farfetched, of explaining why Feuerbach interpreted the predicates of God as belonging properly to the human species rather than to a transcendent being or to an individual human being.) What defines the we in the full range of its possibility is still, of course, the possibility of being somewhere at all, the possibility of being there at all. "We" are there, just as "I" am there, and the concern which limits and defines being in the form of we is the same as that which defines being in the form of I; it is the possibility of having no possibility of being anywhere at all. But the thought "I can die," which singles out the I in the frame of reference of possibility, does not similarly identify the "we" unless the solidarity or the society of human being has as its common concern mortality; but then it takes a form other than that of pure "can be."

The "we" can also appear—if one thinks of Martin Buber rather than Martin Heidegger—not in a common concern but as the occurrence of something "between" the I and the thou in an encounter. In this case, the we that embraces the two is established not through a concern that is common but rather by an event that happened to both and revealed what is "between" them. The society of selves is possible to the extent that those involved can envisage what is between them all and can give expression to it. This is different from the care that is common, for a common concern is still a matter of existing at all, whereas the revelation of something between the one and the others in a society is not a matter of care that is common to existence but rather a matter of what has manifested itself.

These are two different ways of taking into account the being which involves not just the singular being of the self as I but the being of the self as we together. The existentialist way of doing it is through the concept of being-there-too; the way of encounter is that of the disclosure of something which is between the one and the others and which can be grasped or understood as a basis for community among them. The community of the "we" can be a community of common concern; it can also be the community of those who have been grasped by, or who have seen, something that is between the one and the others who are the members of the society. The former is a matter of existing; the latter is a matter of responding to what has manifested itself.

None of the preceding explications of being includes, however, a recognition of the mode of being peculiar to texts and connoted by the word *textuality*. For the way in which the self of a text, its "voice," is with us in the world is neither the same as the way in which others are there too in common concern nor the way in which others are there in an encounter. The self that appears in a text—the voice of a writing—is also in the world, but its mode of being in the world is not that of the being of other selves who, like us, are flesh-and-blood embodiments, nor is it the being of other selves who are responders with us to the manifestation of something "between" the one and the others of us. A text is "there too with" us, but the materiality of its where-and-when is not that of flesh and bones, as is ours; it is, rather, the materiality of linguistic signs. What is, then, the mode of being that is indicated by the word *textuality*? How does the self that is the "voice" of a text appear in relation to the world of concern or the world of a work of art or the self-announcement of being or to any other form? These are matters still needing attention.

Textuality and Self-Understanding: The Inscribed Self

In reflective philosophy, self-understanding serves as the basis for the understanding of the world. The ideal of self-certainty points to the possibility that the self of which we are immediately aware when we understand the meaning of the word *I*, and which emerges from its hiddenness through the method of doubt, is to be perfectly identical with the self as it is objectively grasped. The ideal of self-transparency is the ideal of a subject which has completely incorporated itself into its grasping and constitution of the world so that the creating of the world is a fulfillment of the self. The world then has the form of spiritualized nature, just as the particular human self in its embodiment has the form of naturalized spirit. These are phrasings which indicate the ways in which Romantic idealism understood the ideal of self-transparency. In its most embracing form, this ideal means that the I can be fully coincident with its own predications. The self which does the understanding, as a subject of its own operations, and the self that is understood can be identical with each other. Phenomenology in Husserl and Heidegger broke with this ideal. Although Husserl continued the Cartesian aim, self-transparency provided an insuperable hurdle in connection with what Husserl called the *Lebenswelt*. This phenomenology, as we have seen, abstracted from the question whether the meaning that we understand in terms and in propositions has a reference to an extramental, existing thing. Intentionality—that consciousness is always a consciousness *of*—is an indication that the self as a subject is in one way always already in possession of the formal or essential objectivity of the objects with which it deals. The essence of the physical tree as it is presented to us in the phenomenological apprehension is present to us as an eternal object, and it is independent of our physical sensation. But if this is the case, then the ideal of self-transparency falls short of full realization because it cannot find the selfhood of the self in the sensible world, when the sensible world means that extramental existing reality which lies beyond the intended phenomenon. Thus, the *Lebenswelt*, the real life-world, or the world in which we actually live, is excluded from the sphere in which the self can recover itself. In Husserl's phenomenology, there is no path from the intended objects in their certainty to the material objects of the living world, and, similarly, there is no path from the intending subject to the real subject of the life-world.

Here Heidegger's phenomenology takes a point of departure different from that of Husserl. What Husserl took to be the derivative and the primary is just the reverse of what is really the derivative and the primary. In Husserl's phenomenological analysis, the primary is the subject's intending of the object and the intended object; what is secondary is the actually existing human subject and the actual life-world in which that human subject lives. If, however, the primary is, as in Heidegger's analysis, our actually being in the world, and the secondary is our scientific or conceptual grasping of the world, then Husserl's problem of moving from philosophical, or scientific, understanding to the real world of everyday is turned into the question of the way in which the real world of the everyday can become the world of scientific understanding. In this latter case, there is no problem of finding a bridge between a knowing subject and a known object because the two are involved with each other from the very beginning. Differently stated, the point is that it is possible to show how scientific cognition of the world is a modification of everyday dealing with the world (Heidegger), whereas it is not possible to show how everyday dealing with the world is a variation of the scientific cognition of it. Heidegger's phenomenology starts, therefore, with the fact that we are already involved with the world as subjects who already take care of things in the world. The primary phenomenon is in this case not an intended object which is present to mind in its eternal essence, through the act of an epochal abstraction from the question of transcendent or external reference, but the object given in our ordinary dealing with the world. The primary object is not the reduced object but the real object. Then the question is that of understanding the relation between the conceptual grasp of the world, characteristic of science, and the understanding of the world which we always already have and show in the ways in which we deal with the world. The derivative in this case is the scientific understanding; the primary is the everyday understanding that is exhibited by the way in which we deal with the world in actual existence.

Hence the phenomenon which Heidegger analyzed was the phenomenon of Dasein, or existence as being-in-the-world. The intention of this examination of Dasein is to show what kind of understanding is already contained in the way in which Dasein or human existence deals with the world. The hermeneutical aspect of Heidegger's phenomenology, which supplants noematic reflection, lies in the conception of interpretation as a process in which we put into reflectively formed concepts the understanding of the world that is already contained in the everyday talk of the world. Heidegger II amplifies this hermeneutics by interpreting poetic words as the self-announcement of the meaning of being as such. The poet is one to whom being reveals itself in its own meaning, and poetic words are those words which express the meaning of being. The difference between the language of poetry and the language of everyday talk is, then, that the language of poetry gives linguistic body to an understanding of the meaning of being, whereas the language of everyday talk gives expression to an understanding of the meaning of being there (in the world). The philosopher and the poet dwell, as Heidegger put it through a quotation from Hölderlin, in closest proximity on mountains farthest apart.[5] They are in proximity because both of

---

5. ". . . since poetry and thinking are most purely alike in their care of the word, the two things are at the same time at opposite poles in their essence. The thinker utters being. The poet names what is holy. We may know something about the rela-

them are concerned with the meaning of being. They dwell farthest apart because the poet embodies an understanding of the meaning of being in a text, whereas the philosopher interprets the understanding of the meaning of the being of the world, which is already contained in existence and in the language of everyday that gives expression to the meaning of that existence. But the desire to understand the meaning of the being of existence is, at the same time, the desire to understand the meaning of being, and the understanding of the meaning of existence, which is contained in everyday language and which philosophy conceptually interprets, is also an understanding of the meaning of being; for existence is being, even if it is being in the world, and existence does have to do with an understanding of the meaning of being through being in the world.

For the development beyond even the later Heidegger the concept of textuality is a signal. The difference between text and talk is not an accidental difference between a language which happens to be written down and a language which is spoken; for writing gives autonomy to language, freeing it, at least in part, from the question of an author's intention and a recipient's understanding. The existence of writing makes clear that language is a medium of its own and not only a means of transmitting thought from one self to another. Yet there is more to textuality; and it is not sufficient to circumscribe the meaning of text by Ricoeur's phrasing that a text is "any discourse fixed in writing."[6] A written text is a structured object that is intelligible in its meaning, an entity that is "there too with" us in the world; and the capacity to understand a text is the capacity to understand, to redo in one's own self, the dynamic which has structured the text that is there, or to understand the voice that is inscribed in it. A written text is, we can say, a located self-understanding other than our own; it is an *inscribed self-understanding*, which exists along

---

tions between philosophy and poetry, but we know nothing of the dialogue between poet and thinker, who 'dwell near to [each other] on mountains farthest apart' [Hölderlin, "Patmos"]." So Heidegger wrote in the 1943 Postscript to his "What is Metaphysics?" See Martin Heidegger, *Existence and Being*, introduction by Werner Brock (Chicago: Henry Regnery, 1949), p. 360.

6. "Appelons texte tout discours fixé par l'écriture. Selon cette définition, la fixation par l'écriture est constitutive du texte lui-même," from Paul Ricoeur, "Qu'est-ce qu'un texte?" in *Hermeneutik und Dialektik: Aufsätze II*, Hans-Georg Gadamer zum 70. Geburtstag, edited by Rudiger Bubner, Konrad Cramer, Reiner Wiehl (Tübingen: J. C. B. Mohr [Paul Siebeck], 1970), p. 181.

with the self-understanding that appears in the everyday talk of Dasein. A corollary of this, which we shall indicate but not elaborate, is that through the voice of a text we can also participate in a world other than that of everyday care. This means, too, that the voice of a text can have an authenticity equal to that of the worldly "I" and can, therefore, exhibit a temporality other than that of Dasein's *Sein zum Tode.*[7]

To illustrate this conception, let us think of a brief text, which already makes a connection with acoluthetic reason: "He said to them, 'Follow me!' And immediately they followed him." These words are a text in the sense that they are written down. Whether the writing is done by hand or by machine or by some other means does not matter. That the text is in written form makes it something which I or any reader can read and which stands there on its own, independent of what its author's intention might have been and of what the original hearers of it might have understood it to mean; it can survive not only the writer's act of composition but the writer too. A reader today can read it in the context of a twentieth-century language which is different from the linguistic context of the original author. Moreover, that text can "be there too" with us in a world which we can share with it and which is, or can be, other than the world of care and mortality. Even if we did not know from where this text came, from what time or place, we could read it as a text and find an intelligible meaning in it, and it could be an entity that is there with us. To see a meaning in the words of a text is to recognize that the words say something, that they are not a nonsensical combination of optic marks, words, or syllables; and to be with the text is to understand it as being-there-too in a world, whether or not that world is the world of Dasein's care. It may be true, furthermore, that there is no completely nonsensical text, if evoking puzzlement

---

7. Thus, the text of Paul's letter to the Colossians (Col. 3 : 1–2, or similar words in Romans), which addresses its readers as ones who "have died," can have a voice that sets into equipoise two different world-times, the existential world in which existence is toward death and another world in which existence is beyond death. Must the words "You have died," which can be read by the one or ones to whom they are addressed, be understood only metaphorically or in some other indirect sense? Not if their textuality makes it possible for them to "be there with" us as really as are other human beings. For if they are there in that fashion, they are the voice of an existence as real as the existence of fellow human beings but different in its temporality from that of human existence.

about what can possibly be meant is itself a textual meaning. But, leaving aside that question, we can certainly distinguish between a text that we readily understand to be saying something and a text that we do not understand to be saying anything. Let us suppose, for example, that, instead of reading: "Jesus said, 'Follow me!' and immediately they followed him," the text were to read: "Follow me said immediately and him Jesus followed they." We could read it, and we could try to discern a sense in it, but we would be aware of the difference between reading this wording of the text and the other wording. In one word-sequence, the text makes sense; in the other, it does not do so. The meaning of an unintelligible text may just be its demand upon the reader to rearrange the words so that they make sense. But even that indicates how we can see a difference between a text that makes sense and one that does not do so.

The textuality of texts is their quality of being there in the world as intelligible entities. The significance of this point can be seen better if we retrace the way in which biblical studies developed, over a route familiar to biblical scholars, from the historical criticism of sacred texts to the question of textuality by way of the concept of kerygma. This historical route will show how the concept of textuality can be related to historical critique and to kerygma. We shall sketch, without much detail, the way in which historical criticism yields to kerygma and the way in which kerygma, as the voice of proclamation, leads toward an understanding of textual inscription. No example illustrates the nature of this development more clearly than the biblical narratives of the resurrection of Jesus. Historical criticism, which began with Spinoza and became an integral part of specialized biblical study through the work of Johann Semler, D. F. Strauss, Ferdinand Baur, and Bruno Bauer, differs from philological criticism in recognizing the factor of a point of view, a total perspective that distinguishes one author or one cultural or historical period from another. Reading biblical texts critically meant also coming to terms with the question of myth, when myth is regarded as characteristic of a precritical mentality. A turning point was reached in D. F. Strauss's *Life of Jesus*; for, unlike Semler, Strauss did not call a halt to historical criticism at the resurrection narratives. Indeed, his reading of the resurrection accounts in the New Testament is a paramount illustration of what historical critical research meant. Thus, Strauss could lay down, for a critical understanding of these narratives, the axiom that a dead person does not come back to life. A person who is dead at a certain time cannot later be seen alive. Indeed, if a person thought to be dead is later seen to be alive, then the conclusion to be drawn is that the person was not "wholly dead."[8] What distinguishes a critical understanding from an ancient mythological understanding is the recognition of the irreversibility of death. What then is a critical historian to make of the resurrection of Jesus as reported in the New Testament? The guiding intention is to discover what actual event is being told in those narratives. The answer must be the one that gives the most plausible interpretation of the documents available. What, Strauss asks, would pious Jews of the time have done when the one whom they believed to be the Messiah, who as such would overcome death, was nevertheless put to death and their hopes shattered? They would have read again the prophecies of the coming of the Messiah, for to understand something meant for them "nothing else than to derive [it] from the sacred scriptures" (p. 742). As they did so, they came to a new understanding of what being the Messiah meant, one which brought together the prophecies concerning the coming of the Messianic reign and the prophecies concerning the suffering Servant of the Lord. Consequently, the death of Jesus, far from being a refutation of Jesus' Messianic character, constituted a fulfillment of the promise. This new understanding turned their disappointment into the joy of knowing that the promise in which they believed had been fulfilled. They believed in the crucified Jesus, the Jesus who had died, as the true Messiah. This transformation of understanding was the event that turned the disciples from a fearful band of followers into the joyful proclaimers of the resurrected Jesus.

The New Testament authors do, of course, say that Jesus was raised from the dead. Peter tells his Pentecost audience that the Jesus whom they had put to death God had raised from the dead and that it was necessary for this to happen (Acts 2:22–23). Thus, more is needed to account for the content of the resurrection narratives than simply an explanation of the way in which the disciples could have come to believe that their hopes had been fulfilled rather than shattered by the death of Jesus. It was in order to explain this part of the matter that Strauss had recourse to the difference between a men-

---

8. David Friedrich Strauss, *The Life of Jesus Critically Examined*, translated by George Eliot from the 4th German edition (1840), edited by Peter Hodgson (Philadelphia: Fortress Press, 1972), p. 736.

tality for which mythical imagery is still a natural means of expression and a mentality, the modern critical mentality, for which mythical expression is alien or problematic. If the disciples are thought to have reflected how they might give expression to their new understanding of biblical prophecy, and if they are thought to have arrived at the conclusion that they must use the narratives of the resurrection in order to convey the truth of that transformed understanding, then a critical historian has imported into their perspective something that comes from a later time. The critical historian does not say that the disciples consciously reflected upon the question of the means most adequate to express their transformed understanding of Jesus' new being; for that understanding was mediated to them, and not only to their audiences, by the very language which was integral to the linguistic system that structured their world. Stories of resurrections were part of it. The disciples spontaneously availed themselves of the language which could tell the truth of what had occurred to them. Critical history distinguishes between myth and empirical fact. Myth does not make such a distinction; it is the way of telling certain truths. What that way is Strauss explained by the (Kantian) notion of "Idea"—a concept that can never be filled by a sensory intuition because it embraces empirically incompatible intuitions, in this case the unity of life and death. The resurrection narratives attest—so we might summarize the critical result—that being beyond death does not lie within human power; for the one who raised Jesus from the dead was God. Thus, they give testimony to a recognition of the finitude of human being, or, in more Heideggerian language, to a recognition that human being is a *Sein zum Tode*, but at the same time to the reality of a power that transforms the finality of death into a different kind of event.

Strauss's interpretation of the resurrection narratives is exemplary of historical criticism. It seeks neither to discount nor to defend what a text says. It seeks, rather, to give the most plausible account possible of what the text is about. It works with the distinction between critical (modern) and mythological (ancient) mentalities, and it endeavors to give the best historical explanation available for the data transmitted through documents and remains from the past. Bultmann made a point of the incompatibility between mythical and modern mentalities. That myth and modern science are two incompatible and total worlds Strauss in his own way recognized. But, beyond Strauss, Bultmann sought more than a historical interpre-

tation of the biblical writings. His question with respect to the narratives of the resurrection—to use these again as the paramount
illustration—does not primarily concern making historical sense of
these documents, that is to say, explaining their origin and intention.
Rather, the aim of existentialist interpretation is to make it possible
to meet today the same one whom the disciples encountered through
the word of Jesus, of whom they said that he was resurrected. It may
be true that Bultmann too readily equated the existence mediated
through the encounter with Jesus with what Heidegger calls *Eigentlichkeit*—if for no other reason than that the new being of which
Paul, for example, speaks has death behind it, not ahead of it. But
this is not of importance for seeing the task of existentialist interpretation as such. With respect to the biblical kerygma, the interpreter's
question is not: "What do the texts mean?" but: "How can the reality in them be present to hearers today?" The words written as the
text of the Bible serve as the enduring inscription of the one who
was physically present to his disciples as the man Jesus. The voice of
that inscription can be encountered as a living reality. That is what
kerygma means in the sense that Bultmann gave the term. Kerygma
is the proclamation in which the living reality of the one embodied
in the text—the voice inscribed there—can become present. It is an
oral mediation of the "I am" of the textual inscription. There is no
continuation of the flesh-and-blood person who was Jesus of Nazareth, a contemporary of his first disciples. But there is a textual embodiment of his "I am" and "Follow me!" The written text of the
Bible is not the living body but, as it were, the corpse which can
come alive in the kerygma. Hence, in Bultmann's reading Jesus was
resurrected into the kerygma. "In the word of preaching and there
alone," Bultmann wrote in the famous essay on demythologizing,
"we meet the risen Lord."[9] The aim of preaching, in this conception,
is to present the living summons today. Jesus who is dead in the flesh
can live in the kerygma.

Like Heidegger's existentialism, Bultmann's hermeneutics is fo-
cused upon the distinctiveness of language, as reducible neither
to the thought it bears nor to the signs it uses. It is not concerned
with the textuality of the texts. But one can easily see a connection
with the concept of textuality. Textuality provides two links—be-

9. "The New Testament and Mythology," in *Kerygma and Myth* (New York:
Harper Torchbook, 1961), p. 43.

tween body and language, and between the truth of the world of sensation and the truth of the world of the text. The inscribed self can be "there too with" us because it has its "there" in an inscription—not, as it were, in a body that talks, but in a writing that means. To arrive at this notion of textuality, we need only to eliminate the middle term in Bultmann—the kerygma, which as an oral phenomenon mediates the voice of the writing. Then the textuality of the text refers to the way in which the linguistic signs constitute the materiality of the voice which is "there too with" us in the text and can be a living voice of the exstantial "I am."

Although the history of the interpretation of the New Testament resurrection narratives that has been used here in order to set forth the concept of textuality does have to do with biblical texts, the feature of textuality is not limited to such texts. It refers, rather, to the way in which any text can be the physical location, the embodiment or the "there," of a voice that can be "there too with" us.[10] The textuality of a text is, then, something other than the kerygma in texts because it is a concept of a way of "being there with" us in the world that is different from the way in which human beings are there too with us. There can be a conversation with texts—any texts, not only biblical texts—as there can with other human beings but not with tools or objects or works of art. A text can in that sense be a linguistic structure that gives a place to the voice of the text, an inscription of that voice comparable to the incarnation of the voice that is there in the flesh and blood of another human being. This is to say that a writing is not only a trace of someone who was there as its author; it can also be an inscription of a voice of its own. The interchange with a text is different from the interchange with human beings, but it is an interchange because we can listen to texts as we read them just as we can listen to other human beings when we speak with them. Some writings, of which letters written to carry on a conversation at a distance are an example, are nothing more than another means of carrying on a conversation with contemporaries. To that extent they do not have the kind of textuality meant here, even if their author is an apostle named Paul and the recipients the

10. One might suggest that the concept of textuality is, if not a more adequate way, then at least another way of making the point that Tillich made with his concept of the "biblical picture" of Christ. It is the "biblical picture" itself, not an argument about a historical person behind it, which presents the one of whom it is the picture. Hence, one does not need to get "behind" that picture in order to discover the reality.

congregations to whom he was writing. But even letters can *become* texts; they can become inscriptions of a voice, whether or not identical with the voice of the letter-writer, which can engage attention as really as other human beings. They can do so because of the textuality of their writing; the words in the structure of the text give a place to a being that is there with us in the world.

In this way, the exstantial I can be encountered not only in the person of another human being, not only in a kerygma that can represent the presence of another person from the past, but also in and through the writing that is a text.

8

Christology and Theology

THE ACCOUNT GIVEN OF THE reason of following, or acoluthetic reason, contains no suggestion that this form of reason has a closer connection with theology or ontology than do other forms. If it is true that understanding being and trusting God, and the transcendence between them, are the modes of thinking configured in any form of reason,[1] then acoluthetic reason is of itself no closer to theological thinking than is aesthetic or practical or theoretical reason. But any form of reason can in certain constellations become a more direct theological or ontological expression than the other forms. It can be "symbolic" when at least one of the elements in the relation—the self, the other, the relating—is not only a rational form but also an expression of being *as being* or God *as God* or of both together. In such a case, the rational form is not only a form of reason but also a concrete expression of the understanding of being and the believing in God that are otherwise configured in the rational form but not identified with it. Normally, being is what we understand when we understand anything at all, and God is the one we trust when we trust anyone or anything at all; but this is not the understanding of being as being nor the trust in God as God. It can happen, however, that a particular entity that we understand or a particular one whom we trust is set apart from other entities and others whom we trust by becoming a symbol of being as being or of God as God. The ontological symbol shows being as being, and the theological symbol shows God as God. In such a symbol we not only understand the entity as being what it is but also understand being as being, and we not only trust

---

1. See chapter 3.

God in the one we trust but also trust God as God. Christology is an example of such an occurrence; for the guiding idea in Christology is that the Jesus whom the disciples followed was not only the other in a relation but also the presence of the one whom one implicitly trusts in the exercise of any form of reason and that the following of Jesus was not only a relation of the self to its other, as in any form of reason, but also the manifestation of trust as trust; along with this went the idea that understanding Jesus as the Christ was not only an understanding of the being of Jesus but also an understanding of God as God. The concept of symbol is introduced here to refer to this possibility.

A second idea in the christological discussion is that the following of Jesus is a paradigmatic or preeminent or even solitary case of following. These two ideas need to be sharply distinguished, for the one involves the question of theological exclusiveness and the other the question of christological uniqueness. An analogy with play might be helpful for drawing this distinction. The game of—let us say—basketball is played many times; each of the playings is a case, or occasion, of the game; and we get a sense of what the game means by watching it being played, or playing it, on different occasions. It can happen that among the many playings there is one game played so well that we could say of it, "There you can see what basketball really is." This would be to identify one playing of the game as an exemplary occasion because it made clear what basketball could really be as a game. Even more, the difference between this occasion and other occasions of the game might be so great—we can at least imagine this possibility—that in comparison with it every other playing of the game would seem to be so poor an example as to disguise what basketball really is as a game. This would be analogous to christological uniqueness, when it is said that there is only one case of following that really shows what following is or that "truly" is a following. Such christological uniqueness is different from theological exclusiveness because theological exclusiveness means that the only form of reason which is also a manifestation of trust in God as God is the following that is the following of Jesus. The analogy, in games, to theological exclusiveness would be to say, for example, that only basketball is really a game, all other games are false. "Is the following of Jesus the only true following there is?" is the question of christological uniqueness. "Is the following of Jesus the only true symbol of trusting in God?" is the question of theological exclusiveness. The thesis proposed in the present chapter is that there is a third possibility besides the universalism and particularism by which these questions are answered in the traditional discussions. The intention here is to delineate this possibility in such a way as to include both the question of christological uniqueness and the question of theological exclusiveness.

One answer might be to rule out the possibility, as Herbert Braun seems to do in his *Jesus*.[2] Braun's interpretation of Jesus and the Jesus-tradition is one in which the theological is implicit in a relation but is not one of the terms of it. Indeed, the message of Jesus runs counter to that very expectation. It was the opponents of Jesus who wanted to make of God a term in a relation—construing God as one *to* whom one could speak or pray, whom one could address, in whose name one could act, and the like. And it was Jesus who rejected that effort by showing that service to one's neighbor *is* service to God. How, Braun asks, does the Jesus of the gospels come to demand the radical obedience he demands and to make such obedience possible? What is the source of his authority? The usual answer is to say that Jesus could do so because he was the Son of God; his authority is based on a transtemporal divinity (pp. 146f.). Braun sets forth a different answer, one taking account of the fact that authority cannot be genuine if it compels a response instead of eliciting it freely. Its eliciting a free response "occurs through its representing a content [which] is capable of binding a hearer without compulsion" (p. 147). "Authority lives from the content that it represents" (p. 147), and it can be distinguished from the ways in which that authority is given expression, as when the New Testament expresses it as a faith in the resurrection of Jesus or in the imagery of one who comes from heaven, descends to the world of death, and returns to heaven (pp. 154, 155). These forms of expression are not intended to provide the basis for Jesus' having authority; they are intended, rather, to "express and point to" that authority (p. 156). The importance of this distinction between giving an expression and giving a reason or basis emerges in the contrast between the possibility of encountering the authority of Jesus today and the possibility of expressing its meaning in the biblical imagery. "We today," Braun

2. See Herbert Braun, *Jesus: Der Mann aus Nazareth und seine Zeit* (Stuttgart and Berlin: Kreuz-Verlag, 1969). One could find other examples, but Braun's book, coming from the years of the death-of-God debate, offers as good an illustration as any.

writes, "can become convinced of the authority of a word or action of Jesus as well as ancient Christians did so, but we are no longer able to give expression to our conviction in the cosmic and religious images of the New Testament" (p. 157).

Braun then also raises the question that bears directly on our discussion here. He notes that the attentive reader might well ask at this point: If we make a distinction between authority that occurs in fact and the ways in which expression is given to that authority, can a similar distinction be made when the word *God* is used? In other words, the question is "What is God?" (p. 159); and Braun answers: "God is not the one who guarantees authority, in this case the authority of Jesus; he is the expression of this authority. One can speak of God only in the actual course of obedience and humility" (p. 161). To show what is involved in this statement, he uses the text (Mark 11:27–33) in which the question of authority is put to Jesus (pp. 159f.). By what authority does Jesus do his deeds? Jesus replies with a question of his own: Does the authority of John the Baptist come from God or men? This return question is, indirectly, "a precise answer" to the question directed to Jesus (p. 159). The reason why Jesus does not answer directly, by saying, for example, that the authority is "of God," is, as Braun interprets the passage, that such an answer would in the circumstances not have said anything, for Jesus and his opponents interpret differently what is even meant by the word *God*. Jesus means "radical obedience, total grace" (p. 160), and anyone who agrees with that could say that Jesus has his authority "from God." "But," Braun explains, "such an 'of God' does not add anything essential to the radical obedience and total grace but is rather contained in it; 'from God' is the expression for radical obedience and total grace" (p. 160). This is the reason why Jesus refuses to speak of God directly as the basis of his authority when he is dealing with opponents who do not have this kind of obedience and this kind of knowledge of grace. Appealing directly to God as the source of his authority would in such circumstances not say anything; each side would read into the word *God* a different content

Braun anticipates the question that might be asked of this interpretation. "What then becomes of a love for God" if a true service to God is nothing else than service to human beings? (p. 162). After pointing out the perhaps surprising fact that in the New Testament there is only one reference in a nominal form to the love for God (Luke 11:42)—and its occurrence there is in Luke's later version of a passage which, in Matthew's original version, speaks not of love to God but of mercy and faithfulness to fellow human beings (Matthew 23:23)—and that in verbal form love for God appears in Mark 12:28–34 and its parallels, where loving God and loving others are given as the two most important commandments, Braun concludes that the reason why there are only these few references in the first three gospels to the love for God (p. 162) is that, as he puts it, "what is meant by the phrase is in reality, though not explicitly so, on every page" of the gospels (p. 164). God is loved "in a way of life in which one concretely serves one's neighbor" (p. 164). If the objection is made that this interpretation amounts to nothing but "humanism," Braun replies that one need only replace "humanism" by "love for one's neighbor" and leave out the "nothing but" in order to see that this is not really an objection to his thesis. The meaning of "God" is not such that a person could say, "It may be true that God forgives me, but I cannot forgive myself"; for "only where I do accept myself am I dealing with the phenomenon that is called the grace and forgiveness *of God*" (p. 168). Does this mean, finally, that no importance is attached to the word *God*? Braun answers, "That is correct; nothing depends on the expression itself" (p. 170). What is important, rather, is "the attitude of one who understands himself as called to obedience and as enabled, without his deserving it, to be obedient, or, in other words, what is important is *that* attitude which in the tradition of Jesus is granted and demanded with the use of the word *God*" (p. 170).

The actual authority of Jesus is, thus, not external to his words but is in the very content of what he says and does. It is evident through the way in which his sayings and deeds affect a hearer. They do not elicit ethical respect (to put the matter into our context) but oblige hearers from within themselves. The words do not obligate by formal authority; they obligate because hearers recognize on their own the truth of what is said. Wherever there is a radical hearkening, as there was between Jesus and his followers, that is the occurring of God. For Jesus' opponents, "God" meant the other in a relation, one *to* whom one could pray and upon whom one might call. They could therefore be interested in knowing whether or not Jesus was following divine laws, such as the law of the Sabbath. For Jesus, what is meant by the name *God* is the basis of being human, and one is related "to" God by being related to others in the world—man is not made for the Sabbath, the Sabbath is made for man.

In Braun's interpretation, it is the whole of being in the world and in relation to others in the world that is simultaneously the theological relation. There is no possibility of being related *to* someone or something as *to* God; rather, it is a matter of understanding how every activity of being in relation to others in the world is at one and the same time the occurring of trust in God. That this is a tenable Christology within the framework of the present account of acoluthetic reason should be clear; no form of reason, not even the christological, has to be ontologically or theologically symbolic. But one cannot exclude the possibility that one element in the relations involved in being in the world might not only be the element it is (the subject-term, the object-term, or the term of relating) but also serve as a stand-in for, or an instantiation of, the one in whom it all takes place. The exstantial I can be not only what it is, the I-without, but also a symbol of the God who is trusted (if not also of the being which is understood). The word *God* might come to be not just an expression of what is occurring but also the meaning that acoluthetic reason, or one of its terms, symbolizes. Then the question is one of conceiving how this is possible. How is it conceivable that a form of reason symbolizes a mode of thinking as well?

The history of the formation of the christological dogma concerning the person and nature of Christ indicates the difficulties of conceiving this possibility by recourse to the concepts of Hellenistic philosophy. The dogmatic discussion casts it as a problem of conceiving how one who is fully a human being (and therefore not God) can also be fully divine (and therefore not human); the perpetual threat was the concept of an entity that is more than human but less than divine. Through its several phases, the christological debate and the criticisms to which the dogmatic formulation was and is still subjected indicate the difficulty of the undertaking. The New Testament gospels make no effort at such a formulation; they restrict themselves to such features as the use of the formula of baptizing in the name of the Father, Son, and Holy Spirit. At the heart of the christological dogma lay the conviction that God or, more precisely, the Logos of God, the identity in which God is God, appeared as a human being and appeared uniquely and finally in Jesus of Nazareth. As a brief review of the familiar history shows, the controversies concerned the manner of formulating the unity of humanity and divine identity in him, and orthodoxy tried to steer a course between extremes. In an early phase of the controversy, the Ebionites were

CHRISTOLOGY AND THEOLOGY   195

pitted against the Docetists, the former taking the position that Jesus, born of Mary and Joseph, was at his baptism chosen by the Spirit of God and adopted as God's own son. In the Docetic conception Jesus was a human being only in appearance; he was a human form God had put on, much in way that one can put on a suit of clothes. The orthodox effort was to keep to a middle course between the Ebionitic and Docetic. In Arius and Apollinarius the speculation is already more advanced. Arius conceived of the unity of the divine and human in Jesus as one in which Jesus had a human body but not a human soul and was not in a strict sense God. His soul was divine; his body was human. Apollinarius, on the other hand, held that both the soul and the body of Jesus were human, but a third constituent, the *Logos*, in him, which replaced the human spirit, was divine. Both views were rejected in the orthodox position, which asserted that regardless of which anthropology is espoused—whether human being is constituted by soul and body or by soul, body, and *nous*—one must say that Jesus is simultaneously fully divine and fully human.

With the Chalcedonian formulation of 451, a certain stasis in these and related debates was reached. The council, in reaffirming the formulations from the councils of Nicea and Constantinople, asserted that Jesus is not of like nature (*homoi-ousios*) but of the same nature (*homo-ousios*) as the Father with respect to his divinity and of the same nature as ours with respect to his humanity:

> *homoousios tō patri . . . kai hēmin*
> *homoion hēmin chōris hamartias*
> *ek dyo physeōn asygchytōs, atreptōs, adiaretōs,*
> *achōristōs, gnōrizomenon*
> *eis hen prosōpon kai hypostasin*

He is like us in all respects except that he is without sin. He is of two natures (*physeis*) that are unmixed, unchangeable, indivisible, and inseparable, and he is of the same essence (*ousia*) with the Father and with us. The two natures are together in one person (*prosōpon*) and one substance (*hypostasis*). The formulation, for all its precision and elaborateness, did not settle the controversy. Even the question of what the formulation meant in its own philosophical and linguistic context continued for at least two centuries, although John of Damascus (d. 749), in *The Orthodox Faith*, adopted it as the orthodox formulation. In 680 the same set of problems arose with respect to the will and actions of Jesus, with the question whether there were two wills *(thelēmata)*, human and divine, and two kinds of activity *(energeia)* in what Jesus did.

The further developments in christological doctrine, among which one could include not only these debates about one or two wills in Jesus but also Anselm's proposal of the satisfaction theory in *Cur Deus homo* and early Protestant discussions of the *communicatio idiomatum*, do not really involve alterations in the orthodox formulation at all.[3] But the formulation itself has come under increasing criticism since the Enlightenment. These criticisms are nicely summarized by Schleiermacher in *The Christian Faith* (§95):[4]

> 1. Using the expression "nature" for the divine and the human leads, at best, to confusion. For to say that there is a divine nature and a human nature suggests that "nature" makes reference to something common of which there are two species. God and man are both "natural," as it were, but God is natural in one specific way, man in another. In such a case, the term "nature" embraces two kinds as though they were two species of a genus. But that would mean that the human and the divine share in some third, perhaps "generic," quality designated by the word *nature*. Nature is that from which both divine being and human being arise or of which they are two specifications. In polytheism the matter might be different, for there it was indeed the case that the various deities were born of a common divine nature. But that cannot be the intention in a Christian doctrine of God.
>
> 2. If the term is understood in a modern rather than an ancient sense, other difficulties result. For in modern usage, nature is opposed to God. It is, over against God as the unconditioned, "the summary of all finite existence" or the "summary of all that is corporeal, and that goes back to what is elementary . . . in which all that we so describe is mutually conditioned." A nature cannot be attributed to God because it always means a "limited existence," one opposed to something else.
>
> 3. In contrast to usage elsewhere, in which many individuals or persons share a common nature, here one individual or person has two natures. How, Schleiermacher asks, is it possible for there to be a unity of life together with a duality of natures? "The attempt

---

3. Because of their theory of a thoroughgoing communication of attributes, the Lutherans could assert the position, for example, that one could say not only that Jesus died but that God died on the cross.

4. Quotations are all from Friedrich Schleiermacher, *The Christian Faith*, translated by H. R. MacKintosh and J. S. Stewart (Edinburgh: T. & T. Clark, 1928), §95.

to make clear this unity along with the duality . . . seldom results in anything else than a demonstration of the possibility of a formula made up by combining indications out of which it is impossible to construct a figure"; and, on the other hand, the same writer, when avoiding the formula of two natures, often says something one can follow "and of which the figure" can be traced. So there has always been a vacillating between "the opposite errors" of "mixing the two natures to form a third which would be neither of them" or of keeping the two natures separate but either neglecting the unity of person or making one nature more important than the other.

4. The confusion is increased because either the same terms mean different things in the trinitarian and the christological formulations or different terms are used to mean apparently the same thing. In the Trinity, the unity is spoken of as a unity of essence and not a unity of nature. That gives rise to the question of the relation between "what in Christ we call his divine nature" and "that unity of essence which is common to all three persons of the Trinity" and whether "each of the three persons, outside their participation in the divine essence, has also a nature of its own as well." The confusion is increased when two uses of the word *person* are introduced. In the one case, there are three persons in one essence; in the other case, there are two natures in one person. What is the difference between a nature and an essence? If there is none, as Schleiermacher asserts, what sense is there in the combined trinitarian and christological dogmas? Or, again, how can Jesus have two natures and one *ousia*? How can he be of the same essence as God and man, and yet have only one essence? The term which, in the trinitarian formula, expresses the plurality is the term that, in the christological formula, expresses the unity. The inconsistency is due to the fact that the formulations were adopted as the result of different controversies. But it makes a combination of the two dogmas almost unintelligible. Thus, we cannot find in the traditional trinitarian or christological formulations much help for present purposes.

Theological Christology

A different possibility for understanding how the Christ-figure, the exstantial I, might be a theological figure at the same time is provided by a carefully defined concept of symbol. A symbol points to something other than what the symbol itself is; but, at the same time, what it points to is perceptible or real only there. A symbol differs from symptoms and signs in that way. Fever can be the symptom of a disease, but it is not a symbol; a traffic light can be a sign indicating traffic movement at an intersection, but it is not a symbol. A national flag is a symbol when an attack on the flag is perceived as an attack on the dignity or power of the country itself; for perceiving the attack in that way is an indication that the flag is the material way in which such qualities are present—the dignity and power of the nation exist *as* the symbol. The flag as a symbol does not tell us *what* the dignity and power are but shows itself as a place *where* they are. If the exstantial I is a symbol of God, in this sense of the word *symbol*, then it is *as* the exstantial I that God (who is not I and not the world but not nothing either) exists. The exstantial I is not *what* God is but *where* God is. But a further qualification is needed. Nothing is a symbol in the abstract, without reference to those for whom it is a symbol. The very flag that, for some citizens, is a symbol of the country can be merely a piece of cloth for others. Similarly, the exstantial I, who is the symbol of God in some relations, may in others be nothing more than the exstantial I, the I-without. Symbols do not have an objectivity like that of physical objects. This is, however, not the same as saying that symbols are merely subjective. For we cannot decide what is going to be a symbol for us, and a symbol is not merely a projection of subjectivity. Symbols are objective, but in a different way. Some things do as a matter of fact have the power of symbols, and we can ascertain that they do so, independently of what our wishes might be. But we cannot make something into a symbol by our own volition. We can only recognize and respond to those realities which do in fact impress themselves on us as such symbols.

Some consequences follow from this objectivity of symbols. First, it makes possible a testing of the validity of assertions about symbolic realities, a testing whether something is or is not a symbol. In the classical formulations, there was no way of ascertaining whether Jesus had one or two natures and one or two essences, since the concepts themselves were not clear. To say that Jesus—or anyone as the exstantial I—is also a symbol of God is to say that the person does in fact make perceptible the one who otherwise is the object of the trust that is implicit in the forms of reason. It is possible to distinguish between the exstantial I as only that and the exstantial I as a symbol by reference to the responses evoked. One can, in other words, determine in given cases whether a reality is or is not symbolic.

Second, the notion of symbol places the exclusiveness of religious devotion into a light other than that of theoretical absolutism or relativism. When a symbol is naively appropriated, the symbol is in fact what it presents itself to be; the question of its reality, the question whether it is in truth what it presents itself to be, has not yet arisen. In such a precritical relation, a symbol of God *is* God, it *is* the existing deity; the true God is always the one who is here now in and as the symbol. Critically, however, we can distinguish between refracted and unrefracted symbols; that is to say, the objectivity of symbols is recognized in its difference from the objectivity of physically perceptible realities. Refracted symbols are those recognized in their symbolic reality. In them, respondents for whom the symbols are real symbols can distinguish between the material of the symbol, the "literal" reality that is the symbol, and that which is symbolized; and the symbols can symbolize by being what they literally are and simultaneously being transparent to what they symbolize. Refracted symbols can also take into account the freedom of responses to them, which makes their reality of a kind different from physical objects as such. Symbols do not need to compel the same response from everyone in order to be objectively there; they are symbols because they elicit a free recognition of what they symbolize. This is not to deny that there may be universal symbols; it is only to say that the reality of symbols does not depend on their being recognizable by neutral subjectivities. The duality of this response to symbols is rooted in the structure of finite freedom itself. Unlike empirical objects, which present themselves to perceiving subjects with no differentiation (recognizing a tree as a tree does not depend on the differentiation of one subject from another subject), symbols disclose their symbolic reality differently to different subjects. They are not only culturally and historically conditioned; they are also differentiated by the subjectivities to which they appear. Upon some, they work as symbols; upon others, they have the effect only of the nonsymbolic objects that they are. The exstantial I can, like other realities, be just that; but, if it is also theologically symbolic, then it is not only encountered as the I-without but also elicits a recognition of itself as a realization of the God whom one trusts.

Third, a symbol can be universal in its scope in two different ways. It can be universal in fact if it does elicit recognition from everyone everywhere. Whether there is any such symbol may be doubtful, but the possibility of there being one cannot be excluded in advance. A symbol is universal also if it anticipates both affirmative and negative responses, that is, if its reality is open to the full freedom of response to it. And it can be final to the extent that, in its affirmation, it anticipates its own negation. A final symbol of anything, and hence also a final symbol of trusting God, is one which anticipates even the possibility of its not being a symbol at all. A theological symbol within acoluthetic reason, if it is to include its own negation, must allow for both a critical, rejecting relation to itself (the "No" of those who do not follow) and also an affirmative, accepting relation (the "Yes" of the follower). A universal symbol permits both. It synthesizes critique and devotion. It can do so because part of its meaning is its own being negated. Both the affirmative and the negative responses accord with the meaning of what is symbolized in the symbol. The symbol, qua symbol that it is, elicits not only the yes of the followers but also the no and the indifference of the others; to both ways of responding it is hospitable. A given respondent can know whether the response is a yes or a no or an indifference to both. But the respondent cannot know, for example, whether matters will change in the future—whether the affirmation of today will be the negation or indifference of tomorrow. That a symbol is universal contains no predictions about such future matters of fact. Again, the universality of a symbol gives no indication who will respond affirmatively and who negatively or indifferently. Nor does it suggest that there are any universally efficacious symbols, symbols which evoke a response from everyone, or that all symbols will in the end converge with this one. All it suggests is that those for whom it has once been real as a symbol can understand in it the way in which it comprises its own negation. There is a characteristic in the symbol which gives the symbol a validity even in those circumstances in which it is not, or is no longer, efficacious. Without seeing such a finality in at least one symbol, no one can speak of a universal symbol of this kind as being real. But if at least one symbol has been symbolic in that way—in other words, in the way that the symbol of the cross is symbolic in Tillich's theology—then there is a symbol that is universal because of its radical openness to all eventualities. Indeed, if it is open, as is the symbol of the cross, to its own end as a symbol, then it is both universal and final, for it symbolizes the meaning of finitude in being symbolic at all.

Comparative Evaluation of Symbols

Is it possible to make comparisons between such theological symbols across religious traditions, historical epochs, and cultural differences? Is it possible even to ascertain the meaning of diverse theological symbols? Can someone for whom the symbol of the crucified Jesus is a final symbol, one which is open to affirmative, negative, and indifferent responses and one which anticipates its own end as a symbol, ascertain whether there is a second such universal and final symbol? Can someone for whom something is not symbolic know what is its symbolic reality, shown to others? And if two different symbols are final in the same way, despite the difference in their material content, are they the same symbol or different symbols? These questions are not easy to answer. But the answer that seems most appropriate in view of the preceding discussion is that two such symbols would not be two symbols but the same symbol in two different real places. This notion needs explication.

That comparisons can be made between stories from different religious traditions seems to lie beyond question. It is not difficult to see, for example, how the story of the temptation of Jesus in the wilderness, as given in the gospels of Matthew and Luke, is of a kind with the story of Siddharta Gautama's temptation by Māra (Sutta Nipāta 425–449). The devil comes to Jesus and tempts him with the prospect of overcoming his human limits. If Jesus is hungry, why not turn stones into bread? If Jesus is to gain the world, why not gain it by showing obeisance to the one in whose control it is? If Jesus is to trust God, why not demonstrate the trust by leaping from a pinnacle? To each temptation there is a reply. One does not live by bread alone; one is to worship the Lord God and no one else; one is not to tempt the God whom one trusts. Gautama is similarly tempted by Māra, who offers the world of health, comfort, sensual pleasure; and the Buddha responds similarly in pointing to the spiritual truth of Dharma, to a commitment to compassion for suffering the things of the world. Thus, we might say that both stories make the same point in different ways: finite freedom is the freedom to accept the conditions of finitude, not to ignore them. Or we might say that, in both stories, it is recognized how asceticism or daring cannot as such bring salvation or enlightenment.

But there are objections to the meaningfulness of such comparisons, and, among twentieth-century theologians, it is perhaps Karl Barth who most consistently voiced one sort of objection. It might be objected that looking for such similarities or differences or making such comparisons is of itself to direct one's gaze wrongly. The comparative interest is incompatible with the symbol's own meaning; for it lies in the nature of a symbol to be incomparable, so that undertaking a comparison is to deny the real meaning of the symbols. What has been compared, in the end, is not the symbols but ideas that have been abstracted from them. This is to say, in other words, that what is common to symbols in a group is not what is essential to the reality of symbols. Hence, identifying common elements is in effect, again, to divert attention from the meaning of the symbol as symbol. The results of comparative study are always achieved at a level of generality at which concrete realities or questions cannot be brought into view. So, the conclusion might go, the effort to make comparisons is misdirected because it obliges us to look precisely in the wrong direction. The Barthian objection is of another sort than this, however similar it may at first glance appear. It is based on an understanding of the concreteness of revelation. If Jesus is the revelation of God; if it is the man Jesus who serves as the referent of the idea of God and thus concretely defines it, then his being such is not conditioned upon any prior conceptual content of the idea of God nor upon any characteristic of Jesus. That Jesus, rather than someone else, is the reality to which the word *God* refers is instead an underivable fact. Barth could thus contend that the truth of Christianity does not reside in any such features as its being a more pure expression of grace than other religions. Rather, the truth of Christianity has to do only with the identifying "name" of Jesus and not with any particular qualities of his person or of the religion associated with him. All things are important, theologically speaking, only to the extent that they are associated with that name, which constitutes the revelation, the being there, of God.

Barth thus seems to represent the most exclusivist of theological interpretations, for this theology cannot even undertake apologetic comparisons which might accord other contenders a certain acknowledgement. Yet, despite appearances, there is an opening in it.

For what is important in connection with the self-showing of God is not when and where or how many times and in what forms God has been made known. What is important, from the point of view of Barth's theology, is only that God has become manifest, that is, present as an actual reality with an identifying name, at least once, and present as the one who is for and not against us, and as one than whom we cannot even think a greater.[5] For if this has occurred at least once, then it is a matter of indifference how many other times it has occurred or in what other ways. Barth can therefore castigate, at least indirectly, those who purport to affirm Jesus as the self-showing of God but who then look about elsewhere in other places with the expectation that other attestations will offer additional confirmation. (This is comparable to believing that surrounding oneself with mirrors will make it more certain that "I" am really here.) The Barthian suspicion is directed not against the notion that God can also be revealed elsewhere and in other ways. It is directed against the expectation that finding such other revelations could in any way add to the understanding or certainty of the revelation already known.

The nature of Barth's objection can be seen if we think of the relation between a dramaturgic figure—say the Hamlet of Shakespeare's play by that name—and the different actors who play the role. We can consider an analogy which might seem to elude a Barthian objection. The Hamlet-character can be distinguished from all actors who play it. Yet, despite the extent to which the several actors are different from each other, it is the same Hamlet who appears as identical with each of them in turn. Let us suppose, however, that in a certain performance Hamlet has been played so well that he becomes exclusively identified with the actor playing the role, and we could not imagine anyone else's playing the role convincingly. Now there is an identification not only between the actor and a role but between the person of the actor and the *dramatis persona* that he plays. His performance is "classical"; it is one than which a better

5. "Ein Anderer [als der Gott, der *für* den Menschen ist], ein Gott, der nicht gnädig . . . ist, ist ein Götze, nicht der wahre, nicht der lebendige Gott, nicht der Eine, der in seinem ewigen Wort zu uns spricht, nachdem es in Jesus Christus Fleisch geworden, für uns ans Kreuz geschlagen und in den Tod gegeben ist" (*Kirchliche Dogmatik* [Zollikon-Zurich: Evangelischer Verlag, 1932–67], vol. III/2, p. 741). This is one of many passages in which Barth identifies the one and only God as the God who is not against us but for us.

cannot be thought, a standard by which other performances are measured and beside which others are at best imitations. To say that
what Jesus in his life presented was such a classical performance of
the role of the Christ is to come close to the view of Logos Christology but not by abstracting the Logos from the concreteness of the
person. The eternal Logos became flesh, Jesus, and the identification
is so close that this man is the paradigmatic representation of the
Logos, the one whose being even defines the meaning of Logos.
There are other representations, for the Logos is universal. But there
can be only one "classical" representation. To this, Barth would have
the rejoinder that Jesus is the revelation of God—it is as Jesus that
God shows himself—irrespective of whether his is like a classical
performance of the role of the Christ. Conceivably, the performance
of Siddharta might be a better one, just as Pure Land Buddhism
might offer a better example even than Protestantism of a religion of
pure grace.[6] It is not the classical quality of his performance of a role
any more than it is particular features of his person which make Jesus
the revelation of God. Indeed, nothing about him makes him the
revelation of God other than the sheer, underivable fact that he is it.
That is to say, we have no measure to determine who God or the
Christ is apart from the person of Jesus who is their self-showing. It
is the very concreteness of the person of Jesus which defines what or
who the Christ, what or who God, in truth is.

Let us take the Barthian objection in this strict interpretation, as
meaning that we can no more ask whether the Buddha and the
Christ are the same person in two actors than we can ask whether
the same eternal Logos appears in two different persons. Can we,
nonetheless, ask whether the person Jesus of Nazareth, in all its historically concrete details, might be the same under another name and
in another figure? In the figure of the Buddha, for example? In the
figure of one's closest and nonreligious neighbor? This is not a question of whether the Christ and the Buddha, or other figures, are alike
or different, whether they do or do not have the same teaching,
whether their roles, persons, and character are the same or different.
Rather, it is a question whether the one known to his disciples as
Jesus, the self-showing of God, can also be recognized in another
name with other features, other meanings, perhaps even other teachings. This possibility is one, perhaps the only one, which a radically

6. See Karl Barth, *Kirchliche Dogmatik*, vol. I/2, pp. 372–77.

interpreted Barthian exclusivism appears not to rule out. It too indicates that there is a third possibility besides those of concrete exclusivism and abstract universalism.[7]

These considerations provide an admittedly sketchy account of a theological aspect to acoluthetic reason. They are not indispensable for understanding acoluthetic reason itself, which is the main subject of this treatise; and the concept of symbol, even as shaped by the recent usage in philosophy of religion and theology, may not in the end be able to bear the weight placed on it in this chapter, for there is nothing in the concept itself which indicates the unity of being and not being, of God and not God, that is involved in the symbolic identification of the exstantial I with the being we understand or the God we trust. The remarks are intended, however, to give a minimal account of the way in which christology and theology, or a form of reason and a mode of thinking, are fused in the Christian theological tradition and to indicate the way in which one can see a third possibility besides absolutism and relativism or besides a traditional exclusivism and a traditional universalism.

7. By exclusivism is meant the position that there is one and only one final self-showing God; and by universalism, the position that there is a universal which can be abstracted from every concrete instance, including an instance of the self-showing of God.

Index

Abraham, 9–12
Absolutism and relativism, 129–30
Acoluthetic reason, 86, 93, 116, 125, 154, 167, 174, 182, 189, 200; as related to theology, 189, 200; contrarational expression of, 154–55; contrasted with moral reason, 155–56; definition of, 116, 125; description of, 144–47; nature of, 167; possibility of, 147; text of, 182. *See also* Christological reason; Following
Acts, mental, 103
Actuality, 19, 23, 28; and possibility, 19
Aesthetic and christological identification, 122
Aesthetic distance, vii
Aesthetic experience, 121–22
Aesthetic reason, 121–23
Aesthetic self, 122
Aesthetics, vii, viii, 121–22
Affirmation, 72
Agape, 101
Allgemeinheit, 99. See also *Jemeinigkeit*
Analogical appropriation, 52
Analogy and identity, 156
Analysis, rule of, 154
Anfechtung, 7. *See also* Conscience
Appeal, 124
Appropriation, limit of, 148
Art, 115, 126, 174–75; as secular, 126; as subdivision of theoretical reason, 111
Assensus, 75, 76

Assumption and subsumption, 41
Astronomy, modern, 150
Augustine, 171; on time, 171–73
Authenticity, 1; and ecstasy, 163; Heidegger and Bultmann on, 162–63. See also *Eigentlichkeit*
Authoritarian, 117, 118
Authoritative, 118
Authority, 34, 117, 122, 124, 193; of Jesus, 192–93. See also *Exousia*
Autonomy, 22, 162

Barth, Karl, 1, 20; on comparative judging of religion, 202–4
Bauer, Bruno, 183
Baumgarten, Alexander, vii
Baur, Ferdinand, 183
Being, 15, 36, 63, 132, 134, 149, 164, 170, 174, 189; and entities, 175; and existence, 41; as being, 174; as connecting percept and concept, 38; as connection of individual and universal, 38, 64; as happening and happiness, 71, 77, 141; as living contradiction, 49; as object of understanding, 38, 39, 63; as predicate (Kant), 64; as *Sein zum Tode*, 18; as substance and as understanding, 132; concept of, 64–65; ground of, 72; in propositions and in reality, 164–65; intelligibility of, 70, 78; intuition of, 66; meaning of, 36, 44, 45, 134–35; modes of, 15, 16, 114; of a thing, 64;

creator of world, 98; as everyday and as proper, 7; as given, 139; as groundless, 58; as "I" and as "We," 1, 170, 177; as individual, 1; as isolated singularity, 9; as manifesting itself in language, 143–44; as projecting itself, 48, 96, 99, 100; as relation of self to self, 36; as self-positing, x; as *verfallen*, 148; as zero-point, 98, 102; authentic, 137; calling of, 141; certainty of, 2; characteristics of, 61; christological, 2; coming into being of, 52, 59, 60; conscientious, 137; contrarational in, 153–59; delimiting of, 177; ecstasis of, x; ecstatic capacity of, in *caritas* or *fides*, 100; egoity of, 141; everyday, 137, 146; existence of, 174; existentialist definition of, x; first-order and second-order, 127–28; four places of, 139–40; freedom of, 119; hamartetic, 135–38; in Descartes and Fichte, 97–98; inscription and incarnation of, 170; Kierkegaard on, 36; languages of, 139; manifestations of, 62, 143–44; modern conception of, 5, 7; positing of, 95, 97; possibility and actuality of, 171; projecting of, 171; propriety of, 2, 170; reality of, as I, 6; singularity of, 11, 12; subjectivity of, 12, 59; temporality of, 2, 7; text as materiality of, 176; thrownness of, 60; *topoi* of, 141–42; universality in, viii; ways of appearing of, 96–100; wholeness of, 162; worldliness of, 98. *See also* I, the; Self, being of
Self, being of, 38, 54, 57, 59, 61, 132; as creation and as donation, 61; as unconditional positing, 54; as ungrounded, 59; as unity of subjectivity and location, 52
Self-assertion, 27
Self-consciousness, 108
Self-forgetting, 121
Self-giving, 101
Selfhood, 126, 136
Self-instantiation, 101
Self-negation, 27; possibility of, 27

Self-positing, 38, 101
Self-reception, 101
Self-transparency, 170–71, 178
Self-transporting, 121
Semler, Johann, 183
Silence, 11, 16
Sin, 135; concept of, 135–36; state of, 147–49
Soul, 171; as measuring time, 171
Spiegelspiel, 174–75
Strauss, David Friedrich, 127
Subject, 127; anonymity of, 99; everyday, 99; second-order and first-order, 127
Subjectivity, 4, 12, 36, 41, 98; appearances of, 12; as different from being, 36; infinity of, 50; of the other, 51; universality of, 50
Subsumption and assumption, 40, 41
Summons to follow, 35, 156, 167; compared with moral imperative, 156; distinguished from voice of conscience, 146–47
Swinburne, Richard, on the meaning of trust, 25–26
Symbols, 44, 189; comparative evaluation of, 201–5; concept of, 197–200; finality of, 200–201; ontological, 189–90; responses to, 199; theological, 189–90; universality of, 199–201
System, 106; principle of, 110
Systematic concepts, 95; nature and role of, 94–96
Systematic principle, 108; and rule of procedure, 95, 106–11
Systematic structure, 94–96
Systems, evaluation of, 113

Tathandlung (deed-act), 54, 55, 57
Tautology, 81
Temporality, 170, 171, 182; as meaning of being of self, 173–74; as meaning of care, 15, 170; concept of, 171–74; kinds of, 173–74
Text, 178, 181; as inscribed self-understanding, 181; as "there too with" us, 181–82; definition of, 181–82;